Follow every rainbow

The inspiring stories of 25 women entrepreneurs whose gentle touch created strong business

Rashmi Bansal

First published by Westland Ltd in 2013
Reprinted by **Bushfire Publishers LLP in 2021 (Venture by Rashmi Bansal)**
Core House, Off CG Road, Near Parimal Garden
Ahmedabad 380006

10 9 8 7 6 5 4 3

ISBN: 9788194767909

Cover Design by Idea Spice Design
Typesetting by Ram Das

BULK ORDERS (over 100 copies) for schools, colleges and institutions.
Send your requirement to enquiry@rashmibansal.in

Printed at Thomson Press (I) Ltd.

DEDICATED TO

My mother-in-law, Santosh Bansal.
For her unconditional love and support.

ACKNOWLEDGEMENTS

To all the women who have loved me, nurtured me, inspired and encouraged me.

Thank you, from the bottom of my heart.

My mother, Manorama Agrawal, for loving me through all my moods, my tantrums, my faults and failures.

My *chachi,* Pratima Garg – I think of you as my '*chhoti ma*'.

My *buaji,* Asha Goyal, for her positive spirit. You are an inspiration.

Edith Monteroso – my teacher at Allendale elementary school (Pasadena, California). In your classroom, this writer was born.

Miss Maria, French teacher at St Joseph's High School, Colaba. You inspired me to be more and do more.

My English professor at Sophia College, Miss Colaco. (Wish I had majored in Literature not Eco – an eternal regret!)

Professor Indira Parikh at IIM Ahmedabad, you were warm, affectionate and yet so good at your job.

Kamini Banga, for planting in my head the seed that 'I must write a book'.

Rama Bijapurkar, for being a role model – I love you and admire your work.

My first boss, Chandni Sahgal, for her tough love and bloody high standards.

Ellaeenah Daruwala, for healing my heart and opening my eyes to a 'new world'.

My childhood friends, Shefali Srivastava and Vandana Rao. You are the sisters I never had.

Piyul Mukherjee and Nayantara Chakravarthi – friends, confidantes and let's-have-fun-together pals.

My soul sister, Aneeta Arora. We are always connected, no matter where we are.

Madhuri Y and Shalini Lal, for shared yesterdays and many shared tomorrows.

Supreeta Arya, because we may fight but always make up.

My daughter, Nivedita. You are a beautiful young woman who makes me proud.

My housekeeper, Lata – without whom I would be lost.

And finally, 'Mrs Naipaul'. Though you are far away, you are still with me and within me. Guiding me, loving me, holding my hand.

To all the people who made this book possible.

As always, my deep gratitude to Sunil Handa, friend, teacher, mentor and guide.

To the teachers of Eklavya school – in particular, Principal Rajal ma'am and Principal Nandini ma'am – for reading the chapters and sharing their feedback .

Ravish Kumar, for being such a help and support – in every way.

Pankaj Bhargava, for the generous use of his office, which gives me the peace to write.

Zankhana Kaur (Zee) at TIE Stree Shakti for her enthusiasm and networking support.

Shweta Gadkari Joshi – who did the majority of transcriptions for this book (and did them so well!). Also John BK, Nikhil Sahasrabudhe, Suvadro Chakraborty, Vikash Bakrewal and Aruna Karthikeyan for their excellent work in the same area.

Nupur Maskara for initial proofreading. Astha Gupta and Akanksha Thakore for vetting some chapters.

Aradhana Bisht at Westland for editing and producing the book as I wanted it. I know, I am a taskmaster ☺

Amrit Vatsa for yet another fabulous cover concept.

Durgesh at Core House for DTP work on the cover. Gunjan Ahlawat and team at Westland for final design and layout.

Paul Kumar and Gautam Padmanabhan at Westland for being easy and fun to work with.

Satish, Rajaram and the rest of the sales team, for reaching my books far and wide.

To all my readers, even the ones who complain I don't write in 'English' (in this book I *have* provided translation. Wherever I think you will miss out).

And, of course, to all the amazing women in this book.

I think of you as friends now.

ACKNOWLEDGEMENTS

"Climb every mountain,
Ford every stream,
Follow every rainbow,
Till you find your dream.

A dream that will need
All the love you can give,
Every day of your life
For as long as you live."

– from *The Sound of Music*
(Rodgers & Hammerstein)

AUTHOR'S NOTE

The class of 1993 at IIM Ahmedabad was a special one. There were 30 female students in the batch, and I was one of them.

There was strength in numbers and we were bolder and brasher than our seniors (a batch of 15). We did not hesitate to empty buckets of water on boys making their way past our hostel (a campus tradition known as 'dunking').

When the boys put up their 'joos' magazine on the mess noticeboard with spicy (imaginary) details of girl-boy romances, we created our own magazine. Which took *their* pants down.

In 1993, when we graduated, I certainly felt – we are equal. Man or woman, we carry the same diploma. We are equally capable of 'making it' in the world.

I was terribly wrong.

Women are equally capable. But, the circumstances must 'allow'.

For a woman is like a delicate flower and needs just the right weather, to bloom and come into her own.

She wilts under the heat of disapproval.

She freezes in the ice of resentment.

A woman will simply sacrifice herself, and her ambition, if the 'cost' is too high.

And the family will approve of that – for at the heart of our modern heads lies the age-old belief: 'a woman's place is at *his* side'.

The revolution is coming, but there will be no bloodshed.

Because women will do it their way.

We shall overcome them with our passion for excellence. We shall conquer them with child-like faith. We will show them new ways of thinking and doing things.

Which make the world a stronger yet gentler place.

So lock your boardrooms and sit in your ivory towers. The world of greed and scarcity, the world of yesterday.

Tomorrow holds the fragrance of feminine values. Of courage, of transparency, of grace.

This is that moment in history, when women must seize the day.

January 2013 **Rashmi Bansal**
Mumbai

AUTHOR'S NOTE

CONTENTS

LAKSHMI

These are the '*ghar ki lakshmis*' who brought wealth and prosperity to the home – by co-opting family members into their business. Because success is not something you seek for the self, it is sweeter when shared with all.

CONTENTS

LAKSHMI

These are the '*ghar ki lakshmis*' who brought wealth and prosperity to the home – by co-opting family members into their business. Because success is not something you seek for the self, it is sweeter when shared with all.

CONTENTS

DURGA

Circumstances forced these women to be enterprising, to fight for survival. They rose to the challenge, slaying demons within and without. Tapping into divine energy – or Shakti – which lies dormant in each of us.

DURGA

Circumstances forced these women to be enterprising, to fight for survival. They rose to the challenge, slaying demons within and without. Tapping into divine energy – or Shakti – which lies dormant in each of us.

CONTENTS

SARASWATI

Armed with a professional education, these women are carving out an identity through entrepreneurship. They enjoy an unusual amount of freedom to be who they wish to be, beyond traditional roles.

CONTENTS

SARASWATI

Armed with a professional education, these women are carving out an identity through entrepreneurship. They enjoy an unusual amount of freedom to be who they wish to be, beyond traditional roles.

CONTENTS

LAKSHMI

These are the '*ghar ki lakshmis*' who brought wealth and prosperity to the home – by co-opting family members into their business. Because success is not something you seek for the self, it is sweeter when shared with all.

A CUT ABOVE

Meena Bindra,
Biba

At the age of 39, a navy wife and mother of two started a business to earn some pocket money. With the help of her two sons she turned the humble *salwar kameez* into a national brand with annual sales of ₹ 300 crore.

Millions have heard of Ritu Kumar, but few own a 'Ritu Kumar'.

Few have heard of Meena Bindra, but millions wear her clothes.

Biba is India's largest readymade ethnic-wear brand, with over 100 stand-alone stores across the country. And it all began in 1982, when Meena started a business for pocket money, with an eight-thousand-rupee loan.

I meet Meena at her unassuming corporate office tucked away in Delhi's Chhatarpur area. She sits behind a large desk, wearing a stylish black kurta and cream-coloured stole.

Meena could be your mother or my mother – women who grew up in an India where girls were educated, but never thought of a 'career'.

"I got married at 19," she says, "and I spent the next 20 years raising a family."

It was at the age of 39 that she got into designing of clothes and selling them informally.

Working from home, without targets, without a business plan. But Meena had her pulse on what women wanted to wear – stylish, affordable Punjabi suits.

"I was lucky to be in the right place at the right time," she shrugs. "I never had to go out and do any marketing."

Buyers and retailers lined up at her doorstep to place orders for readymade suits.

And yet, it wasn't easy. Meena's husband was a naval officer with a transferable job. This meant staying in separate cities for 7 years, for the sake of the business. How would she manage it all alone?

A good mother runs a home with co-operation. Meena ran her business on similar principles – with the co-operation of her sons.

Elder son, Sanjay, took over the commercials, expanding Biba from a cottage industry to an industrial scale. Younger son, Siddharth, took it to the next level, with stand-alone Biba stores.

Together, they have built a ₹ 300 crore ethnic-wear empire.

It sounds too good, too easy to be true.

But that is what life can be, if you see the possibilities and not the obstacles.

That is what life is meant to be, for you.

A CUT ABOVE

Meena Bindra, Biba

Meena Bindra was born and brought up in Delhi.

"I grew up in a large family of six siblings – three brothers and three sisters. I was somewhere in the middle."

Meena's father was a businessman, but he passed away when she was only 9 years old. However, he left behind a lot of property so her mother was able to provide and give them a 'normal childhood'.

After completing a BA in History from Miranda House, Meena got married. She was nineteen-and-a-half and in love.

"My husband was in the Indian Navy and almost ten years older than me."

As a navy wife, Meena moved around all over the country – from Delhi to Bombay to Vishakhapatnam. Never more than three years in one place.

"My son, Sanjay, was born in 1965, Siddharth came in 1974. So the first 20 years of marriage, I was just busy looking after home and family."

Only when her kids had grown up, did Meena think of 'doing something'.

"My elder son was in boarding school, the younger one in school. Playing cards was not my scene and I also knew I am not cut out for a job!"

What Meena did enjoy was designing clothes.

"I hadn't done a formal course, but I dabbled with prints and colours. I got a few of my saris block-printed, just for fun."

But to go into business, you need *some* money.

"I spoke to my husband and he arranged for a loan from Syndicate Bank."

Eight thousand rupees is not a lot of money, but enough to buy some fabric and hire a tailor. But as they say, fortune favours the brave.

"My first lucky break was when someone introduced me to a block printer called Devesh. He was a young boy, passionate about his work and he had a big factory."

Every morning, Meena would take a cab to the factory and spend the day there, experimenting with various techniques and colour combinations.

"We enjoyed experimenting with new techniques of printing. Tie and dye, *khari* printing, whatever we did came out really well!"

Through trial and error, Meena put together 40 salwar suits – all casual-wear and reasonably priced (under ₹ 200). Some stitched, some unstitched.

"I had a little sale in my house and everything got sold. I also got a lot of orders!"

This first sale resulted in a small profit of ₹ 3000. With that money, Meena bought fabric for 80 suits and that too sold out quickly.

"So that really encouraged me, and the same money which I made, I would take it, buy more fabric and make more suits!"

It was a business, and yet not strictly business.

"I lived in a huge flat which was like an 'open house'. *Koi chai pee raha hai, koi* coffee *pee raha hai*… It was a very easy atmosphere where women enjoyed coming, sitting and chatting."

And they would also try and buy. Knowing that in case I go home and don't like it, Meena will take it back.

"It was not such a commercial venture, actually," says Meena. "The buyers were my friends, first and foremost, not customers."

Purely by word of mouth, Meena's suits became 'famous' among ladies in the Colaba and Cuffe Parade areas of Bombay. By the end of the year, she had three tailors doing jobwork and started getting enquiries from retailers like Benzer and Sheetal.

"Once I started supplying outside, I needed a name for my bill book. I decided on 'Biba'."

Retailers placed 'large' orders – 100 pieces at a time. And, they wanted new designs and a wider range of fabric.

"I got into terrycots and silks, and quickly scaled up the production," smiles Meena.

From a time pass and hobby venture, Biba was quickly becoming a *real* business. Driven by a force bigger than the creator herself.

"I never did any marketing as such, but I think maybe the time was right. New shops were opening, they needed to stock readymade *salwar kameez* and they heard about me… so I got big orders."

But Meena has only hazy memories of what exactly she earned in that first couple of years.

"I was doing well, but I cannot recall exactly… not lakhs, but definitely I earned in thousands."

Thousands quickly did become lakhs because, in 1986, three years into business, Meena moved into a 1000 sq ft office at Kemp's Corner. An office which was paid for entirely by money earned from Biba.

And yet, there was no business *plan*, as such.

"I was just flooded with orders and had also opened my own boutique in Kemp's Corner."

"Jo ban raha tha bik raha tha – so there were no targets, no deadlines, I never felt I am under any pressure."

Things might have continued in this happy-go-lucky manner, except that, around this time, Meena's elder son, Sanjay, completed his BCom and joined the business.

"I wanted to keep busy and earn some extra money, pocket money. That's why I started designing clothes."

"I didn't encourage him initially. I said – you don't know anything about *salwar kameez* and you don't know anything about business! First go do an MBA and then I'll think about it."

But Sanjay would not take no for an answer.

"I would say, even from his side, initially it was not so serious, but once we shifted to the office he got into Biba full-time."

And he proved to be a big asset. Sanjay quickly took over the 'boring' side of the business – handling the labour, taking orders, keeping accounts. Now, Meena could focus wholely and solely on designing the clothes.

The next few years, Biba grew at a steady pace. More range, more outlets – not just in Bombay, but all over India. Retailers from as far as Bangalore and Jaipur came and placed orders.

By 1993, Biba had become one of India's largest ethnic-wear wholesalers, selling 1000-2000 pieces every month.

"I think our turnover at this point was ₹ 8-10 crore... (*shakes her head*). No, at that time we were selling wholesale so it would be less. It must have been around ₹ 2 crore."

There was money in the business, but it was not the main driving force.

Meanwhile, there were other forces acting in Meena's favour. By the mid-90s, India's first multi-city department store, Shopper's Stop, came into being. They too came to Biba for ladies' ethnic-wear. In the process, Meena learnt many lessons.

"We were forced to become more professional – to stand by our commitments, deliver on time and also bring our costs down, without compromising on quality."

It wasn't easy. From the very beginning, Biba had outsourced its manufacturing.

"When faced with a production problem, my first reaction used to be, 'What can I do? My tailors are like this only'!"

But then, it was a problem Meena would have to solve. Advance planning, control systems and quality checks helped tailors become more efficient. Sanjay handled most of this work.

"I can't say I was 100% involved, but I was not 100% not involved – it was a joint thing."

In 1993, Biba had around 10 employees and worked with around 100 tailors. The tailors worked in groups of 10 or 20, and many of these units produced exclusively for the company. This introduced a measure of accountability.

"Once we were giving 500 pieces to one tailoring unit, we would ask for a date of delivery."

If the delivery date was near and tailors were falling behind, they would be asked to work night-shifts. But scaling up to meet demand was, and still remains, a challenge.

"For men's shirts you can have an assembly line. For *salwar kameez*, 5-6 different *karigars* may need to work on one piece."

What's more, the fabric itself is handmade, not mill-made. So it is not standardised.

"If I order 1000 metres of a particular print from Jaipur, it comes in five different shades. So how do I fulfill a bulk order?"

Working with limitations and yet going beyond limits is the true test of any entrepreneur. And Biba passed that test with flying colours. By the year 2000, production had scaled up to 5000 pieces per month.

Demand was never an issue – as Shopper's Stop and then Pantaloons opened new outlets, they needed more and more stocks.

"We told our tailor masters, 'We have more work for you. Why don't you keep more staff?' so they grew along with us and were happy."

"Readymade *salwar kameez* was a new idea and every shop was looking for suppliers. I never had to go anywhere – people came looking for me."

"I knew when my husband gets a transfer, we will have to vacate the flat. Bombay *mein kahan flat milega* – it's impossible. But I had earned enough to buy a flat so I could stay on."

While tailors expected to be paid in cash, the stores expected credit. But the credit period was 30-45 days and there was generally no delay. So Biba could manage its cash flows without bank limits or overdrafts.

"We never took any outside funding as such. I don't know if that was the right thing – we could have grown faster, perhaps."

The turning point for Biba came when her younger son, Siddharth, joined the company after graduating from Harvard in 2002. Although by then Biba had a wide footprint and annual revenues of over ₹ 25 crore, it was not a well-known brand name.

"Siddharth had a very clear vision – we must have our own retail outlets."

Biba opened its first company-owned outlet in 2004, at In Orbit and CR2 malls in Mumbai. Both shops did remarkably well from day one, with sales of ₹ 12-15 lakh per month.

"That encouraged us and we started booking shops wherever we thought a good mall is coming up. Automatically we get footfalls."

Of course, this kind of expansion requires management bandwidth and funding. These aspects were handled by Siddharth. In fact, the whole company was restructured and, in 2006, Kishore Biyani bought a 10% stake in Biba for ₹ 110 crore.

"Our growth since 2004 has been phenomenal," admits Meena.

In March 2012, Biba's annual revenues stood at ₹ 300 crore, with 90 company-owned outlets contributing 50% of sales. The company continues to outsource manufacturing, but employs around 1000 people in supervisory roles and for retail sales.

A long, long way from a business started to earn some 'extra pocket money'.

"I never imagined it when I started… but as you grow, your vision keeps growing. Now, I feel we can grow to any height, even become a global brand."

But did getting into business mean a compromise in personal life? Meena maintains she was able to achieve that fine balance.

"When I first started, I never ever worked after 6 pm. My husband, being in the navy, we had a lot of evening engagements."

The problem Meena faced was that her husband had a transferable job. When he was posted to Delhi, she stayed back in Bombay – and he was always supportive.

"I would spend 10 days in Delhi, rest in Bombay. We lived like this for 8-9 years, until his retirement in 1993."

Meena then moved to Delhi while Sanjay stayed on in Bombay.

"I had bought a flat at Worli Seaface. Sanjay got married and moved there and I started an office in Delhi."

Meena's deep and continuing commitment is towards great design.

"I rely on my own sensibilities – simple, elegant, wearable design."

Even today, with Biba producing 60-70,000 pieces a month, and professionals to handle all aspects, the one thing Meena oversees herself is designing.

"We have a design team, but I still give the brief, I go through the colours. Samples are made and I give the final approval."

Of course, designs are worked on at least a year in advance. And once samples are approved, a made-for-scale, scientific process takes over. And Meena is happy about that.

"I don't like dealing with too many people and you know I'm not such a good administrator. Frankly, if I had to handle all that, I would not have wanted to grow so much."

"Low cost, good quality and timely delivery – these are the three essential qualities of a successful business."

"I think women always have their family at the back of their mind. For a man, family is important, but it's taken care of by the wife. So in his mind, career is uppermost."

Working with family, she feels, has been a blessing. Because you can trust them. And whatever you are building, you are ultimately doing it with and for your family.

"Of course, it requires certain amount of adjustment," she smiles.

Meena's husband was never interested in the business. Even after retirement, he was busy with consulting projects and authoring a book. He passed away in 2011.

"I think I was happier not having him in the business," she admits.

With her sons, Meena had a clear demarcation of boundaries. Yet, there was argument and friction.

"I thought Sanjay was very radical, he thought I wasn't willing to change. But we always worked things out. As a mother I would eventually give in."

The dynamics changed when Siddharth also joined the business.

"There were differences of opinion on how to take the business forward," says Meena. "Ultimately, they decided to work separately."

In 2010, Sanjay sold his stake and has started a new ethnic-wear label called 'Seven East'.

"We are still close as a family," says Meena. "In fact, it's better this way because conflict is just a waste of energy."

Energy is the force which moves mountains and working mothers.

"I do yoga, pranayama, walking and swimming to keep my energy up!"

And then there are deeper dimensions. A journey within, which, for Meena, began 22 years ago.

"I came across a book called *I Am That* by Nisarga Dutta Maharaj. I didn't understand much of it in the beginning, but I started thinking about questions like 'who we are' and 'what is the purpose of life?' "

Meena read and re-read the book, until the meaning started sinking in. She later bought all the other books by the same author and devoured them. Even today, *I Am That* occupies pride of place on her bedside table.

"It's not something that you can just read 5-6 pages, just half a page at any given time. But over time it has changed me – made me a better and calmer person."

A person who does not blame others because each one is playing their role in life. So you accept the world as it *is*, not as it should be.

And enjoy all the blessings you have.

"I don't enjoy cooking, but I love having a beautiful house and am very fond of interiors, gardening and meeting friends."

All things bright and beautiful, all pleasures great and small.

A woman can be a wife, a mother and an entrepreneur.

Live a dream and have it *all*.

ADVICE TO WOMEN ENTREPRENEURS

If you passionately want to do something, then do it. Every woman has the potential and capability, you must never feel *'hum toh nahi kar sakte'*.

Women are naturally attracted to women-oriented products. We all wear clothes and jewellery, we all eat good food. So it is easier to start a business in such areas.

I have no formal training, either in business or in designing, I had no money and my husband was in a transferable job. So, it seems like this, all the odds were against me, you know, but then, I took the plunge.

Yes, it requires a lot of work discipline. You can't say *ki aaj kar kiya, kal nahin kiya*. There were times when I found it too much, but then I had commitments, I had to honour them. So you have to be focused.

Working with family members is a good way to grow your business. I would recommend it to all women.

LOAN RANGER

Manju Bhatia,
Vasuli

She started working at 16, in a pharmaceutical company. At 26, this chit of a girl from Indore is the Joint Managing Director of Vasuli, a pan-India loan-recovery company which employs only female agents.

Think of a loan-recovery agent and the picture that comes to mind is a 'full-blooded, macho male'. A *paan*-chewing, beefy-shouldered, Ghajini-type villain.

Dragging defaulters out of their homes, screaming and kicking.

Manju Bhatia does not chew *paan*, nor does she have Schwarzenegger shoulders. She is a chit of a girl, looking even smaller behind a giant desk than she actually is.

Just 26 years old.

Manju Bhatia is the Joint Managing Director of Vasuli, a loan-recovery company which employs only female agents.

"That was her idea," beams Parag Shah, MD of Vasuli. "I started the business but whatever the organisation is today, is because of her!"

From a side-business with a monthly income of ₹ 25,000 and one client, Vasuli has grown to a company with 26 branch offices, handling ₹ 500 crore of recovery for 20 nationalised banks. All in a short span of eight years.

Because a 16-year-old girl from Indore decided she could be more than a daughter or wife.

She can be *anything* she chooses to be.

And so can you…

LOAN RANGER

Manju Bhatia,
Vasuli

Manju Bhatia was born into a business family in Indore.

"My father was in the business of electrical appliances. I am the middle child in the family, one older sister, one younger brother."

Manju was a good student, not a great one. But, she had something which very few students have – the desire to get practical experience.

"When I was completing class 12, I decided I must work somewhere. Even if I am paid ₹ 500 per month it's ok, but I want to *learn*."

Manju started appearing for interviews even as she was giving her final examinations.

"CBSE had given lot of leave in between papers, so I would go and give interviews."

Not that there was a lot of choice of jobs in the city of Indore. But Manju wasn't fussy about it. She accepted a job as a receptionist at Tulika International, a small pharmaceutical company owned by a family friend – Parag Shah.

"On 1 April 2003, I completed my class 12 board exams. On 2 April 2003, I started working."

On the very first day, Parag told the 16-year-old something she never forgot, “If you want to become something, learn the basics. *Koi bhi kaam chhota mat samjho*.”

The reception, he explained, is like the ‘control room’ of the office. So, there is scope to learn *everything* about how an office functions. Three days later, Manju was given an additional responsibility – handling accounts.

“I had done Commerce in class 12, with Maths. So what I did was learn how to use Tally.”

Soon, Manju was not only managing accounts, but also trading raw material, which was the main business of Tulika.

“Tulika was dealing in APIs – Active Pharmaceutical Ingredients. We were not manufacturers – only traders.”

Although she had no science background, Manju quickly learnt all the ins and outs of Diclofenac Sodium, Betamethasone and Clobetasol. That, combined with her love for browsing the internet made her a natural.

“In pharmaceuticals, if you trade in unique drugs you get good margins. I had a passion to find these drugs, which are not very easily supplied.”

Having procured an API at a good price, you have to find a customer. Again, Manju would track down which were the biggest factories in need of these drugs. And contact them through the internet.

“In fact, you won’t believe it, but at times I used to buy from suppliers in Mumbai. The product would come to Indore, we used to do the billing, packing and then sell it back to a party in Mumbai.”

Mumbai being a vast city, *nobody* has perfect market knowledge.

Over the next two years, Manju continued with her BA and continued working side by side. In this period, she even learnt how to get an export licence.

“I had to visit excise office, complete various government formalities… each and everything I did by my own hands!”

And then, one day, Parag asked Manju to help with Vasuli, another small firm he owned which undertook recovery for banks.

Something he had started because he had time on his hands, and wanted to diversify into the service industry.

"Vasuli was very small at that time, we had just one client – State Bank of India."

Every month, SBI provided Vasuli with a list of defaulters. One such name happened to be that of a prominent minister. It was a delicate situation.

"If one of our field executives had gone to meet the minister, it would have created a hue and cry in the media. So Parag asked me to go instead."

Manju requested an appointment, without mentioning the issue of default. The idea was to first inform the defaulter and give him a chance to explain.

"People sometimes forget about due dates or, the debit instructions are wrong. The client has no idea that he has missed 3 installments and the bank now sees the loan as 'NPA' or 'Non-Performing Asset'."

And such was the case with the minister. The moment Manju informed him, he called his PA. The next day, the entire account was squared up.

"That day I learnt that something very important – there is a gap between the bank and the customer. It's not like everybody defaults because they don't have money or they don't want to pay." But, when the bank sends a recovery agent to inform the customer, there is tremendous resistance. People take offence, and sometimes even claim harassment. But, Manju had a trick up her sleeve.

"I thought, why not employ more women as recovery agents. Because any office or home we go to, we get a lot of respect."

Manju started recruiting female candidates for Vasuli – young graduates and housewives. The cases being handled at that time were mainly personal loans. But, from 2004 onwards, Vasuli started working in agricultural areas. 'Recovery' now meant seizing of tractors and even JCBs.

"We used to go at 10 at night – all-ladies team – to seize these giant vehicles. JCB cannot be taken on road, so we had to take with us a trailer."

"People used to look down upon me. *Ki* she is ambitious, but doing something worthless."

While this may sound like a daring commando-like operation, it's a part of due process.

First the defaulter is intimated about his outstanding loan. If there is no response, he is warned – your tractor will be seized.

"Some come forward and pay some amount. They also promise to pay EMI regularly. Only when they ignore all requests and warnings for months together, we go and seize the asset."

Even a seizure requires careful planning. Such as a tie-up with a yard, to park the tractors. A driver to manoeuvre the JCB, and a videographer to capture the entire event on film. So that nobody can later claim that they were manhandled or threatened in any way.

"Of course, we also take the local police with us."

In this manner, the Vasuli team seized over 1000 tractors in Madhya Pradesh in a single year. But in 2005, the government came up with a debt-waiver scheme.

"We stopped this line of work completely and shifted to different line of business – seizing and auctioning of property."

The entire *vasuli* business is actually based on a path-breaking act passed by Parliament in the year 2002. The Surfacing Act empowers authorised bank officers and their agents to seize the property of defaulters. And auction it to recover dues.

"Now our focus shifted to the housing loans and default by corporates."

Now in expansion mode, Vasuli opened branch offices, first in Jaipur and Raipur, then in Mumbai. In fact, in 2007, the head office of Vasuli was shifted to Mumbai.

"All the decision-makers in PSU banks sit in Mumbai. We realised that we will get more business only if we have a set-up here."

The entire empanelment process is a lengthy one and the challenge actually begins with even getting a foot into the door.

Manju recalls her meetings with the DGM Recovery at Bank of India. He wasn't very positive about outsourcing the work to this unknown little company. Then, Manju played her trump card.

She said, "Sir, we have only lady recovery agents, we will ensure that your bank does not get a bad image. Trust us, sir, your money will also be recovered!"

The DGM agreed to give Vasuli two accounts, on a trial basis.

"I agreed to start with those two small cases and they were so happy with our work that today, we handle two lakh cases for the same bank!"

Patience and diplomacy are the only two weapons with which you can attack the PSU fortress.

"The CMD of the bank is ready to give you business, but a clerk is powerful enough to stop your work. *Aise* condition *mein kaam karna* is very difficult."

And it's not about offering bribes either. Manju claims that she has never used underhand methods, and never will.

"People have their own frustrations or beliefs. Like sometimes they don't want interference of outsiders. I work to build personal rapport and trust – *kaam ho jaata hai*."

And once work comes in, there is a system and process. Just like in the case of the personal loans and the tractors, the first step is issuing a notice. That is done by the bank. When there is no response, Vasuli is called in to 'take possession' of the property.

"In other words, everyone has to be thrown out."

Isn't it difficult to do that, at a human level? Manju admits to one incident, when she got emotionally involved.

"I had gone with my team to a residential flat at Borivali – I think the building was Golden Towers or Golden Heights. It was a two-

"Recovery is a difficult task because even if you take a toffee from a child, he resists! Imagine seizing a tractor."

"People think recovery agent means *gunde badmaash log*. That's not the case at all, we follow the law."

bedroom house with three generations staying there. One of the elderly persons there was paralysed."

A young girl of Manju's age started crying and said, "*Hamare saath cheating hua hai.* My father's business partner has ruined him."

The elderly paralysed man said, "*Beta*, if I was your grandfather, would you do this to me?"

Manju felt the family had a genuine problem and so she decided to tell the bank to give them more time. Hence she did not start the paperwork or other formalities of 'recovery'.

That same Manju got a call from the Borivali police station.

The officer said, "Madam, there is a complaint against you. You have verbally abused senior citizens, beaten and threatened them."

Manju was shocked.

"I understood that some advocate must have advised the family to file a false complaint. This was the last time that I felt 'sympathy' for the so-called victims."

The bank is a custodian of public money. If you take a loan and cannot pay it back, be prepared to face the consequences.

"We are professionals, just doing our job."

As always, the Vasuli team will take along a videographer and police constable. As well as an officer from the bank and a government-approved 'valuer', to decide what the property is worth.

"Our job is to lock it, seal it and ultimately arrange to auction it."

Since Vasuli is paid a commission only after the bank recovers its money, it also takes care of the sale process. The more the bidders for a property, the better the chances of a good price. The end result is often a win-win situation for all.

Manju recalls one property Vasuli had taken possession of for State Bank of India. A resort in Goa spread over 22 acres. The reserve price for this property was set at ₹ 38 crore.

"We advertised the auction all over the country, contacted all the large hotel chains. We had 12 participants in the auction and the property was eventually sold for ₹ 61.4 crore!"

Of course, not all auctions have such a fairytale ending but the overall quantum of recoveries handled by Vasuli is impressive. In the year 2011-12, the company handled cases worth ₹ 500 crore, on which it earned commissions of approximately ₹ 10 crore*.

"With NPAs like home loans of ₹ 10 lakh, we get a 5% commission. But when we auction assets worth, say, ₹ 30 crore, we may get 0.25% or .5%."

While some agencies refuse to handle small accounts, Vasuli never says 'no' to a client. And, that also makes sound business sense.

The advantage in small accounts is that the average borrower has the intention to pay.

"If the home loan is ₹ 5 lakh, the family will put together ₹ 2 lakh and the case gets closed quickly, we get our commission."

But with 'white collar' defaulters – owners of factories, in particular – the case goes to court and drags on for years.

"The corporates hire expensive lawyers and get a stay order from the court. Then we have to go to the High Court and so on."

So the account is 'big' in size, but when will the auction take place and when will the commission come in, is hard to say. After all, cash flow is vital to any company, and more so, a growing one.

> **"80% cases there is a compromise, meaning, the bank agrees to a settlement less than the full amount."**

* Profit margin in the business is approximately 30%.

"*Mujhe aisa lagta hai ki* family can either be a support structure or a liability. It is up to you how you handle it."

From an eight-man operation based in Indore, with billing of ₹ 25,000 per month and a single client, Vasuli has galloped into a much bigger league. In ten short years.

"We now work with 20 banks through 26 branch offices all over India. And we have 250 agents on payroll."

All the agents are ladies who can speak the local language. The branch head is also a lady, but one of the star performers from one of the two main offices – Mumbai or Indore. Agents are given good salaries, starting at ₹ 25,000 per month. But that's not their only motivation to work.

"You see, in the normal, routine life of a lady, she is not given much say in decisions, even in the home. Here, they have full opportunity and liberty to participate and to use their authority. *Unko accha lagta hai* that someone is giving us so much responsibility."

One such example is Manju's own mother, who was once a housewife. She is now a director in the company, travelling around the country handling tough cases. A woman transformed.

"Actually we have only two gents at Vasuli – one is of course Mr Parag Shah. Second is my father, who has left his business and joined us. He takes care of Karnataka and Tamil Nadu."

With the geographical spread, the complexity of operations has increased. Vasuli now has an online case entry and billing system which makes tracking easier.

"We built the MIS in-house," adds Manju. "That is Parag's contribution. The main 'brain' is his, I am the one who executes everything."

Manju's main focus is on business development. She travels 15 days a month, spends much of her time at bank headquarters in South Mumbai and Bandra Kurla complex.

"I hardly come to office," she says.

It's been quite an adventure so far – what next? So far, Vasuli hasn't taken a single paisa of outside investment, not even a bank overdraft.

"We do have a working capital from State Bank of India, who are our biggest client. But the main thing is we have invested whatever we earned back into the company."

The dream is to transform Vasuli from a recovery agency to an 'asset reconstruction' company. How and when it is going to happen, it's hard to say.

"We are busy with the day-to-day operations," admits Manju.

To get into the next league, Vasuli needs a strong senior management team. And sometimes, it means accepting private equity funding, which Parag and Manju have resisted so far.

Work seems to consume Manju completely, at present. The only thing she has time for, apart from Vasuli, is pursuing her PhD in Law. But what about the future, aren't her parents hinting it's time to 'settle down'?

"No," she laughs. "They know I can take care of myself."

Marriage is not in Manju's mind at all… for the next couple of years.

"I'm 26 right now. When I'm 28-29, then I will see. Of course I want a family, there is no doubt about it. But a little later."

Manju would like to marry a very successful person, and more importantly, a very committed individual. A man who is respectful of her desires, her dreams.

"If I am marrying then my husband has to accept my work. That's very clear. Even if I have kids, I will never give this up. *Jab tak main hoon, yahin hoon*."

Clarity of mind.

Clarity of purpose.

Like the sun, which must rise every day and shine.

Know what you want and that you are born to shine.

Every moment, every day, every year.

ADVICE TO WOMEN ENTREPRENEURS

Whatever the job, no job is too small or too big.

You should have the drive to do something in life and not just sit at home and become a machine to lay eggs, I mean, produce children.

I think all women should be very career-focused and should be not equal, but far ahead of men.

Work hard and be patient, success will follow. A sincere effort will never go waste, *iss liye lage raho, lage raho.*

WORK IS WORSHIP

Rajni Bector, Cremica

Married into a very well-to-do family of Ludhiana, Rajni enjoyed baking cakes and making ice cream. The small business she started in her home kitchen is now a ₹ 650 crore food empire managed by her three sons.

Rajni Bector lives in a magnificent house in Ludhiana's posh Civil Lines area.

I notice the lawn – it is bigger than most public parks in Mumbai.

The doorbell is rung, a servant answers. I enter, slip off my shoes and right there, the first thing the eye falls on is a beautiful black and white photograph of Sri Aurobindo's 'Mother'.

Love, grace, beauty and compassion shine through her eyes.

Illuminating this home.

A home where a housewife created a small miracle.

From a love of cooking, from her *ghar ka* kitchen, Rajni began a small business, 35 years ago.

She didn't have to do it.

Married into a very well-to-do family, money was never an issue. In fact, she need not have entered the kitchen at all, for that was managed by servants.

It was only out of love, out of passion, out of an urge to share herself that Rajni got into business. She simply could not sit idle and 'enjoy life'.

"I am a follower of The Mother.... She always said 'work is worship' and that has been my motto in life."

The result of this devotion is a company which has grown from a tiny acorn. Into a giant oak.

Today, Cremica is a ₹ 650 crore company in which the entire Bector family is involved.

"My three sons completed their studies and joined Cremica. Within 10-15 years, the company grew tremendously."

Give all you have, this is the beginning.

Give all you do, this is the way.

Give all you are, this is the fulfillment.

The words of The Mother to a mother.

And the seas parted, the heavens moved.

WORK IS WORSHIP

Rajni Bector, Cremica

Rajni Bector was born in Karachi, but spent her early years in Lahore.

"My father was a government servant holding a very high position, but then there was Partition."

The family moved to Delhi where Rajni completed her schooling and then joined Miranda House. In 1957, when she was barely 17, Rajni got married into a business family in Ludhiana. A family very different from the 'service' class family she grew up in but still, a broad-minded one.

"I completed my graduation after marriage," she recalls.

Rajni then got busy raising her three sons. In time, all three went to boarding school in Mussoorie, leaving Rajni with an empty nest. And a lot of free time.

"I was very involved with social service projects through the Lions Club. In fact I started the Lioness movement in Punjab and then helped to open the clubs all over north India."

Rajni also worked with the Red Cross and headed the Ludhiana Ladies' Club, which was *the* club to belong to in the city.

"Ludhiana is a small town.
Ladies ka kaam karna bahut bandha hota hai…
and more so in well-to-do families."
(Ladies are restricted from working.)

"Initially I worked as the Secretary, then I was President for two years, then they created a special post of Chairperson so that I could keep contributing."

So much was the energy and enthusiasm Rajni brought in. To whatever she did.

"Still… I felt, I am not doing something very constructive…" she recalls.

The idea of a woman from a well-to-do family 'working' was unheard of. So what more *could* she do?

"I was very fond of cooking. So I enrolled for a course in baking at the Punjab Agricultural University."

And she would keep creating occasions to try out her recipes.

"I used to call people over for lunches and evening teas and dinners. And to the little ones I would say, 'Come over for swimming' and bake them some treats."

Rajni's ice creams, cakes and cookies quickly became the talk of the town.

It was so good, friends would say "You can make a business out of it!"

So just for fun, Rajni did just that. Using a hand-churner she started making different kinds of ice cream and putting up stalls at local fetes and funfairs.

"I remember my first stall was right next to Kwality. I was scared but surprisingly my ice cream was a hit."

In fact, there was such a crowd at her stall that even the Kwality manager came over to taste her ice cream!

"I got a very good response and then people said – 'can you do catering?'"

And so it became a 'business'. Operating from her home kitchen, with one small oven and an initial investment of ₹ 300. Word spread and orders for parties and functions kept pouring in. Sometimes Rajni would refuse but they wouldn't take 'no' for an answer.

They said, "*Mainu kuch nahin pata... hamara order to lena hi padega*."

Rajni recalls one such early order – for 2000 puddings – at the wedding hosted by the local MP.

"It seemed impossible but somehow I did it. I cannot forget how everybody was coming and appreciating me."

Rajni worked with heart and soul, but neglected the 'head' part. She ended up selling below cost price, and incurred a loss. That's when her husband Dharamvir stepped in with the right advice.

"You are working very hard but you need to see this as a *business*," he said. "You must expand, commercialise, do everything properly."

Thus in 1978, with an investment of ₹ 20,000, Rajni set up a small ice-cream manufacturing unit in the backyard of the *kothi*. Now, she could take bigger orders – for marriage parties. And although she could hire helpers, Rajni preferred to do almost everything herself.

"I never believed anyone else can do the job as well as me. So I used to get up early in the morning, sleep late at night.... I used to work much more than 12 hours a day!"

But there was one golden rule – when the children were at home, they should feel their mother's presence.

"I was very particular... I have to be there with them for every meal, for their studies, whenever they want me."

In 1983, Rajni formally registered the business.

Her husband called one afternoon said, "Tell me the name you want to register."

"I used to do everything on my own...
I used to work for hours and hours.
12 hours was very less for me!"

"*Family neglect kar ke main apna kaam kar rahi hoon*, that was not possible. Children always came first."

Rajni wanted some time to think about it.

He replied, "No... I can't wait... the person has to go *today* and register the name."

The name that came to Rajni's mind was 'Cremica'. Inspired by 'cream' which she used in so many recipes. And that's how a company was born.

Soon, Rajni diversified into making bread. The response was so good that she decided to set up a bread-making automatic unit with the help of her husband.

"We had a place at G T Road, so we started a unit there. Then, we went to Phillaur, we started making biscuits..."

Rajni is a bit hazy about exactly *how* it all happened. The important thing is that it did, and it was successful.

"Equipment came from Delhi, we took a loan from HDFC. But you know it was not all that planned."

Giant ovens were installed in a shed-like building, and production started. With increase in production, a marketing team had to be set up. The most important thing, which Rajni personally monitored, was the quality.

"Naturally we want to do it the better way, *na?* I looked into every detail."

Should the bread contain more milk? How much fat content should be in that milk? Small things which make a big difference in taste.

"I never used to compromise on the ingredients.... So people started saying – what Cremica can make even Britannia and Parle cannot make!"

1990 was a turning point. Terrorism was still flourishing in Punjab and there was a lot of tension between Hindu traders and Sikh farmers. The Bectors' 107-year-old business in trading food grains, oil and fertiliser was badly affected.

"There was an attempt to kidnap our eldest son – Ajay. Then we thought, maybe this business is not our cup of tea and slowly we wound it up."

By this time, Cremica was a respectable ₹ 5 crore business. The family decided to put all its eggs into this new oven and bake a bigger cake. Rajni's eldest son joined soon after graduation, followed by her middle son Akshay who completed engineering from Manipal. The youngest – Anoop – was preparing for his CA, but left it midway.

"He said, 'Why waste time on qualifications – let me join the business and grow it'."

Do se chaar, aur chaar se aath haath – business badta gaya family members ke saath.

With the involvement of her husband and sons, the passion-led business started by Rajni turned ambitious and professional. The business grew phenomenally, touching a turnover of ₹ 20 crore.

At the same time there came a new and very big opportunity. In 1995, McDonald's decided to enter India and was scouting around for local suppliers.

The company zeroed in on Cremica, for supply of buns.

"We did a lot of trials initially, but we were not getting the proper result. I remember we must have wasted thousands of kilos of buns trying to create the 'perfect bun'."

The East Balt Commissary in Chicago are the 'original' bun-makers for the McDonald's franchise – since the times of Ray Kroc. Their expert bakers were flown in to train the Cremica staff on the secret behind that soft sesame-seed bun.

"Our is a business family and my husband encouraged me. He said, 'If you want to do something big you will have to expand... bring in new machinery and new methods'."

"Instead of two hands if four hands are working... it makes the difference. So it is good if family members join your business."

However, American techniques did not work with Indian wheat, which has low gluten content. Ultimately, a whole new process had to be improvised.

With the partnership working out well, McDonald's threw another challenge to the young company.

"Can you make batter and breadings for us?"

Cremica tied up with UK-based EBI foods to manufacture international-quality breadcrumbs (used to coat burger patties). McDonald's was pleased and wanted more.

"Can you supply us with tomato sauce?"

A 50:50 joint venture with Quaker Oats USA followed, to set up a sauce plant. Apart from tomato ketchup, chilli sauce and mustard sauce, Cremica also supplies 'vegetarian' (eggless) mayonnaise to McDonald's. A uniquely Indian concept.

"McDonald's standards are very tough. Every month samples are sent to Hong Kong for testing and grading. We also have our own testing labs at every factory."

Keeping high standards is a hard thing. But it also makes it easy to get more business, especially from multinationals. Cremica's factory in Phillaur began making the biscuits sold by Cadbury's and ITC Sunfeast.

"We also sell biscuits, sauces and condiments under our own brand name – Mrs Bector's Cremica foods."

The scale and size of the business grew rapidly. By 2006, Cremica was clocking revenues of ₹ 100 crore, with 30% year-on-year growth. Goldman Sachs took a 10% stake, for ₹ 50 crore. The funds were used to further energise and expand the business.

"We now have a unit in Greater Noida and in Bombay. All very modern, fully automated plants."

Another new plant with a capacity of 5000 tons per month was recently installed at Una in Himachal Pradesh. In 2011-12, Cremica crossed annual sales of ₹ 650 crore. The company now employs over 4000 people across locations.

With highly skilled professionals in all important functions.

"To be frank… I am almost retired now," says Rajni. "The children are managing the business very well."

However there is one thing she still looks into personally – new products and new recipes. After all, taste and quality are the two pillars Cremica stands on.

"I am most involved in the biscuits and bakery section. I am still there to see what we are making, how we are making, let us experiment something – can we do it better!"

At 71, Rajni has some health issues – such as a back problem – which she takes in her stride.

"I never bothered about myself at all…. There were so many days I used to sleep 3-4 hours only. I was balancing all my relations… all my family… work… everything…"

The result has been phenomenal. And so has the recognition. Awards from the government and industry bodies have come raining down on Rajni.

"I have got so many awards that I have lost count," she smiles.

Though she does remember fondly the one she received from the President of India, Abdul Kalam, in 2005.

Abdul Kalam said, "Oh… so you are the ice cream lady, *na?*"

No matter how big Cremica gets, that is how Rajni will always be remembered.

The lady who stepped into her kitchen yet stepped out of the boundary.

Because evolution *is* revolution.

And it can quietly start, wherever you are.

ADVICE TO WOMEN ENTREPRENEURS

You must work but you must also give priority to your family. It is better to start once your children are a bit grown up and can handle themselves.

Divide your time between children, family and work. Try to work in the hours when your children are in school or late night/ early morning. Of course, you need to be a very motivated and hardworking person.

Take help from family members. I always took help and advice from my husband in business matters.

Run the business professionally. In the food line, you have to be very particular about ingredients – whatever business you do, never compromise on quality.

Dharamvir Singh (husband):

Men should always co-operate and encourage the talent of ladies and not be jealous. In fact, encouragement of the whole family is required.

I remember Rajni working at midnight, at times even 2 am. I admire her talent and her dedication. That's why we wanted that her name should always be in the forefront.

I also believe that when one works hard and has good intentions, blessings come to you. With Cremica, some super power is working somewhere… I am sure of that.

HUM SAATH SAATH HAIN

(We're all in it together)

Nirmala Kandalgaonkar,
Vivam Agrotech

A housewife in a small town, Nirmala decided to 'do something' when her children grew up. Combining her background in science and social work, she entered and found success in the unusual business of vermicomposting.

Gururaj Deshpande has just finished his inaugural address at the annual TiE Conference in Nagpur. The next speaker is Nirmala Kandalgaonkar.

"*Waise maike ki main Deshpande hoon* (my maiden name is Deshpande)," are her first words, addressing one of the most successful serial entrepreneurs in the world.

Nirmala proceeds to give a thirty-minute presentation in Marathi, the language she is most comfortable in. She explains the intricacies of vermicomposting and biogas, with confident command over her subject. And the passion of an entrepreneur who truly believes.

That her idea can change the world.

Nirmala started this unusual business ten years ago, at the unusual age of 50.

"*Bachche bade ho gaye toh maine socha ki ab main kuch karoon!*" (With the kids all grown up, I decided it was time to do something.)

Not the usual small business ventures ladies get into – like making *achaar* and *papad* – but something different, something of benefit to rural India. Where she was born and brought up, and had experience of social work.

"*Bachpan se hi mera sapna tha ki Marathwada region jo itna backward hai, uske liye mujhe kuch karna chahiye*." (It was my childhood dream to do something for people of Marathwada, where I was born, because it is so backward.)

Nirmala is educated, but not sophisticated. With her synthetic sari, large red *bindi*, *mangalsutra* and slightly dishevelled hair, she reminds me of the countless middle class working women you see in Mumbai's local trains. The kind who wake up early, complete all household chores, put in a full day's work and commute.

And still find the energy to look after the family, when they get home.

Because family is the *source* of all energy.

It is the foundation of existence, a bedrock of support.

If we're all in it together, we *can* conquer the world.

HUM SAATH SAATH HAIN

(We're all in it together)

Nirmala Kandalgaonkar, Vivam Agrotech

Nirmala was born in Mhalakoli village of Hingoli district in Maharashtra.

"*Chhote se gaon mein mera janam hua hai*... (I was born in a small village). Both my parents were teachers."

It was a big family, a joint family. But education was a priority for both the boys and the girls.

"School *ke baad,* I went to Aurangabad for higher education."

Nirmala did her BSc in Biology and then took up a job as a social worker. She worked with an organisation known as Akhil Bhartiya Vidyarthi Parishad. There, she met her husband Girish.

"Unki mataji meri teacher thi (His mother used to be my teacher). We liked each other; he proposed and I accepted."

The year was 1978. The couple was quickly blessed with a son – Nilesh – In 1979. Daughter Neha was born in 1984, while the youngest – Kaivalya – came in 1986.

Like most young mothers, Nirmala was fully occupied, raising the family.

"We decided that I should not work, *bachchon ki parvarish acchhi honi chahiye* (so children can be brought up properly)."

Girish was in 'service', working with a company called Bemco Sleepers, which manufactured railway sleepers.

The Kandalgaonkars were a typical small-town middle class family, until one day Nirmala decided it was time for her to 'do something'.

"Vo aise shuru hua ki bachche padh likhkar bade ho gaye. Bade ho gaye bachche toh phir unki jimmedari utni nahi rahi mere upar." (It happened like this, that the kids grew up and one day I realised they don't need me as much as before.)

"Toh phir maine socha ki kuch accha kaam karoon." (So I thought, let me do something now, something useful, something good.)

The question was – what? Nirmala's only experience was with social work, which involved going from village to village spreading awareness among women on various issues.

"I decided I must do something for the villages only. And whatever I manufacture and sell, it should create a positive effect, a ripple effect."

At the time, Girish was posted at the factory, which happened to be in a rural area. Thus it was easy to observe and understand the lifestyle of the farmers, and their problems. Clearly, the biggest problem they faced was economic viability.

"*Humne dekha ki zyadatar farmers ka business loss mein ja raha hai.*" (We could see that most of the farmers barely made any profit.)

The main reason was that they had to invest a lot of money in buying seeds and chemical fertilisers. In addition, the farmer sweats and toils in the field. But, cannot decide the price at which to sell his crop. That price is fixed by the government.

Nirmala proposed to change this equation, through the use of vermicompost.

"Traditional method *mein kisan khud apni khaad banate the. Lekin modern zamane ke naam se yeh sab chhod diya.*" (Traditionally farmers made their own manure. But to be modern they stopped doing that.)

The idea was simple: to make natural manure fashionable again. And the first step towards that was studying techniques that had been passed on from generation to generation.

"Traditional method *hai zameen mein ek gaddha khod dete hai. Usme sab waste daal dete hain aur kechven chhod dete hain*." (Traditionally one makes a pit in the ground.The pit is filled with waste material and earthworms are let loose in it.)

The method works, but it's not very scientific. You don't know how many earthworms you should ideally use. And how much manure can you expect, or when it will be ready for use.

Using her science background and a large pinch of common sense, Nirmala began conducting 'experiments'.

"To measure results I needed a controlled environment. Hence, instead of a hole in the ground, I devised a metal box or 'cage'."

Through trial and error, Nirmala gradually learnt the ins and outs of earthworm excretion. The optimal temperature and soil conditions required to produce good quality and quantity of organic manure.

"*Is kaam mein poora ek saal lag gaya*..." she grins. (This process took an entire year.)

Girish chipped in with his technical skill. The manure-making 'system' is a box with steel sections and chain link mesh. The bigger challenge was portability.

"We quickly realised that the box had to be lightweight and folding."

Nirmala provided the ideas, Girish the engineering. Initially, the boxes were fabricated in a nearby workshop.

"Our initial investment was ₹ 20-25,000," says Girish. "We have a small piece of land in a village nearby so first of all we tried making the manure over there."

The experiment was successful, and word spread.

"*Aaju baaju ke log aakar kehne lagey, hamein bhi chahiye*." (Farmers from around the village came and said we want to have this too.)

So Nirmala manufactured a few pieces and sold them at cost price. It was a test-marketing phase of sorts.

"*Product theek hai, chal raha hai, logon ko pasand hai Mera confidence badh gaya*." (The product is okay, it works, people like it. My confidence grew.)

"Karodon ka turnover hona chahiye, aisa mere dhyan mein hi nahi tha. Bas yeh tha ki jo karungi, kuch alag karungi."

(I never had dreams of doing turnover of crores, only that whatever I do it will be something with a difference.)

As did the demand. Finally, Nirmala decided it was time to go commercial. A sole proprietorship by the name 'Vivam Agrotech' was thus born on 5 June 2001.

The business, however, was more of 'concept' selling, of convincing people about the benefits of organic manure.

"People did not know that they could make *khaad* (manure) themselves, and what are the benefits. *Pehle unka mind taiyyar karna padta hai, unka man jeetna padta tha,"* recalls Nirmala. (First I had to prepare their minds and then win their hearts.)

Farmers were given demonstrations. Invited to touch and feel the vermicompost. And, of course, given free samples.

"I used to hand out small-small packets of vermicompost and ask them to use it in a small pot, and see the result."

Many would come back and relate miraculous tales.

"I used this *khaad* in the tulsi plant in my home. Within three days the colour of the leaves became greener!"

The trick was to sell *one* unit in a village. But to do this, one had to do continuous demos across the countryside. That never fazed Nirmala, after all, she'd done exactly the same kind of thing as a social worker.

"*Mera kaam tha gaon gaon jaakar sharaab aur gutke ki aadat ko chhudvaana.*" (My job was to go from village to village, spreading awareness about the ill effects of *gutka*.)

It was therefore relatively easy for Nirmala to win their trust. What's more, Vivam Agrotech provided 'full service'. Each unit came as a 'set': 200-cubic-foot box, earthworms, free transport and installation, as well as training at the customer's residence.

"We had to educate the customer to be patient," adds Nirmala. "*Khaad taiyyar karne mein do-teen mahine lagte hai.*" (It takes 2-3 months to prepare manure.)

The price of each set was ₹ 20,000, a considerable sum for rural India. Bank loans were not easily available, but Nirmala worked out a system of installments.

"We never had repayment problem. *Log acche the* (people were good,) *kabhi dhokha nahi diya* (no one cheated me)."

The fact is, the vermicomposting system quickly paid for itself. The cost of 1 ton of chemical fertiliser was ₹ 3000 at the time. The farmer using Nirmala's system could expect a yield of 8-9 tons of manure in the first year itself. A clear 'profit' of ₹ 4-7,000 on his initial investment.

Despite these obvious benefits, sales moved at snail's pace.

"In the first year, I managed to sell 3 units, *woh bhi badi mushkil se* (with great difficulty)," she says, breaking into a big-toothed smile. "*Mera poore saal ka turnover tha chaalis hazaar.*" (My entire year's turnover was ₹ 40,000.)

Things improved in the second year, with word-of-mouth publicity bringing in customer. Around 25 units were sold, yielding revenues of close to ₹ 5 lakh.

"*Aur phir ye aisa badhate hi gaya.*" (And like that, it kept growing.)

Yet, the company had only one 'employee' apart from Nirmala herself. The business did not *need* manpower as such.

It needed willpower and boldness. Which Nirmala had plenty of.

In 2002, she happened to go to Delhi, accompanying Girish on a business trip. On a whim, Nirmala decided to pay a visit to the Ministry of Agriculture. She walked in – without any contact or appointment – and managed to meet a senior IAS officer – Vandana Dwivedi.

"*Ladies hain to maine socha baat kar leti hoon* (She was a lady, so I got the courage to approach her). I told her about my product, and what I do. *Bas utna hi* (That was about it)."

Three days later, Nirmala got a pleasant surprise. A fax from Vandana Dwivedi, appreciating Nirmala's work. And offering her a stall, free of cost, in the Agriculture Pavilion at Pragati Maidan's international trade fair (14-27 November 2002).

> ***"Biogas mein ek akeli mahila hoon. Mujhe kehna bhi bohot garv hota hai ki all India mein kachre se electricity banane ka kaam kisi mahila ne nahi kiya hai."***
>
> **(I am the only woman in the field of biogas. It gives me a lot of pride.)**

"I had never been to Pragati Maidan, never participated in an exhibition," she laughs.

But Nirmala seized the opportunity with both hands. She roped in Girish and daughter Neha to help out and made the most of the experience.

"Much later I learnt that other companies had paid more than a lakh of rupees to be there."

Numerous enquiries were generated at the exhibition, from all over India. Vivam Agrotech also came into the *sarkaari* (government) radar. Organic farming was an idea that government agencies were trying to promote, hence in year 2004, farmers buying Vivam Agrotech's vermicompost system were given a special subsidy.

"This brought the price from ₹ 20,000 to ₹ 15,000 for the customer," explains Girish. "The government paid us the difference of ₹ 5000."

The reason for the support to Vivam was its scientific method. Earthworms have a tendency to migrate – the mesh system takes care of that problem. They are also known to 'drown' in excess water, reducing output of *khaad* in the traditional method.

"Another practical advantage of Vivam's sytem is *ki baithke kaam karne ki zaroorat nahi hai* (you don't have to sit down and work). It is built to be used while standing."

Understanding the pain points of the customer is what elevates a product from good to great. And makes it *work.*

Word of mouth continued to be the main marketing method for Vivam. But instead of going from village to village, Nirmala started attending local agriculture exhibitions. Where stalls were available at reasonable rates. Girish often travelled with Nirmala for exhibitions, especially on weekends and holidays.

"*Wahan pe kya problem aate hai, kya nahi... thodasa guide karne ke liye.*" (What problems and issues can come up, just to guide her a little, that's all.)

Quiet, continuous moral support.

In 2004, Girish was transferred back to the city office. Living in Aurangabad, Nirmala got enquiries from owners of bungalows. Could the system work for their gardens?

"*Kyun nahin*! (Why not)," said Nirmala.

She modified the vermicomposting system, made it smaller in size.

"I also made a more compact model to fit into window-sills of flats," she adds.

Urban sales added zing to the bottom-line. By 2005, Vivam Agrotech had notched up sales of ₹ 20 lakh per annum. The company also employed a team of five responsible for installation and training, travelling wherever required.

More business and employees also meant more working capital. For the first time, Nirmala approached the bank.

"We had invested ₹ 3 lakh of our own savings by then and *kaam chal raha tha* (work was going on)," says Girish. "But now we had to take it to the next level."

That next level included expanding into new areas, like municipal waste disposal management. Making good use of wet garbage – or kitchen waste.

"*Hamare dyaan mein aaye ki vermicompost ke saath hum biogas generation bhi kar sakte hain,*" says Nirmala. (We realised that along with vermicompost we can get into biogas generation.)

While *gobar* gas was commonly used in rural areas, biogas from kitchen waste was a new concept altogether. Vivam Agrotech devised a mini biogas 'plant' which could be installed on the terrace – like a Sintex tank. The experiment began with the building where Nirmala and Girish were themselves living.

"*Hua yeh ki kachra daalne ke liye bahut door jana padta tha* (We had to go very far to dispose of our garbage). So it became convenient for society members to just go to the terrace and deposit their kitchen waste in the biogas unit."

"Humare ghar mein khana bananawali dusri koi nahi aati hai. Main hi banati hoon. Toh speed mein karna hai, pura karke phir 8-10 ghante Vivam ke kaam mein active rehna hai."

(I don't have a cook, everything I do myself. I work with speed knowing I have to finish and put in 8-10 hours of work in my business.)

Again, it was an adaptation of the traditional method. But smaller in size and more efficient.

Of course, it was a small society so hardly 2-3 kg of waste were generated per day. Producing enough biogas for just a single family's use. But bigger the society, more the potential benefit. Vivam began marketing the concept to housing societies.

"*Aapko pata nahin chalega ki biogas hai ya LPG. Koi badbu nahin aati,*" beams Nirmala. (You can't tell the difference between biogas and LPG. There is no foul smell.)

By and by, the scale and scope of work was increasing. In 2006, Girish decided to quit his job and decided to become a consultant for concrete products.

"I had more time on my hand so I also got more involved with Vivam."

The biogas idea got the Aurangabad Municipal Corporation excited. Can it be done on a bigger scale? The answer was yes, there must be some technology which could be adopted. Nirmala and Girish came to the Bhabha Atomic Research Centre (BARC) in search of that Holy Grail.

"BARC *ke paas techonolgy toh thi magar wo implement nahin kar sakte the*," she says. (BARC had the technology but could not implement it.)

A three-way partnership was quickly hammered out. Using BARC's knowhow, Vivam proposed to the corporation a biogas plant serving an entire ward. One ward generates 2-3 tons of kitchen waste per day. Taking this waste 20-25 km outside the city and disposing it is expensive and time-consuming.

Biogas was a beautiful – and urgently required – solution. Vivam's first biogas plant came up in Chandrapur in the year 2006.

The Chandrapur facility was designed to handle 1.5 tons (1500 kg) of waste per day. The problem, however, was that residents refused to segregate their dry and wet garbage.

"*Humne phir SHG* (Self Help Group) *ki madad se segregation ka kaam karwaya.*" (We trained an SHG or Self Help Group to segregate the waste after it came to the biogas plant.)

The biogas generated was provided to a ladies' hostel nearby. The project outlay was ₹ 12 lakh, including installation and training. The cost was borne by the municipal corporation.

With these kind of bigger projects under its belt, Vivam's revenues jumped. By 2009, the company's annual turnover had gone up to ₹ 90 lakh.

"We have installed 15 large-scale plants for various corporations," says Girish.

The biggest project is in Kondhwa in Pune where biogas is used to power 300 streetlights! A similar power generation project has also been set up by Vivam in a village near Chiplun, in Ratnagiri district of Maharashtra.

"BARC *ke jo Chairman hain*, Anil Kakodkar, *unhone khud inaugurate kiya*," says Nirmala proudly. (The Chairman of BARC, Anil Kakodkar, came to inaugurate the plant.)

Biogas now constitutes 70% of Vivam's business. Now, Nirmala has a 15-strong civil construction team handling on-site work and training and maintenance. Employees are on contract basis while labour is hired locally, on daily wages.

Bigger contracts are coming in the vermicompost business as well.

"European countries are very particular, they do not want any fruits or vegetables grown with chemical fertiliser," says Girish. "So we have set up large projects for exporters, generating up to 100 tons of compost a month."

In 2006, older son Nilesh joined the business, along with sister Neha. Vivam now has multiple offices – one in Aurangabad, another in Pune and a third in Mumbai, where youngest son Kaivalya is studying. However Aurangabad continued to be the manufacturing base.

"Swimming karti hoon, driving karti hoon, yoga karti hoon. Mentally aur physically acchi rehti hoon toh bachche bhi khush rehte hai."

(I swim, I drive, I practise yoga. When I am mentally and physically fit my family is also happy.)

Vivam is now appointing agents on commission basis, to market and sell its vermicomposting units, under the brand name 'Swaroop'.

"I think the future lies in large-scale mechanised composting," says Girish. "Then, we can handle hundreds of tons of mixed waste per day!"

However such projects require large investment outlay. Banks have not been very forthcoming. Vivam currently enjoys an overdraft limit of ₹ 15 lakh from State Bank of India, but it is against a small flat the family owns in Aurangabad.

"*Humein work order ke against OD chahiye*," sighs Nirmala. (We would ideally like overdraft against work orders.)

Until then, Vivam raises money – as and when required – from informal sources.

"Like recently, we made a bid for a mega project with the Pandharpur Municipal Council worth ₹ 2.5 crore," says Girish. "We managed to raise private finance."

Vivam's requirement, essentially, is working capital. Profit margin in the business is relatively low, at 10-15%. Payments are often delayed – a hazard of working with government agencies.

Another 'necessary evil' is *chai-paani.*

"Dena padta hai..." admits Nirmala. (We have to give commissions to government officials.)

Though many hesitate to 'ask' a lady outright and simply dilly-dally and don't pass work orders.

Yet, overall, Nirmala sees a bright future for this baby. With environmental issues gaining more attention, waste management is expected to see phenomenal growth.

"*Do-chaar saal aur lag sakte hain par aage scope bahut hai*," admits Nirmala. (It might take 3-4 years but there is a lot of scope.)

Vivam's annual turnover is now nudging ₹ 1 crore, with modest profits of ₹ 12 lakh. The company recently instituted a tie-up with Ayurvet, a subsidiary of Dabur, for marketing of its products. What's more, Nirmala has converted her sole proprietorship into a 'private limited' company.

A signal that this is a serious business, a professional business. Which can and must attract talent.

"Mr Prasad Dahapute has recently joined us. He has vast experience in finance and power projects... So hereafter I am confident finance won't be so much of a problem for us," grins Nirmala.

The next generation is also raring to carry the company forward on its able shoulders. In fact, younger son Kaivalya took up MBA in Finance with the objective of understanding and applying what he learns at Vivam.

"*Usne dekha hai ki dus saal mein Maa ki kitni bhag-daud ho rahi hai paise ke liye*," grins Nirmala. (He saw how much I had to run around over the last ten years, to raise money for the business.)

Just a statement of fact, not a complaint. Running around is something Nirmala accepts as part and parcel of her life. *Aakhir life ki saari responsibilities poori karni hain.* (All of life's responsibilities must be taken care of.)

"*Savere saade chaar baje se raat gyarah baje tak main khadi rehti hoon... karna padta hai, koi badi baat nahin hai*." (From 4.30 in the morning to 11 in the night I am on my feet... one has to do it... it's no big deal.)

Very first thing in the morning, Nirmala takes out an hour for yoga and pranayama. Then, she goes about preparing meals – both breakfast and lunch.

"*Dus baje tak sab complete karke phir business ka kaam shuru ho jata tha. Aur maine office ghar mein hi rakha tha*." (By ten I used to be done with the housework and ready for business. I kept my office in the home itself.)

Sounds good, but what about the postman, dhobi, *aaju baaju se* neighbours. Is it really that easy to switch out of 'housewife' mode?

"*Inka accha co-operation tha. Bachchon ka bhi bohot accha co-operation tha.Voh kuch takrar karte hi nahi the. Unko aisa lagta tha ki mummy jo kar rahi hai voh accha kar rahi hai.*"

(My husband co-operated, my kids co-operated. There were never any conflicts, always they felt our mother is doing something good.)

"*Woh sahi baat hai magar atmosphere create karna padta hai*." (It is a problem but one has to create the right atmosphere, and have self-discipline.)

The work Nirmala has chosen involves travelling. And she has absolutely no problem with that.

"*Mere paas gaadi thi – Omni van. Khud chala kar main gaon gaon jaati thi*." (I had a vehicle – an Omni van. I used to drive it myself from village to village.)

At times, she returned as late as 11 in the night.

"*Woh din main do samay ka khana banake chali jati thi. Bachche so jate the!*" she says matter of factly. (On such days I would make both lunch and dinner before leaving. Children would go to sleep.)

And the family co-operated fully. No typical Indian expectation of hot chapattis on the table. Nor any *kit-kit* from the extended family about 'neglecting' home and hearth.

"*Understanding hamara accha tha. Meri saasuji ka bhi aur meri mummy ka bhi hai*." (We had a good understanding. My mother-in-law and my mother also were understanding.)

Girish smiles benignly.

"*Support to dena hi chahiye. Thoda financial support, thoda ghar mein. Nahin to aagey nahin badh payengi*." (One must support one's spouse. Some financial support, some with respect to home duties. Otherwise she will not be able to get ahead in life.)

Which is a problem in itself for the Average Indian Husband. A wife who is 'better known' for her achievements than he is...

"*Jab maine kaam shuru kiya to inko accha laga. Jab mera naam hua inko aur accha laga.*" (When I started my work he was happy for me. When I became known for my work he was even more happy.)

The understanding and encouragement goes back a long way. After Nilesh was born, it was Girish who forced her to learn to drive a car. It follows, then, that he holds the fort for Nirmala at a family wedding, while she is in Mumbai to attend an event honouring women entrepreneurs.

"*Rishtedaaron ko thoda bura laga to sahi ki baahar ke program ko ghar ke program se zyada importance de rahi hoon.*" (Relatives felt a bit upset that I am giving more importance to a program outside the home instead of a family function.)

But when Nirmala actually won the Stree Shakti Puruskar from TiE, all was forgiven. And it was Girish who kept the 1 lakh rupee cheque in his pocket. To display with pride, to friends and family.

"*Tees saal mein kabhi jhagda bhi kabhi nahi hua hai na... dono ko beech mein*," says Nirmala shyly.

I ask Girish what it was about Nirmala that attracted him to propose to her in the first place.

"*Inka jo svabhaav hai, rakh rakhaav hai...* it is very different. *Sab ke liye accha karna chahti hain, sab ko khush rakhna... Aur talented bhi hain. To yeh sab mujhe bahut accha laga.*" (Her nature, her way of dealing with people is very different. She always wants to do something for others, keep everyone happy. And she is so talented also. I liked all these qualities.)

Nirmala gently teases him, "*Accha hua aapne poochcha... itne saal to mujhe kabhi nahin bataya.*" (Thank you for asking him all these years he never told me this.)

Everything need not be *said.*

When it is understood, at a deeper level.

Everything need not be a struggle.

When you're in it together, in heart, in mind, in spirit.

ADVICE TO WOMEN ENTREPRENEURS

Kuch na kuch karna chahiye. Social work karo ya business karo, ya ghar se kuch karo ya padhaai karo. (Women must do something beyond normal household duties – whether it is social work, business, home-based enterprise or higher studies.)

Samay nikalna chahiye aur job hi karti hai dhyan lagake karna chahiye. (They must take out time and do it seriously, just like a job.)

Aap shuru kijiye, kaam accha hai toh support karne vale log tayyar ho jate hai. Ye mera khud ka anubhav hai. (You start the work in a small way. If it is good, people will come forward and join you.)

Apni family ka mind develop kijiye, ki yeh kaam mere khud ka, ek ka nahi hai. Poori family ka hai, family ke liye hai. (Prepare your family mentally, that this is not just your work but something which belongs to the entire family.)

Har ek lady jab dil lagake kaam karti hai na to successful hoti hi hai. Ye mera 100% vishwas hai. (Every woman who puts her heart and soul into her work is successful. I am 100% confident about that.)

Hum jab bachchon ke liye kaam karte hai, apni family ke liye kaam karte hai to kitne vishwas se kaam karte hai. Usi tarah se business bhi sacche dil se karo. Sirf profit ke liye nahin. (When you do anything for your kids or the family, you do it with so much interest. Pour yourself into business in the same way, not just for the sake of profit.)

Mere business mein pehle paanch saal bilkul hi profit nahi hua. Paisa dalti gayi dalti gayi aur bas yeh dekhti gayi ki product accha hai, logon ka fayda ho raha hai. (I didn't earn any profit in my business for the first 5 years. But I earned a lot of goodwill.)

Paisa aur naam aata rehta hai... vo to hamare kaam ke peeche peeche aata hai. (Money and recognition will follow... If you do good work that will happen on its own.)

BIRDS OF A FEATHER

Ranjana Naik,
Swan Suites

Ranjana started a call centre to generate leads for her husband's direct-selling venture. But this super-saleswoman then diversified into hospitality and now dreams of making Swan Suites the 'Taj' of service apartments.

A woman cannot have it all. That's what the world would have her believe.

She may step out of the home and show her mettle, but that action comes with a heavy burden. The burden of guilt.

"Am I neglecting my child?"

"Am I neglecting my husband?"

"Am I really allowed to pursue my own dreams?"

Ranjana Naik is a wife, a mother and a hard-nosed businesswoman.

"I went back to work after 40 days, I had to. But I don't feel bad about it. I made proper arrangements."

Ranjana is clear, focused and no-nonsense. She is also very ambitious and constantly trying to grow. Both the company and herself.

Networking, reading, observing and even attending courses. The '10,000 women entrepreneurs' program at ISB, in particular, made a big difference.

"Finance was so difficult for me – numbers would dance before my eyes," she recalls.

Now she knows the ins and outs of balance sheet, profit and loss, raising capital from banks and institutions. And I think to myself – why can't more of us do this?

Why can't we share, support, motivate and encourage each other? To learn more, to seek more, to believe more.

To lead blissful, guilt-free, queensize lives.

We can, we must, we will.

BIRDS OF A FEATHER

Ranjana Naik,
Swan Suites

"My mother was a school teacher and my father was employed with IDPL – a public-sector pharma company. My extended family also is all doctors and engineers."

Studying hard and 'doing well' is what was expected of Ranjana also. But, life had other plans.

"I always liked my friends who were from business families. In fact, I was keen to drop out in class 10 itself and start my own business!"

Naturally, her father would have none of it.

"Then I said, ok, after the 12th I will not go to regular college, I will do some business."

Ultimately, Ranjana gave in and enrolled for a BSc in Microbiology at Vanitha Mahavidyalaya. But, as a final year student, she did dabble in business once again.

"I was fascinated by Public Relations, so I took up a course at Bharatiya Vidya Bhavan. And I thought of starting a firm of my own. "

Ranjana got together with a group of friends, many discussions took place. But the venture never took off.

"We decided to get into the fabric business instead."

This time, they bought material, got it dyed and stitched. Even set a date for the grand exhibition. But as soon as they graduated, the group disbanded. Some took up jobs, others got married.

"We managed to sell what we'd made among our own friends and that was the end of the business!"

Ranjana was left with the question – what do I do now? Although her heart was in corporate communications, she decided to go for a sales job.

"I thought that will help me learn more about the real world."

The job was with 'Apex Institute of Professional Selling' – it involved selling programs on 'how to sell' to companies. The modus operandi was to visit colleges, visit companies, and get enrolments. Ranjana enjoyed the job thoroughly and was promoted to 'centre head' within two years.

"I was one of those very aggressive types," says Ranjana. "If the target was to get 50 people to the centre as walk-ins, I would plan out for 150-200."

That way, at least a hundred footfalls would happen.

Around the same time, Ranjana met her future husband – Nitin. He was her brother's colleague. What's more, he had just quit his job to become a Direct Sales Associate (DSA) for Standard Chartered Bank. The idea was to generate credit card applications for the bank, but as an entrepreneur.

"That was very exciting for me! I remember begging him to give me a job in his company so that I can understand how to do business."

While that didn't happen, what did happen was the decision to get married. In 1997 – at age 24 – Ranjana tied the knot with Nitin. But, she continued with her job.

"My husband was not very comfortable with me joining him. He said, 'You have this public relations thing which you want to start. You should do that.'"

In fact, even Ranjana's father-in-law encouraged her to think of starting on her own. Despite this unusual amount of support, Ranjana was hesitant.

"I was still like... 'let's see' kind of a thing."

Meanwhile Ranjana shifted companies – first to NIIT, then to Pentafour. The job profile was similar – centre head, sales and management. But more promotions and more opportunities were coming her way. In addition to Pentafour's Hyderabad centre, Ranjana was managing the business of all its franchisees in Andhra Pradesh.

"I was even given an option of opening a new branch in Malaysia... but I refused. I was very sure I want to stay in Hyderabad, my husband is settled here. I cannot leave him and go."

Meanwhile, Nitin was facing a major challenge. So far the business was working with 'feet on the street' – go door to door, to popular shopping areas, get forms filled up. Leads did come in but it was hard work. Could there be a better way to grow the DSA business?

"We used to discuss these things – how to get more leads, more numbers. One idea we came up with was 'telemarketing'."

Around this time Nitin went to Bangalore for a dealer meet and learnt that the call centre model was working well for many DSAs.

He came back and said to Ranjana, "Let us start our own call centre. You are from sales background, so let it be your baby."

Ranjana quit her job and jumped right into it. Although part of Nitin's business, it was to be an independent set-up, a separate location.

"We rented an apartment in Panjagutta and started the operations of Swan Finmart. See, at that time, for that kind of a business, setup cost was not that much – mainly staff and telephone lines."

The couple invested their own money, confident that it would be recovered quickly. And Ranjana used all her ingenuity to make sure that happened. The main challenge was to get a good database of potential credit card customers.

"I would have either been in service or I would have done my own business. I would never ever like just being at home."

"It needed marketing... lot of marketing. When I was on bed-rest I used to feel bad that you know I can't follow up companies the way I would have. "

It was the year 2000 and retail chains like Shopper's Stop and Lifestyle were just setting up shop. Ranjana approached them and in fact, they were interested.

"We have customer data but it's all in physical format – can you digitise it for us?"

It was hard work, donkey work and yet Ranjana accepted.

"I remember we literally carried the 'data' in bags and suitcases to our office. But we got a database of around 25,000 people this way."

Two birds killed with one stone.

Ranjana hired data-entry operators to handle digitisation. The telemarketing team then used this database to sell credit cards to high-potential customers. But it wasn't just a case of making cold calls and hoping for the best. There was a *method* to the madness.

"Payment was based on the percentage of applications approved. So we worked backwards to pinpoint which customer profiles get the maximum approvals."

Ranjana requested the bank for data of customers whose cards were approved. This was fed into the database and soon a profile emerged. Those employed in software companies, for example, were almost certain to get their cards.

"Before sending each application we would check if it met parameters favoured by the bank in terms of age, income, employer and so on."

Naturally, a high percentage of Swan Finmart's applications got approved. Which meant higher commissions.

"That year we managed to be pan-India No.1 in the Standard Chartered DSA network. I mean, in number of cards issued."

Swan Finmart expanded rapidly. By 2004, the company had a 2000 sq ft office and 50 employees. 35 female staff – for telecalling and setting up appointments, 15 male staff – to collect the documents and signatures. Revenues crossed a crore of rupees, with an average of 1500-2000 applications a month getting approved.

Then, things started changing. The bank changed its policies and commission structure, making the venture less profitable. On the other hand, costs were rising.

"GE set up a call centre in Hyderabad – they were paying 3 times the salary that we were paying. So, we lost many quality people."

Somehow, Ranjana hung in there for a year but business continued to decline. Upgrading the telemarketing option to a GE-like call centre was an option. But the investment and risk was too high. That's when the partners decided to actively look out for some new line of business.

A friend had just started the business of service apartments in Bangalore and it was picking up well.

"Why don't you do something similar in Hyderabad?" he said.

In fact, he made a generous offer.

"Let's do the business in partnership. If it works out, continue with me or then, venture on your own."

The partnership model made sense. The sales team in Bangalore would bring in clients while Ranjana would handle the ground operations in Hyderabad. In fact, the company sent a 'Resident Manager' to help set up the new branch.

"I got to learn a lot from him – how to source apartments, furnish and maintain them, and much more."

The service apartment business is capital-intensive. You need to

"Ishani never clung to me, maybe if that had happened I would have felt guilty. So I can say she too was supportive!"

"It helps if you have a working mother – I literally grew up with my grandparents in a joint family. That made me independent."

put down a deposit and invest ₹ 1 lakh per room* in furnishing. And you must have at least 20 rooms to begin with. Then there is the monthly rental and staff cost. Both partners invested an equal amount of money – around ₹ 23 lakh.

"We started in one of the good complexes which had a swimming pool and all such extra facilities. Such complexes were very new in Hyderabad back then."

The first six months were great, with 80% occupancy. It seemed like a good time to expand when, all of a sudden, business in Hyderabad dried up. The partners went their separate ways and much soul-searching followed.

"Where did we go wrong?"

After surveying the market, Ranjana realised that the Hyderabad market was dominated by real estate agents. These agents would furnish vacant apartments to a bare minimum and peddle them as 'guesthouses'. There was no concept of 'per day' rate, only 'per month'. And that too not for rooms but entire three-bedroom apartments.

"I realised that the Hyderabad market was different from Bangalore. We should have done some marketing in Hyderabad rather than rely only on Bangalore office."

Every business goes through its tough phases. When the partners split, Ranjana took over the lease in Hyderabad, as well as the furnishings. But high rentals and low occupancy made it a loss-making business. Side by side, the telemarketing business was also in trouble.

"Targets were not being met so, we had to sit down and discuss with the team."

Then, along came another life challenge. After 7 years of marriage, Ranjana was expecting and it was a difficult pregnancy.

* The furnishing cost per room is now ₹ 1.5 lakh.

"Since I had high BP the doctor asked me to take bedrest for three months. But I continued to work on the phone."

During this period, Ranjana's main objective was to secure a lower rent property. The new set of rooms had to be refurnished with the old fixtures. The housekeeping and service staff had to be constantly supervised.

"I was back at work exactly 40 days after my daughter was born but we had lost a good six months."

On the positive side, there was 50% occupancy. Ranjana knew that if she could increase the occupancy to 70%, the operation would at least break even. Giving up was not an option – over ₹ 25 lakh had already been invested in the business.

"I am a very bad loser," smiles Ranjana. "Besides, I could see that it was just a matter of time before business had to pick up!"

A service apartment reputation is built on the quality of its property and the quality of its service. To cater to guests, you need a supervisor, two cooks, housekeeping staff, a room service guy – a team of 8-10 people working in shifts.

"I was very lucky that the supervisor from the joint venture joined me. Deepen was very hardworking, sincere and also doubled up as the cook!"

Ranjana was also fortunate to get a good maid to support her at home. As soon as she got pregnant, she hired full-time help and trained her to be fully capable and responsible.

"My mother-in-law was also with me, but from time to time she needs to travel to our native place or to Australia, where my brother-in-law lives. I did not want to tie her down."

An entrepreneur mom cannot take six months' maternity leave. But she can take mini-maternity breaks, every day of her career. Ranjana timed her work outside the house with the baby's sleeping and feeding times.

"I would make surprise visits to keep the staff on their toes. But a lot of the monitoring and follow-up work could be done online or via phone."

A working mother cannot be 24×7 with the baby, taking care of all her needs. Was there ever an element of guilt – of missing out on the early years?

"Earlier I use to have doubts – am I going on the right path, is this the correct thing? After the ISB program I became much more confident."

"I never saw any abnormal change in her, that she was missing me or clinging to me more... I think she took it fine, so I can say she was also supportive!"

With all this support, Ranjana pushed forward. The key to turning around the business was better rates and better occupancy. Getting some customers who would take rooms on a quarterly or annual basis. But corporate deals remained elusive.

"I realised that to get bulk deals we would have to give some kickbacks to HR managers."

Something Ranjana had no idea how to deal with. So instead, she decided to focus on retail customers. But how to reach out to these individuals?

"I decided to tie up with event managers. They would send me people who were in the city for 3-4 days on training or with exhibitions."

What's more, retail customers pay in cash, whereas corporates expect 45 days' credit (but often take longer). For a small company, chasing up money is a major challenge.

"When you have cash crunch you wonder whether it's good to be in this business or not... So in a way retail clients are much better."

This way, little by little, the company grew. In time, a couple of corporate contracts also came in and occupancy went up to a healthy 85%. Ranjana decided to expand and by 2008, Swan Suites had 28 rooms on offer. And yet, Ranjana often felt confused and alone.

"I used to feel that neither am I from a business family nor do I have any formal business education. So am I doing things correctly, efficiently?"

Ranjana joined various Google groups to connect with fellow entrepreneurs. Because there is much to learn and share, from those on a similar life path. On a friend's advice, Ranjana applied to the '10,000 woman entrepreneurs' program at ISB Hyderabad. And she got accepted.

"I used this opportunity to focus 100% on learning as much as possible!"

The program touched on various theories but the emphasis was on practical application. One very important learning for Ranjana was 'how to negotiate'.

"We had a very good professor who made us do role plays. So, I actually understood how the other person thinks and how to plan before you get into any negotiation."

Ranjana actually applied what she learnt in that class to secure a 'dream property'. A high-end building which was already with another service apartment company. But Ranjana remained on the lookout.

"I knew the only way to get better clients was to have a better property on offer. So I used to scan the *Deccan Chronicle* classified section every week."

One day Ranjana came across an ad which said: 'Service apartment lease' for sale. It was the very same building she had shortlisted earlier.

"When I called, the service apartment company quoted a very high price – ₹ 1 crore deposit and ₹ 40 lakh monthly rental for 30 rooms."

Knowing this was way too high, Ranjana decided to speak to the owners directly. They revealed that the service apartment company was vacating the premises from the following month. The business was going bust due to high rentals.

"The other company was paying ₹ 70,000 per month for each apartment whereas the going was ₹ 35,000. So I had to bring it down."

The deal was eventually sealed for ₹ 40,000 per apartment.

Market research was another area Ranjana was never comfortable with.

"I used to run away from my customers earlier, thinking he's going to give me a complaint or problem," she laughs.

At ISB, Ranjana realised that market research was about talking to customers – not once a year, but continuously. Because that's how you grow, how you learn and improve.

And finally, Ranjana tackled her biggest weakness – finance. Like many women running a business, she had little inclination for *hisaab-kitaab*.

"Numbers would literally dance before my eyes," she recalls.

Before the ISB program, Ranjana relied on Nitin to handle the company finances. Now, she knows as much – and more.

"Being in a service industry, getting finance from banks or any institutions is difficult. But I learnt how to keep the books in place, fulfil the statutory requirements."

Today, Ranjana can calculate her working capital requirements. Confidently walk into a bank, and get an overdraft.

"In fact, in certain areas of finance, I know more than Nitin!"

Meanwhile, Nitin's business was once again facing challenges. In 2006, Standard Chartered wound up its credit card business, hence Nitin became a DSA for Barclays. While Barclays had a lot of big plans, in September 2008, the global economy suffered a setback and the plans were cancelled.

"See, the business was too dependent on external factors. So he decided it was time to move on."

In February 2009, Nitin exited his marketing business and formally joined Swan Suites. He took over the operations 100%, while Ranjana focused on marketing. Which was just what the business needed, to grow and prosper.

"Prior to Nitin joining, there was a lot of pilferage – it was very difficult for me to keep an eye on everything. Besides, we saw there was a lot of potential waiting to be tapped."

The last 3 years have seen that happen. Swan Suites has grown from 24 rooms to 125 rooms. Funded mostly through internal accruals and a small investment by a friend. But more than anything it's the combined energies of Ranjana and Nitin. The extra management bandwidth and teamwork that's grown the business.

But is working together all smooth sailing?

"As long as your roles are different, it's fine. But at times there is overlap and there is friction," she admits.

Each blames the other for being stubborn.

"When a suggestion goes from sales (my domain) to operations (his domain), there is resistance. And it's vice versa also."

But with discussion and deliberation, decisions get taken. In the best interest of the company.

Swan Suites now employes 46 staff members and a senior management team, including a General Manager. And in the near future Ranjana sees the company expanding further, even outside Hyderabad. With the budget hospitality segment growing at a rate of 70% year on year, the scope for growth is huge.

"In China there is a concept of 'branded service apartment'. I think that is the way to go, even in India."

The vision is that Swan Suites should be like a 'Taj' of service apartments. The first choice for a budget business traveller.

"6000 people every month search for Swan Suites on Google according to the search reports. Now we need to replicate that in cities across India."

In all this, where is the time to spend together – as a family? Ranjana follows a fixed schedule now, arriving in office at 8:30 am and getting back home at 4:30 pm.

"Ishani is now six years old and more demanding. I try to spend more time with her, and with her studies."

And less time discussing office issues at home with Nitin. Though calls and emails from the office do keep coming in, late into the night.

"I love what I do so… *yeh sab to chalta hai*," she laughs.

Love is each human being blooming into a fragrant flower.

If work be a woman's fragrance, let it explode with intensity.

And fill the home, the workplace, the entire world.

ADVICE TO WOMEN ENTREPRENEURS

Women can do a lot. We underestimate ourselves a lot. Even if you do maybe a small fraction of what you are capable of, that will be very big.

You really need to have a supportive family but we need to work towards getting the support also rather than just saying 'I'm not getting support'.

So, once that is taken care of, once you are out of the house, especially once you have a family and kids, your efficiencies are very high. You would not like to waste even a minute.

Make sure you have someone taking care of the basic household needs. Like food, if you can hire somebody who can cook, do it! We're in India so we can still take that advantage and we can manage that part rather than get bogged down.

Treat your maids the way you would treat a valuable employee.

A working mother is good for the kids also. The confidence, the independence that they get is very important. Had my mother been around, giving me everything, I wouldn't have gone and got what I want.

There was a phase when my daughter was young and business was young. I used to be very hassled. Now I work very hard but I have also learned to relax.

TRUE BLUE

Leela Bordia, Neerja International

A *bahu* from a Marwari family ventured into the slums of Jaipur with the idea of doing social work. Her passion and imagination revived the traditional art of blue pottery and improved the life of artisans.

Imagine yourself as the daughter-in-law of a traditional Marwari household. A little modern because you don't wear a *ghunghat*, only a *pallu* on your head.

In this community, women enjoy respect but within certain boundaries. Their place is in the home, in the *rasoi*, in the *pooja ghar*.

Now imagine a *bahu* from such a family, visiting the slums. Sitting on the floor, in the heat, with the artisans. Creating beautiful blue pottery to export to foreign lands.

"I started this as a social work more than 35 years ago. But it grew and grew and became a business."

And a fascinating one at that. At the Neerja International showroom in Jaipur, blue and yellow pottery items are displayed from wall to wall. Cups, tiles, hooks, beads, lamps – anything and everything you can think of is there.

"I am still designing, creating more and more products," adds Leela.

Keeping villagers in their villages. Bringing a dying craft back to life.

That is the power of one woman, who shook off the *pallu*.

And took bold, new strides.

TRUE BLUE

Leela Bordia, Neerja International

Leela was born in Rajasthan but grew up in Calcutta.

"My father was an executive with Hindustan Motors and my mother (Nagina Devi) was a homemaker, but very involved with social work."

Leela vividly recalls holding her mother's hand and visiting the slums of Calcutta, along with a sari-clad lady with a kind smile. Much later, she realised that lady was Mother Teresa.

Nagina Devi campaigned against social evils such as dowry, purdah and discrimination in all forms.

"My mother disapproved of inequality among male and female children, rich and poor."

Although born in a privileged family, Leela attended an ordinary school. She was sent without a 'lunch pack' so that she would eat bread and chai like all other children. Not stand out as an 'officer's daughter'.

"I was taught to be equal and fair to all."

Leela resolved that she too would grow up and 'do something'. But her mother died young and she took on the responsibility of three younger siblings.

“I wasn’t that good in studies and even left them in between.”

Later, however, she went back and completed her graduation. In 1974, Leela got married and shifted to Jaipur.

“It was an arranged marriage. My husband used to be into construction line. No lunch time, no dinner time, because the construction line is always like that.”

Leela thought it was best to utilise her time, instead of complaining. She started working as a Montessori teacher in a nearby school. But the ‘social work’ bug remained, so one fine day Leela ventured into a slum area close to her house. What she saw was sad and shocking.

“The slum – Hida ki Mori – was full of men and women who had migrated from the village in search of work. They worked very hard, in very bad conditions, just to survive.”

Leela started visiting regularly and she would always take something with her – money, food, clothes. But she found it was never ‘enough’.

“*Jaise maine dena shuru kiya, unki demand badhti gayi.*” (The more I gave, the more they demanded.)

Surely, there was a better way to ‘help’? It was then that Leela noticed the beautiful blue pottery which the slum-dwellers made in their tiny homes. There was something beautiful and fascinating about it.

“This was the traditional art, inherited from their forefathers. But which people did not value in the city.”

The patronage of Maharani Gayatri Devi had given the craft a boost in the 1960s. But the market for blue pottery was limited. There wasn’t much demand for the heavy urns, vases and plates the potters were making. But the art itself, and the distinctive blue colour held potential.

“I told them, ‘*Aap isko thoda badal dijiye*.’” (Change the way you are working.)

But the potters were adamant – this is the way it’s *always* been done.

In 1976, Leela gave birth to her daughter Aparna. But her visits to the slums continued. There was no concrete idea except to help the people to help themselves. Certainly, it was never a ‘business’.

For more than two years, Leela kept trying to convince the potters to try something new. Finally, a young potter named Kailash agreed to work with her. Together, they experimented on the wheel.

Meanwhile, the Wheel of Fortune itself was turning – both for Leela Bordia and for the future of blue pottery. The school she was teaching in was connected to an export house (now well-known as Anokhi). It was here, in 1977, that Leela met Paul Comar, a buyer from France.

"When Paul came to know of my work, he was very appreciative. And he gave me some new ideas."

He asked Leela, "Can you make like this, some beads? I can sell bead curtains in France."

Although she had no idea how to do it, Leela agreed. She sat wih Kailash, and his potter friends, for many weeks, to get the proper shape, size and colour.

"What temperature to heat, how to glaze them on all sides – we learnt all this by doing again and again."

When the curtains were ready, Leela proudly packed them off to France. Paul promptly sent across the payment and Leela was overjoyed – her potters were finally getting the 'help' they so badly needed. But, she soon discovered a disturbing bit of news through a mutual friend.

"Our entire consignment of curtains was rejected in France because of poor quality, rather uneven quality. It was actually sold for a throwaway price."

Leela realised she lacked experience. She was so excited to get an order and fulfil it that she didn't look into the finer details. And yet, Paul said nothing. In fact, he returned the following year and said, "Let's try again."

The second innovation was a 'doorknob'. Again, the idea came from Paul and Leela sat with her potters, in the open-air 'laboratory'. But this time it was different. Everyone had heard that *baiji* is getting orders from 'foreign', doing something good.

"The *karigars* themselves came forward and said – we want to work with you."

> ***"Mujhe ye tha ki logon ki madad karni hai.... Business ka to A B C bhi nahi malum tha."***
>
> **(I only wanted to help people, I didn't know even the A, B or C of business.)**

One such artisan was Lalaram, who was originally from the village of Kotjewar, 50 km outside Jaipur. But why should these artists leave their villages and live in slums, to do the work they can easily do in their village?

"I told Lalaram, you go back to the village, *main aapke saath judungi* (I will support you). *Kaam waheen se hoga* (Work will be done there)."

Now this meant that Leela would have to visit the village – across bumpy road, come rain or shine. But it was a conscious decision on her part, and a major milestone.

"*Maine apni strategy banayi – ki jo bhi kaam aayega, main gaon mein doongi aur logon ko jitni help ho sakegi hum karenge.*" (I made it my strategy that I will give whatever work I get to the villagers and help them as much as possible.)

And thus, with Paul's faith, Leela's imagination and Lalaram's perseverance, the 'ceramic doorknob' was born.

"This product was a hit and it is our speciality even today!"

Around this time, Leela's sister Manju Lodha was living in Mexico and she said to her, "I have seen pottery like this here also. Why don't you come to Mexico and see how do they do it?"

Leela liked the idea. In 1979, she spent a month in Mexico, understanding the local style of pottery. To do this, Leela had to travel every day from Mexico City to Puebla village, 100 km away.

"The village was too small and not safe for me to stay overnight, especially since I didn't know the language."

But the language of art needs no words. Leela spent her days observing the artisans, their techniques, their glazing. There was no formal 'course' as such, you just pick up what you need to know.

Leela returned to India and the following year, she gave birth to a son. Work continued side by side. So how did she manage two young children, duties of a wife and daughter-in-law *and* this grand passion for pottery?

"My husband and mother-in-law were very supportive. Besides, our pace of work was quite slow."

There was no fax, no telex, no email or mobile phone. No pressure to execute orders quickly – you could do it over weeks or months. But slowly and steadily, things were moving along.

As word spread, artisans came to *baiji*, looking for work.

As Leela supplied to the market, she understood what would sell.

Based on the demand, more items were produced and sent off to the market.

"*Ek aisi chain banti gayi aur is tarah se humara kaam chalta gaya.*" (A virtuous cycle came into being and our work went on increasing.)

The co-operation of villagers in Kotjewar was crucial. It started with Lalaram's family, but one by one other families came and became a part of the project. Each family was an independent 'unit', so eight families became eight units.

Leela had registered a proprietary concern in 1978 – only because she needed it, to export goods. She called the firm 'Neerja International', after her sister. But it was only in 1983-84 that she felt this is more than social work.

"I realised I have created a business platform and I need to become more professional."

And at this point comes a twist in the tale. Traditionally, Jaipur pottery is made from ground quartz. The addition of cobalt oxide gives it the trademark turquoise blue colour. So essentially you had two colours to work with – blue and white.

Leela introduced a new colour into this mix – a sunshine yellow. Why yellow?

"I don't know really... But yellow is a colour so much associated with Rajasthan. And I felt it goes very well with blue."

Leela instinctively realised that people would not fill up their homes with single-colour objects. Blue doorknob, blue bedcover, blue

"I learnt many techniques from all over the world but didn't change the ingredients, so that we retain our unique identity of 'Jaipur pottery'."

lamp – blue *everything* would get boring. But when you change something – anything – people do not accept it immediately.

"I was criticised by many for what I was trying to do. But I had belief in myself and continued."

In 1984, Neerja International was a small enterprise with sales of about ₹ 4 lakh. The turnover grew very slowly because firstly, production was slow. Every piece was made by hand, in a many-stage process. Exactly as it was done a hundred years ago.

Since Kotjewar was the production centre, Leela made weekly trips to the village, to take stock of the work.

"Generally I went on Sunday and my husband used to go with me. I would sit with the potters while he would take rest on a *charpai*."

I wonder how many spouses would do this, week after week!

The life of an entrepreneur is always uncertain. You might set off on an adventure to India and reach America instead. But that's the fun of it.

The early disaster with the bead curtains had its own happy ending. Leela fashioned necklaces out of the leftover beads and stocked them at Anokhi. At that time the movie, *Far Pavilions,* was being shot in Jaipur.

"The actresses of that film came to the store and loved the necklaces so much, they bought the entire stock."

Similarly, Mrs Kelkar, wife of the Taj Hotels' CEO Ajit Kelkar, noticed Leela's work. At that time, Taj was building the Rambagh Palace property in Jaipur.

Mrs Kelkar said, "Leela, I want you to make some murals at Rambagh Palace."

Leela spent 6 months on this 'thrilling' project. The artwork she executed can still be seen at the Rambagh Palace coffee shop – Neel Mahal.

"I really admire Mrs Kelkar and thank her because she has been a patron of Rajasthani art and of my work."

The Chairman of the Export Promotion Council visited Kotjewar. Subsequently, Neerja International was invited to participate at export promotion fairs in Pragati Maidan and elsewhere.

"After this I realised that if you want to grow then you have to expose yourself. For the first time, I made a brochure and visiting card!"

In 1988, Leela recruited her first employee – a lady by the name Nirmala.

"Till then I was doing the packing, I was doing the paperwork, I was looking after production. But it became too much because business was growing."

With growth comes money, with money comes the issue of 'accounts'. Leela admits that part of the business has never been her cup of tea.

"From the very beginning my husband is taking care of the finance part. I don't know much about it… If I get my pocket money I am happy!"

The business grew organically, without outside funding.

"We invested only the initial ₹ 500 in buying materials. Then we just put back whatever money was made."

In the early days the foreign buyers Leela worked with were also happy to pay an advance. Though times have changed. And so has Leela herself.

As her art got recognised internationally, Leela started travelling abroad. In 1994, she was invited by Globus, a famous Swiss department store, to hold an exhibition of Jaipur pottery. She stayed in Berne for 6 weeks, as their guest.

"Whenever I used to go to the store, the staff members would fly India's tricolour to greet me. I felt like an ambassador for India."

In 1996, Australian author Michael Caudle wrote a book called *Business in Asia*. He featured the Hyundai motor company

"Hum unko design batate gaye, woh kaam karte gaye... aur iss tarah gaonwaalon ke saath ek bridge ban gaya."

(I gave them designs, they took on the work... And thus I built a relationship with the villagers.)

from South Korea, Changi airport from Singapore and Neerja International from India.

"This book is used by class 10 students in Australia as a part of their curriculum. So we had many teachers and students coming here, to visit the village and see how we work."

The entire operation is a decentralised one. Neerja International does not 'own' a single production unit. Every unit is free to work with or supply anyone, but they choose to work with *baiji*. Because there is mutual trust and mutual benefit.

Neerja International procures orders – the artisans fulfil the orders and get paid on time. They bring their wares to Jaipur where it is checked, packed and despatched to the buyer. What's more, they do not have the headache of sourcing the raw material from Beawar. The company arranges for it.

"The most important thing is that I keep innovating, creating new designs and new products to sell."

From beer mugs to bathroom sets, tables to wall tiles – the Neerja International catalogue has it all. The sheer range of 'apps' is amazing. Moving from 'decoration' to utility, the market for Jaipur pottery expanded manifold.

Yet in 2003, Neerja International experienced a crisis, with turnover falling by half. There was no recession or reduction in demand. Just a sense of *thakaan.* Both the children had grown up and left Jaipur for their work and higher studies.

"I felt the business was becoming something of a burden and if they don't wish to carry it on – what is the point?"

At that time Apurv was in America, first studying and subsequently working in an IT company. He decided to relocate to India with a two-fold objective – help his mother with her business and start his own software company. And that, in a sense, was a turning point for Neerja International.

Today, the company sources products from 15 village-based units, employing close to 500 workers. The amount each unit earns is variable – it depends on how much time and effort they are willing to put in. It ranges anywhere from ₹ 20,000 per month to ₹ 2 lakh per month.

Apart from that, Neerja International employs about 50 people in Jaipur itself, to handle quality control, packing and administration. Exports remain important but sale within India now constitutes 50% of the business. The overall turnover of the company fluctuates between ₹ 2 crore and ₹ 5 crore, depending on favourable weather conditions and rain.

"*Turnover bahut bada nahi hai* (Turnover is not very big). It's a labour-oriented work... hands are more."

The important thing is that these hands are not doing menial or factory work in the city. They can sustain themselves as farmers, with additional income from the craft. What's more, members of the second and third generation are also joining the units – choosing the traditional way over city life.

"Both my daughter, Aparna, and daughter-in-law, Nupur, have also joined the business."

New generation means new thinking, new ways of doing things. This includes generating export orders through the internet as well as starting a chain of exclusive retail stores to sell blue pottery products. The very first such 'Neerja' store is situated at Jacob Road in Jaipur.

**"Whosoever is working with me,
you will find they are buying the land,
not selling the land.
That is my success story."**

If your house runs perfectly, you can win anywhere in the world.

Working with the children has been smooth.

"They know more than me, they have seen the world. But still they respect my views also."

And Leela believes that change is good, but old ways work best with the production of blue pottery. The 'ERP' she uses is her own brain.

Orders are assigned to the heads of various units on a simple piece of paper. Depending on their level of expertise and size of the *bhatti* (kiln). Delivery of handmade goods is always a little variable and Leela will only accept a deadline when she knows it can be fulfilled.

"I tell the buyers a firm yes or firm no, I don't keep them hanging. It could mean refusing an order or working all night to fulfil a commitment."

Commitment is an attitude and it extends to all areas of life. As much as Leela cares about her work, she cares for her family.

"I married into a very traditional community but I have been lucky to get the full support from my mother-in-law and my husband Kamal who were very open-minded."

There were people who asked, "*Kya zaroorat hai Leela ko kaam karne ki? Kamal kamaate nahin kya?*" (Why does Leela need to work? Doesn't her husband earn enough?)

Leela's mother-in-law would smile and shrug it off. What's more, she said to her *bahu, "Aap kaam kar rahi hain, chupchap karti rahiye. Jab kahi pahunch jaaye tab sabko bataiyega."* (Whatever you are doing, keep doing it quietly. When you reach somewhere then you can talk about it.)

Sometimes, a relative would drop by while Leela was away, busy with some work.

"Where is your daughter-in-law?" they would ask.

Maaji would ring Leela in her office and tell her, "Please pick up some fruits on the way back. I have told them you have gone to the market."

Leela has a simple and pragmatic take on how to 'have it all'.

"In married life there are 2-3 important things. One is that 'ego' should not be there. Second is that family comes first. You should not be too ambitious, in a hurry to get ahead."

When her children were young, Leela worked limited hours.

"Initially for two hours, then three, then four hours. When they started school, then during the school hours."

For many years she worked from home, then shared office space with her husband. It was only when the enterprise grew fairly big that she got her 'own place'.

And she continues, at her own pace.

"I have started learning vocal classical music because I thought I should little diversify myself."

For the wheel of life must keep turning.

The life you mould is in *your* hands.

Go on, set your intention – seize the clay!

ADVICE TO WOMEN ENTREPRENEURS

If you need to work for money it's a very different thing. Otherwise our first responsibility is our house. If we can run the house properly, we can run the world, I tell you. We really can run the world. But, our first duty or responsibility, whatever you call it, is our house.

Nowadays girls have studied, they have the knowledge... they should work. But when you have children, keep less working hours. As they grow up you can gradually increase. After some years you will automatically feel that everything is in position. Your children are also in position and you can give more attention to your work.

And second thing is ego. That shouldn't come in between you and your family. Other than that every person has got a different life situation, different understanding, different way of thinking.

Ek cheez aur ki kitni bhi bade bade kaam ho relax and dheere dheere ek ke baad ek vo kaam hote jaate hai. (One more thing I would say is no matter how big the task in front of you, relax and slowly, slowly, little by little it will get done.)

Apurv Bordia (son):

I am very proud of everything my mother has achieved. But yes, when I was growing up, sometimes I wondered why she is not like other mothers. Why does she have to work?

There was a particular buyer, whenever he came she would have to work late. When I would know this person is coming I would always get angry.

Now I realise what she has done is very special. In our community for a woman to do all this for more than 30 years ago is remarkable. Hats off to my father and my *dadi* for supporting her all the way.

CROUCHING TIGER, HIDDEN WOMAN

**Han Qui Hua,
Guangzhou Guanyi Garment
Label Accessories Ltd**

At 16, Han cycled around Jianxi town selling rice cakes, to support her family. In 1999, she entered the label-making business and has taken the company turnover from $5,000 to $250,000, with the help of her extended family.

I have never been to China but I know it is richer, more powerful and more 'successful' than India.

And the same appears to be true of Chinese women.

8 women appeared in the 2012 Forbes list of '100 Richest Chinese'. Of these, 6 are self-made billionaires.

I don't think we have a statistic to match that in India. And yet, I wonder, does this indicate a change in an ancient culture and civilisation?

That culture – in both our countries – where men have always dominated women.

The story of Han Qui Hua is poignant. It reminds you that things change, but mostly on the surface. There are many opportunities in China today for a woman to be strong and successful. And yet, she must never forget her 'place'.

The man, the family, the customers and the world – all must be happy.

Too much pride spoils the family broth.

Stir gently, tread softly.

This interview was conducted by Shivi Sabharwal in Guangzhou, China, and translated by his colleagues, Ms Sherry and Ms Eli. My heartfelt thanks to all three of them.

CROUCHING TIGER, HIDDEN WOMAN

Han Qui Hua,
Guangzhou Guanyi Garment
Label Accessories Ltd

Han Qui Hua was born in 1967, in Jie Yang City near Chaoshan (Guangdong Province).

"My father was a daily wage worker in a factory while my mother was farming on a very small land we had in the village."

It was a tough life, the family was poor and there was never enough food or heat in the house. Han's childhood was much tougher than most kids as she was the eldest in the family.

"I always had in my mind to do housework and take care of sisters and brothers. So I can share burden of my parents."

The only spare time was at night from 8 pm to 10 pm, to play with other kids from the neighbourhood.

One of the happiest memories Han recalls is the birth of her first brother. The male child is valued far more than the female in traditional Chinese society.

"I saw my parents are smiling more than ever before."

Han entered elementary school at the age of 9, when she joined grade 1 along with her brother. As her mother was busy working, it was Han's responsibility to look after him and it was better for them to study together in the same class.

Han studied up to grade 5 though she says her 'knowledge' was only up to grade 3. At that point, she dropped out of school.

"Though I did like to study, it far exceeded my ability. I couldn't understand much of what teacher said in the class."

The real reason, however, was that the family needed more income. And Han always put family in 'first position'.

Finding a job in China, back then, was not easy. You had to be patient to get one and work very hard, just to survive. But Han was not one to complain. She started doing odd jobs in factories and in some shops in Jianxi Town.

One day, while walking along the street, Han noticed some peddlers selling homemade desserts. She went home and asked her mother, "Can we not do this also?"

Han's mother thought she was crazy and refused. But Han persisted.

"Why not you make rice cake, and I sell them?"

The family eventually agreed and 16-year-old Han started selling rice cakes along the roadside. It was her first taste of 'business'.

Every day, after breakfast, Han got onto her bicycle and pedalled through the streets, looking for customers. If the cakes were not selling, she would move to the next village, and the next. Until she had sold every last rice cake.

"Each day I would sell 60 pieces, each piece only for 0.1 RMB (87 paise)*. Like that I did for two years."

Han then took up a job in a hardware factory, near the airport in Shantou city. The work was tough and the environment harsh.

"Every time when the aircraft flied by, the earth shaked for a while with some plane noise as well."

Most workers fled within a week or two but Han would not give up so easily. With great difficulty, her father had arranged for the 30 RMB required for her passage to Shantou city. It would be shameful to return empty handed.

"I worked in that factory for one month. It was being the longest any person stayed in that work."

On receiving her 200 RMB (₹ 17,500) salary, Han quit and returned home. She gave the full 200 RMB to her father.

"It was first time I had seen such a large amount (of money) and I was so pleased that I can help my family."

* I RMB (Chinese currency) = ₹ 8.72.

In 1990, when Han was 23, a cousin recommended her name for a job in a department store in Shenzhen. The job was to attend to buyers in stalls selling cigarettes, wine, sugar, rice etc.

"I like this job so much, as there I learned how to be patient, how to be calm down, how to be humble."

Shenzhen was a new and exciting experience for Han. Compared to her hometown, it was like a 'foreign country' or a very fancy place. Even though Han worked from 6 am to midnight, she found the job easy, compared to factory work.

There was just one problem. Her boss had a younger sister, a tart and mean lady who liked to pick a fight for nothing. Many of Han's colleagues left because this lady was nasty to them. But Han stayed on.

No doubt she too was treated harshly but it was not in her nature to gossip or complain.

"I always feel grateful to my boss to give me new chance in life."

Han finally left after serving for more than two and half years. She was the longest working staff member.

"When I left, my boss was very sad and his wife also cried. Both of them always very good to me and stayed friendly relation with me."

Another important thing happened in Shenzhen – it was here that Han met her future husband, Wu Da Jian. In the village, due to her family's financial condition, no boy came near her or liked her. But in Shenzhen, she was just one of the millions of men and women looking for a better opportunity.

"I met my husband in 1991 through his cousin's sister, who was from my village. It was a blind date."

Wu Da Jian worked as a butcher and he and Han met just four times before they got married in 1992.

"I realised that he was a responsible man and I think I made a wise choice."

Life was going at a slow pace, neither Han nor her husband had any high ambition.

"We were always working and didn't think about too far ahead."

"I have a calmer attitude so I will mostly handle customer part. But I know everything about handling machine also."

The young couple shifted to Zhuhai and a few months later, her first daughter Wu Hui Ting was born, followed quickly by another daughter and a son.

From 1994 to 1998, Han stayed home to look after the kids while her husband worked as a taxi driver. This meant less income and they struggled to get through at times. But, mostly they managed.

The 90s was a 'boom time' for small manufacturers in China. Her husband's childhood friend gave them the idea of starting their own business

"He told us that there is good money in making labels and also assured that if we lose money, he could help to sell the plant."

The label machine cost 60,000 RMB (₹ 5.2 lakh), excluding materials and plant. The total amount needed was more than 100,000 RMB (₹ 8.7 lakh). Han cobbled together money from friends and relatives.

"Part of the money to start this business came from my old boss and his wife as a 'friendly loan'."

The label-making machine was bought from Guangzhou and on 1 May 1999, Han went into business from one very small room. Han was in the factory from 6 am till 1 or 2 am, the next morning. Her husband helped, but most of the jobs were done by her.

In addition, she had to look after the children.

"My son was 1 year and 3 months, younger daughter was 3 years old. Our house was near to factory so somehow I manage both."

Running a factory was not an easy task. The machine master / supervisor was a cheater and thief, so they were losing money each month.

"I realise I must have knowledge to operate machine without master's help."

When you are pushed into a corner you find hidden strength. Han and her husband found that strength, and survived.

It took about 3 months to make the first profit yet at the end of the year, they had earned more or less nothing. In fact, the company incurred a small loss. Yet, the couple persevered.

"We both have left our job, we have borrowed the money, so we must go on."

In April 2000, there was a serious fire in Beijing city. As a result, fire safety became a major concern. The department of urban management in Guangzhou started conducting checks on all the small units in the area, forcing many to shut down. Han's was the last plant standing in the Zhongda textile wholesales market.

"I had to work at night to avoid the inspection and just to continue."

Pressures continued mounting. Handling finances, inspections and also the machines – all at once – was difficult. At the same time, her husband's health became an issue. Han decided to give up and quit the business.

She went back to the friend who had promised to help them, in case the plant was in trouble. He was quite rich at the time and owned a large property. Yet, when Han handed over the materials list, he questioned her about 3,000 RMB (₹ 25,000), a very small amount.

"I was shocked to realise that he is not going to save us. I need to run this business, on my own, no matter how hard it was."

At that time Han's brother Han Hai agreed to join her in business. Together, they worked on many problems.

For handling machines, she took the advice of the machinery company and employed operators recommended by them. Han left the production and delivery work with her brother and husband while she went out to get more and bigger customers.

"In business one should always follow the rule of 'Good quality & Integrity."

"I work for family. Family is to love with your heart."

There were dozens of factories making labels, so how could Han do more business than others? It was on the basis of relationship, good quality and integrity.

"My first customer was a shop in the accessories market. They are still doing business with me and it is more of a friendship now."

By 2002, the problems had been ironed out and the company grew rapidly. "Actually it became bigger than we ever planned or thought."

After each season, Han and her husband would evaluate their earnings, think about what are the new trends and on that basis, add more machinery. Always using their own earnings from the business, never taking loans.

Thus from one large unit with a few machines, Han expanded to another, bigger factory. Demand increased and in 2003, they bought a third factory and were employing more than 70 workers.

"We have so much work so I call my sisters, other brother and my husband's brother to join the business and help me."

At this time, Han developed a new 'swing tag' which became very popular. In 2005, she gave this business to her cousin brother to run directly, as she had no time to spare.

After all, what is the purpose of running a business? To take care of and make your family happy. But is it easy to work together?

"Yes, my husband fight when we started business, lot of arguments. But we always preferred to talk it over as we respect each other very much."

With growth, they have matured and take it 'more easy' than before.

Other family members are handling different operations – one brother manages 'hang tag' factory, while sister handles printing. Han handles labels, customer relations and overall finance.

Han has the last word in all matters, yet she prefers to stay low-key.

"I will seldom show this to my relatives back home; that actually I am in charge."

For to be humble is in her blood, and it is in her upbringing. It is the natural fragrance of a woman.

From just over USD 5,000 turnover in 1999, Han's company has reached an annual turnover of more than $250,000 (₹ 1.4 crore) in 2012. It is not highly profitable at present, but Han is satisfied.

"Time is very bad for manufacturers in all over world, including China. Considering that, I feel we are not doing bad."

The business currently employs 150-200 workers. There are plans for expansion into trading business or 'export line', but after 4-5 years, when her children can join.

"Right now they are still in school or university. I will let them decide what they want to do, once they are ready."

After all, they have seen Han's struggles and been part of it all. The kids handled the cooking and household chores while Han put her heart and soul into her business.

"My eldest daughter cooks the gravy, son cooks rice, second daughter washes dishes. Like that we managed, only now we have maids."

Han is still young and full of energy. She has no plans to 'hand over' the business, any time soon.

To 'retire' means her life is not valuable any more.

"I would like to die with my 'Boots On'."

ADVICE TO WOMEN ENTREPRENEURS

Just follow your heart; and try to be happy and positive, always. In business, if you keep integrity high and be honest to your work and customers, you can never fail.

Try to be tolerant, hardworking, insistent and have a broad vision.

If you could not get high education, still you can do good business. Rather I feel hard work and determination are most important.

Most Chinese do value male more than female (though many Chinese women are doing better than males now).

Advantage in business: if women and men are in equal ability, customers prefer to choose female, as while working they're more exquisite / responsible / careful.

Wu Hui Ting (daughter):

My mum is a so kind woman. Because she think much about her families, her friends and her co-operation partners.

She is so persistent. She did her work well when she was young. She earned more money than other workers who worked for the same boss. Many things what she has decided she will try her best to do them well. And she really does some things perfectly.

She is so filial piety. She often looks after her parents. When she is free, she often comes to her parents' home and talks with them. She often gives money to her parents. She wants them to buy things what they like.

She loves talk with her friends who are younger than her. What's more, she has a young heart.

She reads some books now and watches some history television dramas. These can let her to learn more. She loves learning from the people who is successful.

CLIMB EVERY MOUNTAIN

Premlata Agarwal,
Mountaineer

In May 2011, this 48-year-old housewife from Jamshedpur became the oldest Indian woman to scale Mount Everest. Premlata's grit and determination prove that age is no bar, for any kind of enterprise or achievement.

I know many, many Premlatas. They are my aunts, first cousins and second cousins.

Agarwal girls whose matrimonial ads describe them as 'wheatish' and 'homely'.

Girls who cheerfully live up to that description to please our *samaaj*.

Premlata too bowed to the wishes of her parents when she had an arranged marriage, at age 18. She carried out her duties to her husband, in-laws and children like a good Indian housewife.

Never dreaming dreams for herself.

Until one fine day, the legendary mountaineer Bachendri Pal noticed her climbing talent. And convinced her that even at 35, she could start on an adventure.

To look up and away from her little world and aim to conquer the mountains.

"Kabhi socha na tha ki ek Marwari ladki, aur wo bhi iss age mein, yeh sab kar sakti hai."

Par ek baar socha to phir kar ke dikhaya.

13 years later, Premlata Agarwal scaled the summit of Mount Everest. At 48 years of age, she is the oldest Indian woman to have achieved this incredible feat.

An inspiration for anyone, anywhere who wonders 'do I have it in me?'

But most of all 'wheatish' and 'homely' women.

You are *more* than the labels that were given to you.

CLIMB EVERY MOUNTAIN

Premlata Agarwal,
Mountaineer

Premlata was born in Sukhiapokri, a small place near Darjeeling.

"We are seven sisters and two brothers. I am second number in sisters."

Premlata studied in a Nepali medium school, but only up to class 12.

"My father did want me to study further but *gharwalon ne kaha – kya karogi padkar. Naukri karni hai kya*?" (Others in the family said what's the point, you're not going to work, are you? Just get married.)

Thus in 1981, at age 18, Premlata moved to Jamshedpur to start a new life. Her husband belonged to a Marwari business class family. But a little different from usual.

"Our family is not as conservative as most Marwari families. When I said I want to study further my in-laws did not mind."

But within a year Premlata gave birth to a baby girl and the study plan was abandoned. Premlata settled into her life as a wife, mother and *bahu,* taking care of all in the family. Doing the 'best possible' for her two daughters was the main priority. Education, sports – all-round development.

"In the evenings I used to take my daughters to the J R D Sports Complex to learn tennis. Since I had to wait there while they practised, I joined the ladies' gym – mainly for yoga classes."

At the J R D Complex, Premlata came to know of the 'Dalma Hills Walking Competition', organised by the famous mountaineer Bachendri Pal. She took part and – unexpectedly – won the third prize.

"When I went to collect her certificate from Bachendriji's office, I saw her photographs on Mount Everest. I was so impressed that I told her – 'I want my daughter to join adventure line'."

Bachendri replied, "*Beti hi kyun*? Why don't you take it up yourself?"

Premlata was astonished. At 36 years of age? For a housewife? How would it be possible?

"Age is no bar," replied Bachendri. "*Agar kuch karna hai to koi bhi age mein aa sakte hai*."

And that's how Premlata's mountaineering career started, in the year 1999. The very first stop was the Nehru Institute of Mountaineering in Uttarkashi, for a basic course of 21 days. Most of the trainees – including Premlata's own daughter – were half her age.

The instructor mocked, "*Iss age mein mountaineering karne aayi ho*? You won't be able to do it."

Premlata replied, "Bachendriji has sent me, *kuch sochkar hi bheja hoga*."

"This is not Dalma Hills of Jamshedpur," said the instructor. And, it surely was not. The one-month course involved trekking in the Himalayan mountains, up to a height of 13,000 feet. The trainee must secure an 'A' grade – or repeat the course. To everyone's surprise, Premlata not only secured an 'A' grade but also the 'best trainee' award.

"*Hoon to main Darjeeling ki*, I was used to walking in the mountains," she smiles. "But I never thought I will join mountaineering!"

One month, one victory, one giant leap in confidence. Premlata went on to do the advanced course at the Himalayan Mountaineering Institute in Darjeeling.

"*Mera hausla badhta gaya*. (I gained confidence.) Then, I started going with Bachendriji for mountaineering expeditions."

These annual expeditions – ranging from 21 days to a month – took Premlata to the Karakoram pass, Stok Kangri (Ladakh) and

Island Peak (Nepal). Getting permission from her in-laws was an issue in the initial period. But her husband always stood by her like a rock.

"You don't worry – *hum sab sambhaal lenge*," he would say.

Luckily, the expeditions were always in the month of May when schools shut for vacation. So the girls would be packed off to their nani's place.

"One thing I was sure that *unki padhaai kabhi affect nahin hui (their studies were not affected)*."

Another small mountain Premlata conquered was the freedom to wear what she wanted. And it started much before she began climbing the other mountains.

"When I first got married I wore only saris, that too with *pallu* over my head."

That was sheer torture in the heat of Jamshedpur. So one day her husband said, "You can stop covering your head."

Over time, *salwar kameez* started becoming common. Premlata wanted to adopt this practical dress in day-to-day life. But her mother-in-law objected.

"Dadiji (grandmother) won't like it."

Dadiji was sitting right there so Premlata innocently asked her, "Do you have any objection if I wear salwar suit?"

Dadi was very fond of Premlata so she was in a dilemma. She could not object but she could not approve either – she stayed silent.

"Donon ek doosre ka mooh taak rahe the, main jaldi se andar jaakar suit pehen kar aa gayi." (Each was waiting for the other to

"Jabse main shaadi karke yahan aayi sari pehenti thi. Aur pallu bhi dhakke rakhna padta tha."

(After marriage I always wore a sari and also covered my head.)

"Uss samay sunke to bohot hi hairani hui ki is age mein aur ek housewife ke liye adventure sports join karna."

(Taking up adventure sports at my age, being a housewife, it was a shocking idea.)

say something, in the meantime I quickly changed into a *salwar* suit and came out.)

A clean heart with clean intent produces clean results.

"I married young so I did not know much about *duniyadari*," she laughs. "I always took things at face value."

Once Premlata took up mountaineering, she started wearing pants. But it wasn't an issue any more. What remained an issue was the amount of time she could give to the sport. Always, it was a question of balance.

"Many times I would come home after training in the gym for 2-3 hours and rush straight into the kitchen."

Without even changing out of her tracksuit and sports shoes.

"My husband used to say do everything you want to do but make sure you don't neglect *ma-babuji*. They must get their food on time."

How Premlata would do it was her problem to solve. And like a resourceful Indian housewife, she did.

Yet, there were dilemmas. In 2004, when she completed the Island Peak expedition, Bachendri Pal told Premlata, "You are extremely fit. Now you must train for Mount Everest."

"*Main haske reh jaati thi*," says Premlata. (I would laugh it off.)

Both her daughters were in school and she could not afford to be away from home for months on end. Which you require, to train for Everest. So she never even raised the topic at home. Five years later, during an expedition to Mount Kilimanjaro, Bachendri Pal put forth the challenge again. This time, circumstances were different.

"My elder daughter was married while my younger one had completed class 12 and was studying in a college outside Jamshedpur."

This time, Premlata asked her husband, "Bachendriji is asking me to train for climbing Mount Everest. Will I get three months 'leave' from home… maybe even more?"

Premlata's husband immediately said, "Yes! You must do it."

Her father-in-law added, "*Beti, tum ja sakti ho*. You have my blessings."

At that moment Premlata *knew* she would do it. She *had* to do it. She was now 47.

Training started with rigorous morning and evening sessions at the gym. Jogging, weights, yoga, pranayama, aerobics – everything. This was followed up with another advanced course at the Himalayan Mountaineering institute in Darjeeling. Technically, Premlata was not eligible for the course as the cut-off age was 35.

"I told them my age is 35 only and they believed me."

Premlata then went to Sikkim for training in 'snow climbing' and 'ice climbing' in December 2010. This involved 8-10 hours of continuous trekking – ascending and descending on the same day. The sherpa she was training with pronounced – "You are ready for Everest!"

Many climbers reach the base of the summit. It's conquering the summit that needs true stamina.

"When you go for summit, oxygen is very less and you can't carry extra with you. So you have to be able to climb at a fast pace."

Premlata was confident – she could do it. On 25 March 2011, she boarded a flight for Kathmandu and onwards to Lukla. This is where the trekking for Everest begins, at 8000 feet above sea level. The journey to the peak would take approximately 3 months.

"Every day I would go for jogging carrying a 20 kg load. You have to build that kind of stamina for Everest."

"In any expedition you can see the summit but it still seems very far *Lekin mujhe aisa kuch feel nahin hota tha.*"

(But I never felt disturbed by that.)

"First we climbed Island Peak and Kala Pattar as a pre-Everest expedition. Finally, we reached the Everest Base Camp."

This is where the adventure *really* starts. There are four camps on the route to Everest. Climbers must acclimatise themselves for 45 days by going back and forth from Base Camp to Camp 1 and Camp 2. Spending one night at higher altitude and then making the descent. And right from this point, you are in danger.

To reach Camp 1, you have to cross treacherous glacial crevasses using a flimsy aluminium ladder. The ladder sways in the wind and the mountaineer must maintain balance. A task all the more difficult for Premlata due to a childhood injury to her ankle.

"I was finding it very difficult to balance, especially while descending. At times there is no ladder and you just have to jump across. *Woh toh aur bhi mushkil tha*."

The sherpa accompanying the group would constantly taunt, "Where have you done your course? If you don't know how to position your leg why have you come here?"

In fact, right from Kathmandu, the sherpa was having doubts. Premlata's elder daughter had come to see her off. After she left, the sherpa asked, "*Aapki beti kahaan gayi*? Doesn't she want to climb Everest?"

Premlata replied, "No, I'm the one who will be climbing."

The sherpa was shocked – an Indian lady, at *this* age, attempting such a feat? For the rest of the trip he did nothing but discourage and demoralise Premlata. But, she was made of sterner stuff.

"I knew I have set out on a mission. *Kuch bhi ho jaye, kaise bhi ho, mission ko poora karna hai*."

The sherpa would constantly say, "Why have you come here, you can't do it!"

But Premlata's only focus was all those who believed in her.

"I had so much support at home, from husband and family. Tata Steel had spent so much money on my training. Bachendri didi had so much confidence in me. *Vo saara vishwaas, sari shakti mujhe push kar rahi thi*."

A hidden reservoir of strength lies dormant in each of us. Waiting for a challenge, a difficulty, an 'impossible' task.

"Whenever I was having difficulty, I would keep reciting Hanuman Chalisa. I must have recited thousands of times."

The group of six climbers, which included a husband-wife team from the police force and one other woman, reached Camp 2 without incident. Both women took oxygen from Camp 2, whereas Premlata waited to reach Camp 3 (24,000 ft). But here's where the trouble started. The weather on Mount Everest is highly unpredictable and it suddenly took a turn for the worse.

"There was *aandhi-toofan*, strong winds of over 100 km per hour. Snow was flying all around and onto our faces…"

Taking a single step became an ordeal and yet, the climbers continued. Because they were *almost* there. But then the sherpa got news on his satellite phone that the weather was expected to get even worse. The climbers protested – they were ready to battle it out.

The sherpa said, "*Everest yahin rahega, jaan bachegi to phir chad lenge…*" (Everest will remain here, we can return to climb it another day.)

"Gharwalon ka, Bachendri didi ka, Tata steel ka, sabka jo vishwas tha vo upar tak leke gaya. Laga mujhe mere aim tak pohochna hai kaise bhi."

(My family, Bachendri didi, Tata Steel – all of them had so much confidence in me. That gave me the strength to reach the summit, no matter what.)

"Mujhe lagta hai ki hamare undar itni shakti hai... jo day to day life mein 10% bhi use nahi hoti."

(I believe we have so much power hidden within ourselves. We don't use even 10% of that power in day to day life.)

Reluctantly, the group descended to Camp 3, thinking they would spend a couple of nights and make another attempt as soon as the weather cleared. But all the tents at Camp 3 had been swept away. There was no choice but to descend to Camp 2 (21, 500 ft). And from there, back to square zero – Base Camp (17, 500 ft).

"We had no oxygen, no rations, so we had no choice… It seemed like our Everest expedition was over."

Premlata – suffering from dehydration – lay in a tent for three days. At this point she spoke to her husband on satellite phone.

He said, "All the newspapers have reported that you have returned without reaching the summit… It's okay, you come back safe and sound, nothing is more important."

But before ending the conversation he added, "*Lekin phir bhi dekh lena… matlab try karna*." (But still, see the situation… give it a try.)

Premlata spoke to her brother in Darjeeling. He said, "Don't put your life in danger… but just see, in case weather improves…"

In fact, the weather had started clearing.

Her elder daughter had words of encouragement, "Mummy, you can do it!"

Finally, her father said, "*Jab ek kadam aage badhaya hai kuch karne ke liye to peeche kyon hatna*. (You have taken a step forward, now why are you stepping back.) You could die any time and any where. In a road accident, or train accident. Don't be afraid of death!"

All these words energised Premlata and convinced her, there was no turning back. The team leader warned that the weather was not 'great' but they could make a second attempt. The group decided to take its chances. Once again, they started the ascent. This time, the problem occurred at Camp 4 (27,000 ft). Premlata's oxygen started malfunctioning.

"The sherpa was walking ahead of me. I was afraid to tell him as he might say – *vaapas chalo*, turn back."

So, Premlata attempted to fix the problem herself. She removed the washer and put a cotton tissue paper in its place. That made it far worse and more difficult to breathe. Just beneath the famous 'Hillary step,' the group took a moment of rest. Premlata tried to adjust her oxygen mask but the heavy gloves she was wearing made it hard to use her fingers.

"I took off my right glove and kept it on the ground. In a second, it had flown off..."

Oxygenless, gloveless, Premlata was in a dire situation. At 27,000 ft, at minus 45 degrees centigrade, your fingers will turn blue in minutes, without protective covering. Premlata realised that this was truly 'the end' for her. Yet the words of her family, the trust of Bachendri didi, the expectations of her country – all weighed on her.

"*Bas yehi khayal aaya ki mujhe kaise bhi climb karna hai.*"

The next step she took produced a miracle. A cream-coloured woollen glove lay on the ground in front of her. It was not insulated, it was not the proper recommended equipment, but it was good enough.

"I put on the glove and it gave me so much *shakti* that I reached the peak."

Premlata scaled Mount Everest on 20 May 2011 at 9:30 am. She spent 20 glorious minutes on 'top of the world'. *Maano, chaaro taraf swarg.*

"I had taken two cameras – quickly we took some pictures. This is the 'proof' of reaching summit!"

Premlata wanted to do some video recording but the sherpa insisted they had to start descending – the weather was once again worsening. Sheer grit and determination had kept Premlata going. Now, pain and exhaustion started kicking in.

"Our ration of biscuits and chocolate were over... My stomach was empty as I had not eaten for 24 hours!"

"Abhi bhi bohot log samajh nahi pate ki Everest chadhne ka 'fayda' kya hai. Koi inaam mila? Ya phir Bhagwaan mila?"

(People don't understand why I climbed Everest. Did I get any prize? Did I meet with God?)

Another miracle came in the form of a foreign climber, who shared his ration of liquid chocolate. Thus fortified, Premlata continued the descent. As she sipped on her only remaining thermos of precious water, it was her turn to 'pay it forward'.

"There were so many climbers, *sab to ek ghoont paani ke liye taraste hai vahan*."

In sharing, the thermos was quickly exhausted. The sherpa scolded Premlata for her foolhardiness. But by now, he knew she was far stronger than he had reckoned. The group reached Camp 2 and then, Base Camp. It was then that Premlata took off her gloves and realised that her fingers *had* turned blue.

In addition, her shoes were causing trouble, so she decided to take them off.

"I walked down to Lukla only in my slippers."

In Kathmandu, Premlata's husband, daughters and *bhaiyya-bhabhi* were waiting for her to arrive.

"My success is not mine alone… *sab ka saath tha*."

Premlata's husband pipes in, "*Mera kuch role nahi hai*… only that I did not object to her taking up this path."

And, he stood by her, when anyone in the family or community objected.

"I feel, if I could not do something big in life, at least let me not stop her from achieving."

And the quest continues. In 2012, Premlata conquered Mt Elbrus in Russia and Mt Aconcagua in South America. Her dream is to climb the 7 highest summits across 7 continents, which will be another first for an Indian woman.

And back on firm ground, Premlata would like to start a fitness centre. Teaching yoga, aerobics and meditation to the women of Jamshedpur. Already, she has held a month-long fitness training camp for ladies of the Marwari comminity. And it has changed attitudes.

Many used to ask her mother-in-law, "Why does Premlata want to climb mountains? *Kitna paisa kamaati hai*?"

Premlata's *saasu* would reply, "It's not for money… in fact we have to spend our own money for training."

And they would be horrified.

"After one month training with me they got a lot of energy. And they stopped asking such questions."

When Premlata returned from Mount Everest, the same ladies gathered at the station with *aarti ki thaalis* and garlands. Not that they truly *understood* why she had to do it. Or, what it takes.

Nothing, no matter how small, can be taken for granted.

"Being a vegetarian, I had to survive on *dal-chawal. Wo bhi height par kade kade bante hain*."

No matter how many layers of clothes you wear, you are *always* cold.

"*Jaise fridge ke andar so rahe hain*," laughs Premlata.

And regardless of how well-trained you are, ultimately it boils down to Faith.

"Every day the ice shifts, the routes change… every day the ladders are put in place but really, they are for your mental satisfaction only."

In front of Premlata's eyes, a sherpa fell into a crevasse. His body disappeared*, never to be found.

"The sherpas are responsible for the safety of the climbers… and they do their job well. But they don't actually hold your hand or 'help' you as such."

Khud hi jaana padta hai – each man, each woman on their own.

Climbing Everest then, is like life itself.

Whatever the mountain you set, as your goal.

---

* 10 climbers were killed while attempting to scale Mount Everest, in the year 2011.

ADVICE TO WOMEN ENTREPRENEURS

Main to yehi bolungi sabhi ladies se... ladies hi kyon, male members ko bhi bolungi.

I would say to all ladies... and why just ladies, men also...

Duniya bohot sundar hai. Uske liye aap apna shareer ko fit rakhiye aur positive attitude mein rahiye, to aap duniya ka ek ek pal jee sakte hai. Aap present mein jiye. Past ya future ko bhul jaaiye aur humare andar ek power hai... aisa power hai ki hum kuch bhi achieve kar sakte hain.

(The world is very beautiful, all you need is a fit body and positive mental attitude to live every moment of it fully. Live in the present. Forget the past or the future. We all have tremendous power within... such a power that we can achieve anything we desire.)

Agar aap dil se chahte ho kuch karna aur usmein 100% lagoge koi bhi field mein, aap zaroor safal honge. Agar usmein aap safal kahi bhi nahi hote hai to aap dil se usko paana nahi chahte hai aur usmein aap apna 100% nahi laga rahe.

(If you want to do something with your whole heart and put in 100% – in any field – you will definitely be successful. If you are not successful then it means that either you did not desire it deeply enough or you neglected to give it your 100%.)

Ek aur cheez hai ki kabhi bhi koi bhi success hota hai... to akele uske bas ki baat nahi hoti, bohot logon ka support chahiye. Is liye sab ko, family ko, saath mein lekar hi aagey badhna chahiye.

(One last thing which is that success is never an individual achievement. You need the support and blessings of many people. Let your family share your dreams and ambitions, take them with you, as you move ahead in life.)

DURGA

Circumstances forced these women to be enterprising, to fight for survival. They rose to the challenge, slaying demons within and without. Tapping into divine energy – or Shakti – which lies dormant in each of us.

I WILL SURVIVE

Patricia Narayan,
Caterer

An alcoholic husband forced Patricia to leave her cocoon and step out into the world. From a stall on Marina Beach the enterprise has grown into a food-court chain, proving that women can do *anything* – if they put into it their heart and soul.

The room is sparsely furnished. A gilded photo frame with a picture of Jesus Christ hangs prominently on the wall.

Patricia is simply dressed, she has deep dark circles under the eyes. She has had a tough life, and it shows.

Married at 19 to a man who turned into an alcoholic and wife-beater, Patricia was left with the job of raising two young children. Not wanting to be a financial burden on her parents, she decided to go out and earn a living.

"I did something on my own to prove a point. I didn't want people to say, see she got married on her own and became a failure," she says calmly.

If it meant running from pillar to post, working 24×7 carrying huge responsibility on frail shoulders – so be it. The motivation was different but the struggle just the same.

There are millions of women like Patricia, suffering in silence. But they are not as helpless as they might feel. Economic power changes many equations. Brings respect, recognition and self-esteem.

Others can offer a helping hand or a shoulder to cry on. But the best course of action is to wipe your tears, don your *dupatta* and create a new life and new goals for yourself.

Because you have more power in your gentle hands than you think....

I WILL SURVIVE

Patricia Narayan, Caterer

Patricia Narayan was born in Nagarcoil, a small town in the Kanyakumari district of Tamil Nadu. But both her parents were government servants, so she was brought up in Chennai.

"I belong to a very conservative Christian family. I am the eldest, with a sister and a brother younger to me."

In fact, it was a joint family, with grandparents, uncle and aunt living together. A close-knit one. After completing her schooling at St Thomas Convent, Santhome, Patricia joined Queen Mary's college for the BA course. But in her second year of college – 1977 – something happened. Patricia fell in love.

"He was running a restaurant right opposite my college. I was half in love with the man, and half in love with his kitchen!"

Right from her childhood, Patricia had a passion for cooking.

"I was always doing something or the other, trying out new dishes. So to me – apart from the thrill of romance – there was the thrill of entering a commercial kitchen."

In those days, cutlets or *chhole-puri* was a novelty in Chennai. Something you rarely – if ever – made at home. Patricia made it a daily habit to go to the restaurant at lunchtime, just to watch what was going on.

Another thing you didn't do back then was simply have an 'affair'.

"After 3-4 months I decided to get married."

Both families were opposed to the idea – Patricia being Christian and the boy, Hindu. So the couple had a registered marriage.

"For two months after the marriage, I sat at home quietly. I didn't have the courage to tell anyone."

But how long can you keep such a secret? *Baat nikal aayi* and with great reluctance, Patricia's family 'accepted' the boy. They held a 'proper' wedding.

At the end of it her father said, "I have done my duty, now you are on your own."

"I know, he had many dreams for me. I shattered them all. But then I thought ok, at least I have married the person I love!"

But is love enough? Not in this case. Very soon, Patricia realised that the man she had married had a lot of issues. Serious issues like addiction to alcohol and drugs. Physical and verbal abuse became an everyday affair.

"The minute I realised that my life came to a full stop, there was not even a comma there. I knew I have done the most stupidest thing on earth... by marrying this man."

The one silver lining in this dark cloud was the support of her mother.

"Everything had happened so fast... I was pregnant with my first child. My mother stood by me like a rock during that difficult time. If I am sitting here and talking to you today, I owe it to her."

Patricia bared her heart to her mother. And without judgement, without blame, her mother took her back into the family fold.

"My dad was working night shift, so somehow Mom managed to get me, my husband and child into the house to stay. And she said, 'We will get him out of all these bad habits'."

Emotional support was abundant, but finances were tight. For the first time in her life, Patricia felt the burning desire to earn money. Fuelled by hunger, fuelled by want.

"Till the day I got married I never knew what problems were. I never knew the price of vegetables or dal or what it was like to 'not have money'. I knew I had to go out and earn."

But what kind of work can a 19-year-old college dropout do? There were no call centres, no malls.

"My exposure was also so less and I was very demotivated. But it was a 'live or die situation' … I had to do something to survive. Not for me but for my child also."

So Patricia turned to the one skill she had – cooking. Since her mother was working, she had a lot of friends in the office who lapped up the homemade goodies.

"That gave me courage. And I started thinking – what next, what more?"

Patricia had another passion – making artificial flowers. She took up a course to perfect her skills, and then started supplying decorative pieces to hotels.

"I could stay up all night making the flowers, I loved it so much," recalls Patricia. "But, it did not bring in much money, you know."

It was then that a family friend – a doctor – gave her an idea. The doctor was associated with a school for the handicapped and knew that the government was giving out stalls in public areas. On one condition – the stall owner would have to train and employ the handicapped.

Patricia right away said, "I am interested!"

"But where do you want your stall?" asked the doctor.

"Marina Beach," she replied, without hesitation. It was a place she was familiar with, where she knew large crowds came on weekends.

"And one thing for me is that when I want something, I always think of something which I definitely know I can get. But this thing, I had no idea. Where to start, even."

"I felt like killing myself at times but I had a small baby. I said to myself, 'I got into this, I will have to get out of this'."

"It took more than a year to get approval for my first stall but I fought for it ... I did not allow anything to dampen my spirits."

It was the PWD (Public Works Department) which would have to be approached, for permission. A Mount Everest of a task for a soft-spoken, timid young Patricia.

"I went to meet the secretary, his office was on the 8th floor I think. You won't believe this but I was so terrified of getting into the lift, I climbed up the stairs!"

Carrying the little one. But, there was more to come.

The secretary said, "You can't just walk in and ask to see so-and-so officer. You need an appointment or a reference, at least."

Patricia said, "I don't know anybody... I don't have any contacts... but I have to meet him."

She said, "Okay. but he is in a meeting till 3.30 in the afternoon. You will have to wait."

Patricia sat there, for hours. Finally, Madhavan Sharma – IAS – arrived.

He asked his secretary, "Who is that lady with a child sitting outside?"

And he called Patricia in first, ahead of the folks with appointments and referrals. After hearing Patricia's story – and her request – he called up the executive engineer of the relevant sub-division and said, "I am sending this lady to you. Do whatever is possible for her."

Nothing happened immediately – there was running from pillar to post for almost a year. But, Patricia believed, and she persevered.

"It's like you get the blessings from God but then the *pujari* doesn't allow you to enter the temple... But I didn't mind. I completed all the procedures, met various people."

Without hesitation, whenever an officer would call, Patricia would go.

"But mind you, I did not spend a single *paisa* as bribe. And ultimately I got the approval."

To sell snacks and drinks from Marina Beach, between 3 pm and 11 pm. The menu included cutlets, *samosa*, *bhel*, tea, coffee and ice cream.

"We started on 20 April 1981 – it was a Friday. I spent the whole morning preparing the food – and about 80 cups of coffee."

And she stood there, waiting for customers.

Nobody came.

"Finally at about 7:30 in the evening, one gentleman bought a coffee for 50 paise. That was my only sale of the day!"

Patricia went home and cried her heart out.

It was her mother who consoled, her "Don't give up hope, give it some time!"

The next day was a Saturday and from the moment Patricia set up her stall, the food and drink was flying off the counter.

"I did not have a moment to catch my breath even!" she grins.

As promised, Patricia employed two young students – both deaf and dumb – as assistants.

"I taught them everything, right from how to peel onions. They were very sincere and learnt quickly."

To stand on one's own feet is a wonderful feeling. When in doing so you also help others, you are truly fulfilled.

The Clarke Snack Bar became a popular hangout on Marina Beach. With time, Patricia got additional facilities like permanent electric supply.

"So I started selling juice and ice cream also."

Patricia had the knack of understanding customers.

"My memory was very good, you know. So if someone orders the same item few times, the next time I keep it ready for them!"

And she would constantly introduce new items, kind of 'test marketing' what people liked, what she could add to her menu.

"When you see people eating, when they relish it, they don't even

"I did not go to a catering college, so every day on the job I was learning new things."

have to tell you. You look at them and you know. That gave me a lot of encouragement!"

When you put your heart and soul into something – no matter how small – it creates a path. To something bigger.

Marina Beach had a 'Walkers' Association'. Top bureaucrats, ministers and CEOs came each morning, and many were regulars at Patricia's stall. One such customer opened up a new opportunity.

"This officer worked with the Slum Rehabilitation Board and they were looking for a caterer."

He said, "Your food is good, why don't you try for it?"

The Slum Board catered not only to its own officers but to visitors as well. Wednesdays and Fridays were public grievance days – more than 2000-odd people thronged the building. That could be big business!

So, Patricia applied and she got the contract.

"They gave me a good kitchen with a nice counter. I got some more people to join me and soon I was making really good money."

The Marina Beach stall was already doing well.

"The maximum sale on a single day – it was a *bandh*, I remember – it was ₹ 15,000."

Leaving the stall in the able hands of her assistants, Patricia decided to focus all her energies on the new catering business. There was just one problem: her husband.

"Sometimes he would come and create a scene, or just take away the cash box and vanish. If I didn't give him money, he would beat me, abuse me..."

But whatever it was, Patricia accepted the situation stoically.

"I felt that I had disobeyed my parents and so I deserve this punishment."

Her only aim, her only priority was to look after her children.

"In 1982, my daughter Sandra was born. Both the children were looked after by my sister, brother and mother while I was working, day and night."

The canteen served breakfast, lunch, dinner and snacks. So preparations would start at 3 in the morning,

"It was very tiring. But then, once you start liking your work you don't really feel tired. Only thing I felt is that 24 hours is not enough!"

Managing a kitchen operation – no matter how big – was the easy part. Managing the accounts was quite another story.

"I really don't know what profits I made, my focus was only doing business and whatever my needs are, they should be taken care of."

After a lot of prodding, Patricia ventures a rough estimate.

"I think Marina Beach stall, probably we were making sales of ₹ 1.5-2 lakh per month..."

A pretty large sum of money back then!

"Yes, but I was also expanding the business. For the canteen business, I had to buy my own equipment. So like that, I kept investing the money in new projects."

The next offer came from Bank of Madurai. And Patricia had to make a tough call.

"The bank was in a different area, so I had to choose which business to do. Slum Board was good, but I thought the bank will have a better atmosphere, better clientele... I can price my food a little higher!"

Thus in 1986, Patricia took over the canteen operation of the Bank of Madurai, Mount Road branch. While the sun was shining through on the professional front, dark clouds remained in her personal life.

"My kids were in school, my husband however was just the same. I took him to de-addiction centres but he was so stubborn, he would never complete the treatment."

Despite all this, Patricia bravely carried on. And, another new path opened.

"I was a tough taskmaster – my boys were terrified of me. They knew I would never take any nonsense in the kitchen."

"I heard from my uncle that the National Institute of Port Management (NIPM) is looking for a new caterer. So one fine day, I hopped into a bus and went there."

NIPM is situated on the East Coast Road, 25 km outside Chennai city. It was rather impractical to travel that far every day. And yet, something inside Patricia said, "I must go there".

By the time she reached, the office had closed for the day. But the administrative officer was there, and he was kind enough to meet her.

"He showed me the canteen – it was like a 5-star hotel kitchen! The boilers, the freezer, everything was huge."

Patricia was reeling with shock and excitement.

"The way he was talking to me it sounded like I would have to start the next day..."

The officer asked, "Can you handle this place?"

Patricia summoned all her strength and replied confidently, "Yes, I can".

The officer gave her the rates – they were subsidised, since NIPM was giving the space, as well as free equipment.

"I went home and did all the workings. The margins were low but it was such a big opportunity, and so thrilling! I wanted to do it."

The next day Patricia met the Chairman. An elderly man, in a big office. Patricia felt small and nervous. She sat at the edge of a large sofa, her legs almost trembling.

The Chairman asked, "Do you know who you will be catering to here? We have young boys who have just come out of school. They do vigorous physical training from 5 am till 7 am."

At 7.30 in the morning breakfast was to be served.

"They are like lions who come out of the jungle and attack anything you give them!"

The Chairman doubted Patricia would be able to handle the pressure.

"This is not a housewife's job."

Patricia replied, "No, sir – I can manage it. At least give me one trial!"

The Chairman abruptly got up and said, "Nice meeting you, you can leave now."

Patricia came out, disappointed. The administrative officer was more sympathetic.

"Let me see what I can do."

A few days later, the officer and some of the staff came to Bank of Madurai. But nothing happened. Months passed by, when suddenly in the April of 1991, Patricia got an SOS from NIPM.

"We are having a problem with our caterer, will you be able to take over?"

It was a Monday evening, and they wanted Patricia to start by Friday!

The officer added, "I am putting myself on the line by giving you the contract. Please don't let me down!"

Patricia assured him everything would happen smoothly. On Wednesday, she released an ad for cooks and workers. On Thursday, she conducted the interviews. On Friday, she was at NIPM – lock, stock, staff and barrel.

"The previous caterer served the evening dinner and left the place – in a huge mess!"

Luckily a couple of the old staff stayed back. And Patricia had her own people as well. Overnight, they cleaned up the kitchen and set into motion the next day's work.

"Morning 5.30 I have to serve bed coffee, which I managed without any major problems."

The weekend provided a bit of a breather, by Monday morning everything was absolutely no problem. The lions came, they saw and they had their fill.

"Only one thing I was very particular, that on the 5th of every month I have to pay the salaries. Not a day late."

"Yes, it really was like that (*laughs*). Everything was unlimited, they would eat 10-12 *phulkas* at a time!"

Catering to 500 such stomachs was a challenge, but a manageable one.

"The Chairman was very particular that *phulkas* should be *phulkas* and not *papads*. He never had any cause for complaint!"

However, this was not the case at the Bank of Madurai.

"I had to be at NIPM 24x7 so I left the other canteen in the hands of my staff. My husband just had to go there and sit there – the boys were managing all the work."

Although there were no problems with the food service, the bank was not happy with the supervisory arrangement.

"My husband was deteriorating. Now that he had money, he behaved even more badly."

A month after she took up the NIPM contract the Bank of Madurai called and said, "If you want to run the business, you are most welcome. But we don't want your husband to come here."

Apparently he was coming to work in an inebriated condition. With a heavy heart, Patricia gave up the bank canteen. And she became a more hard-nosed businesswoman.

"Until then, I used to take contracts in my husband's name because I used to think it's better to have a man's support, even if only on paper."

Let not the male ego be hurt!

"But everywhere he created problems, it became too much for me. So I signed the NIPM contract in my own name."

And Patricia was most particular about her name.

"My main focus was on providing the best quality".

It was tough, because she got a fixed price per person per day, but the quantity was unlimited. Still, Patricia never compromised.

"Like, if something went wrong I would not even think for a minute. I would simply throw 300-400 litres of gravy in the gutter and ask the boys to cook again."

Patricia was also very particular about the quality of her ingredients.

"I would go to the beach at 4 o'clock in the morning and personally buy fish in the auction. I would buy the costliest and the tastiest variety and only serve the centre pieces."

Hearty seafaring men were known to gobble down 6-7 slices at one sitting.

"I would stand there watching them and feel tense. Because it should not be less, you know... But just seeing them relishing my food was the biggest satisfaction."

Little wonder then that at his farewell party, the Chairman came up to Patricia and complimented her.

"You have done a wonderful job – you have made us all proud."

Of course, Patricia was earning more than compliments. The NIPM contract was bringing in annual revenues of over ₹ 1 crore. Patricia now had a kitchen staff of 70, as well as a manager and an accountant.

"Ya, but you know my focus was always on the work."

The one stress factor was the distance.

"I used to first go daily by bus. Then, they gave me quarters so I would stay for 2-3 days at a time, then come home and take the children there for weekends."

With a huge private beach and plenty of running around space, the kids were more than happy to tag along.

"My work time I never compromised. The children were mostly under my mother's care, my sister and my brother helped also."

In 1992, Patricia finally filed for a divorce. The couple had already separated but the legal formality became necessary for the sake of the children.

"I used to travel up and down every day, roads were bad. One of

"You can call it micromanagement but I am fanatic about details, I look into everything."

my friends said one day – what if something happens to you? Everything you earn will go to your husband, your kids will be left with nothing!"

Liberation is more in the mind, than on a piece of paper. But sometimes, the paper is that final act which frees the soul. To sing its song stronger and sweeter.

"I took up one more contract at a dental college and a medical college hostel. Both were right outside the NIPM gate."

Of course, the rates were lower and menu limited, but Patricia was happy enough to cater to 500 more stomachs. What's more, she got a free hand to set up the kitchen with her own equipment. And manage it as she liked.

"I had never learnt the 'right way' to do things, I had created my own systems!"

This was especially in the area of procurement. Patricia would go to the market on Wednesdays and Sundays and make all the purchases.

"On Sundays I would buy provisions as well as vegetables, so I hired a 407 (matador). On Wednesdays I would pile up my perishables in an auto."

By this time, Patricia had a 'permanent auto guy' who would also ferry her between work and home.

"I did not feel safe travelling late by bus, so I switched to auto. Then I found I am spending ₹ 300-400 per day on auto. So somebody suggested to me I buy a vehicle and hire a driver."

So Patricia bought a second-hand car. But it was more a matter of convenience than personal comfort.

"NIPM had many short courses, so every week the number of people I was catering to will change. So, my entire thinking would be what I have to purchase, what will be the menu."

Like milk on the stove, minor crises will boil over – if left unattended.

"The main cook will suddenly go on leave, or there will be a small accident in the kitchen. It's all a part of life, you learn to deal with it."

But something quite unexpected happened in 1996. NIPM decided to float a tender and invite other caterers to bid for the contract. There were no problems or complaints with Patricia, but some people were envious of her success.

"You see, people saw me first coming by bus and auto, then by second-hand car. And now I had a new car. So they started making comments like 'Oh you are earning so much', without realising how hard I am working!"

Also, by this time, East Coast Road was no longer on the outskirts of Chennai. NIPM itself had expanded, making the catering contract more lucrative.

"The lowest bid was 10% below my price. They told me I can continue if I am willing to work at that rate."

But Patricia refused.

"I was already providing the best quality at the lowest price possible. Where could I compromise?"

Giving up the kitchen she had run for seven years was hard. But not as hard as giving up her principles.

Besides, Patricia still had her beach stall and catering contracts for three colleges. At the same time, in 1996, she dabbled in setting up a restaurant.

"It was a small place called Chef Suzanne. What was different is we had an open kitchen – a full glass kitchen – and we served tandoori, which was something new in Chennai!"

The restaurant became popular but the location was not suitable.

"We were operating from a basement and the drainage was poor. The whole place would get flooded everytime it rained."

Patricia was willing to spend ₹ 50,000 and get repairs done. But the landlord was unwilling to sign a 3-year lease. Around the same time, her son – Praveen – was going to the UK for further studies.

"So, I decided to shut shop and go with him, settle him in."

"I did feel guilty about neglecting my kids but my son knew what I had been through, he understood everything."

On her return, Patricia got involved with another restaurant, this time as a partner.

"I used to attend this exhibition on food in Singapore, that's where I met a very renowned restaurant owner. As we were visiting the various stalls, suddenly he made me an offer!"

Patricia was a bit taken aback, but then quickly accepted. It was a vegetarian restaurant – a new concept for Patricia. But, why not!

"I also gave my inputs for the decor, and it was very much appreciated. Actually, my partner gave me a lot of respect and recognition for my work because he could see – 'here is another workaholic like me'!"

Life finally seemed to be turning a corner on the personal front as well. Patricia finally bought her own flat and moved out of her parents' place.

"I always preferred to live jointly but my kids had grown up and needed space. So I decided to become independent."

While daughter Sandra was in college, son Praveen was now an officer in the merchant navy. What prouder moment for a mother than to see her kids well settled?

Patricia also fulfilled a long-cherished dream – of owning a small flower shop.

"I'm a person who loves to give flowers instead of gifts. I used to visit a particular shop and used to think, 'How nice if I could sit here surrounded by all this beauty of nature.'"

One day Patricia got a call from the lady who owned the shop.

She said, "I'm planning to leave the country – would you like to take over my place?"

Patricia jumped at the opportunity.

"Actually I did not see this shop as a business. I took it just so I could sit there and enjoy the touch and feel and smell of fresh flowers!"

There remained a thorn in the rose bush – Patricia's husband. Although divorced, Patricia felt compelled to once again reach out to him.

"I knew he would be out there somewhere, on the road. Still addicted to his habits. Even his parents didn't want him!"

Call it love, or guilt, or simply duty, Patricia could not see him suffer.

"I took a house for him, sent him to a rehabilitation centre."

However, on 11 September 2002 he succumbed to a massive heart attack. And thus a difficult chapter finally came to an end.

"We performed the last rites also. I think I have been a good wife. Of course, I could not succeed in changing him..." she trails.

The same year, Praveen got married. In 2004, daughter Sandra completed her college education. Patricia fixed her marriage, a few days after the final exams.

"It was on 29th of April, 2004. Everything went off well. I was very proud... I had conducted two weddings and settled both my kids!"

And that's where this story might have ended, had it been a fairy tale. But in life, as you ride into the sunset, suddenly you encounter a storm. And for Patricia, it was a devastating one.

"My daughter had just returned from her honeymoon, she was on her way to Dindukal, after visiting some relatives. I spoke to her at about 5.30 in the evening..."

Exactly half an hour later, Patricia got a call.

"There has been an accident."

All four passengers – including Sandra and her husband – died on the spot. Patricia and Praveen rushed to the spot – two and a half hours away. The bodies had been taken to the hospital.

There are no words to describe the sea of emptiness, the grief and the despair which swirl in a mother's shattered heart. Even after seven long years, tears stream down Patricia's face as she recalls the scene.

"I pray that my worst enemy should not go through what we did."

"When I took the NIPM contract I had to do everything professionally. Every payment was made by cheque, I hired an auditor and a full-time accountant."

The next few months, and then years, went by in a haze.

"My son had come home for the wedding – he never went back."

Patricia would not eat, she could not sleep. She could not *accept* what had happened.

"Why? Why did you take *my* daughter??" she beseeched the Lord.

But, there were no answers. One year was spent in this paralysis until, finally, Praveen decided to pick up the reins of the business.

"I was of no help at all. He had to fight it out on his own."

People whom Patricia had worked with – and believed in – tried to thwart him. Luckily, the loyalty of some staff members remained. And with their help, Praveen slowly learnt the ropes, took over and expanded the operations.

"Today we run four brands – all named after my sister," says Praveen. "The first is Sandeepha – pure vegetarian. Another is San's Kitchen, which serves non-veg food. We also have a counter selling juices and mocktails, and recently we started Chinese as well."

The business is now focused mainly on food courts, with 12-13 units across Chennai.

"We don't do canteen contracts any more, unless it is in the food court format."

The company employs 200 people and clocks revenues of around ₹ 2 lakh per day, on average. Enough to keep Praveen's hands full – and then some.

"He is continuously on phone. If you switch it off for a couple of hours there will be a hundred missed calls!" exclaims Patricia.

Terrified with the idea of Praveen taking calls while driving, Patricia nowadays accompanies him as often as she can. To the office, and even to the market to buy provisions – like before.

"Actually all these years I always told her to come out of the house, spend some time in the kitchens. But she would never agree."

But that was to change. In January 2010, Patricia received a surprising New Year gift. An award from FICCI for 'Woman Entrepreneur of the Year.'

The award recognised three decades of work Patricia had put into her enterprise, under difficult circumstances. Suddenly, Patricia found herself in the limelight.

"At the award function I didn't know what to say. I had not written any speech!"

So Patricia simply spoke, from the heart.

"Thank God I did not shake or tremble or anything. I just told them whatever I felt, what I had gone through and it was easy after that."

A profile of Patricia appeared on rediff.com, and that opened the floodgates for many more interview requests.

"I never talk about myself you know... But maybe my story helps some people so I am speaking."

And as she speaks, she relives the past. In some sense, coming to terms with it. She still questions God, but she is also grateful for all the good in her life.

"My grandchildren, my friends and family, my staff... All these good things happened and I did not question God. So I have to accept everything, even the bad..."

And sometimes, the only thing you can do is give back. In whatever way you can.

"When Sandra died, no ambulance was willing to take the bodies to the hospital. They were taken in the boot of an Ambassador car," she chokes.

Patricia is now running a charitable ambulance in that area. An act of kindness which has saved countless lives.

"The main thing is that whether dead or alive, people should be treated with dignity."

A life with dignity, with head held high.

ADVICE TO WOMEN ENTREPRENEURS

First you need to have an inclination towards a particular line of work. If you love what you do then regardless of all the initial hassles, you will be able to perform.

Second, you have to get your hands dirty. Like in the catering business, you need to know everything from how to wash vessels to cooking – only then you can command work from others.

Next, without the support of the family, I don't think any woman can stand out. Either it should be from the husband and in-laws or it should be from the parents. With support, women can reach any heights.

Being a woman has its advantages. For example, there are many government schemes and loans for women entrepreneurs.

But at times people also try to take advantage of you – especially when they know you don't have a husband. Only thing I advise is, you simply brush such incidents off and stay focused on your work.

ANOTHER KAHANI

Sudeshna Banerjee,
P S Digitech HR

When her marriage broke down, Sudeshna woke up. From a steady, low-paying job as a schoolteacher she became an assertive businesswoman, proving herself in the male-dominated world of engineering services.

The first thing you will notice about Sudeshna is her large round *bindi*. Then, her lustrous hair and expressive eyes. The kind you associate with poets, singers and dancers.

"You are right," she laughs. "I was a dancer in my younger days. I had to give it up after marriage."

But that was not the only thing she gave up. Self-respect, self-esteem and self itself were sacrificed. In a union with a man who was never committed to his marriage vows.

Ultimately, she walked out. And learnt to fend for herself in a hostile world.

"To rent a house… as a single woman… is the most difficult thing I have ever done," she says, the pain evident in her eyes.

Sudeshna could have remained a victim. Somehow eking out a living on a schoolteacher's salary. But from somewhere within came a desire to not just survive, but to thrive.

This desire propelled her to make unusual choices. Like leave the security of a job to enter the world of business. Not just any business but the male-dominated world of engineering services.

Despite having no training as an engineer.

"Only I had the faith, I can do anything I really want to do in my life."

Sudeshna speaks in a sweet, lilting Bengali accent. There is absolutely no bitterness in her voice. She relates events and incidents from her life which would ordinarily make one feel sad. But she laughs heartily and I laugh with her.

Because a woman can be powerful and passionate and ferocious.

But real power comes when she can stick her tongue out.

Transcend victimhood, transcend womanhood and become a living form of Kali.

ANOTHER KAHANI

Sudeshna Banerjee,
P S Digitech HR

Sudeshna was born in Santoshpur in South Kolkata, in a family of teachers.

"My father was a professor in Calcutta University and head of the department (BEd) of Bijoy Krishna Girls' College. My mother taught Bengali in a school. I have one younger brother."

Sudeshna wanted to be a doctor but when she didn't get through the entrance exam, she took up BSc. Following that up with a Master's in Zoology.

"I went to do my MSc at Muzaffarpur University in Bihar, where I stayed in a hostel."

Subsequently, Sudeshna did her BEd as well as a Post Graduate Diploma in Computer Application (PGDCA).

"I started teaching in a school but I was never really serious about a career," she admits.

After a six-year-long love affair, Sudeshna was happy to get married and 'settle down'. She was 27 years old.

"I moved to Bangalore with my husband. There I was teaching biology and computers in a local school."

Some time later Atanu* took up a new job and was transferred back to Kolkata.

"We moved back to his home in Golfgreen. I loved to stay with my parents-in-law and it was just 5 minutes walking distance from my parents' place."

Sudeshna once again took up a teaching position at Loyola High School where she was a popular and well-respected teacher. She also joined a theatre group.

"Actually, I have been a *Kathakali* and *Odissi* dancer since childhood and given many performances. But after marriage, all that stopped."

Ghar ki bahu dance kare, yeh accha nahin lagta hai.

But Sudeshna never made a fuss about it. What she did object to was something quite different.

"From the very first day of my marriage I realised that my husband is attached to some other lady."

And this became a regular affair… or series of affairs.

"Each time, I kept thinking that he will change."

She swallowed a bitter pill and stayed in the marriage.

In the year 2001, her mother-in-law was diagnosed with cancer. Sudeshna put her heart and soul into looking after Ma – whom she loved dearly.

"This was the time when I got a rude shock. I learnt that my husband is in love with a very good friend of mine, who is also married. In fact we even used to go on holidays together."

When Atanu was confronted he created a big scene. As if it was all *her* fault.

In the midst of this drama in March 2002, Ma passed away.

"The following month we found out that my father-in-law has cancer. So now I was busy looking after him."

When Sudeshna told her parents about her plight her father responded, "Whatever it is, you stay there. Don't come back."

* Name changed.

So she had a discussion with her husband.

"If you love her, then marry her. You don't have to be with me your whole life."

But he fell to her feet and cried, "No... no... I can't live without you. That was just an infatuation. It's all over now."

Famous last words, because a few months later Sudeshna learnt that her friend had conceived. And the child was fathered by Atanu!

"They came to me and said, 'This child will be brought up by all four of us.'"

This was the last straw on the wife's back.

"Yes, I cannot have children and Atanu was against adopting a child. But this was too much… just too much!"

At this time, Sudeshna's father-in-law lay on his deathbed, blissfully unaware of what was going on.

"He had an idea that my husband is having an affair with somebody. But… after all he is the son and parents are always a little blind."

Shortly after that, he too expired. Again, Sudeshna went to her parents and explained the situation.

Her father once again said, "No... no... you stay with your husband. It may be also be your fault."

Meanwhile, the baby was born.

Sudeshna went to her friend and said, "This child should not be known as a bastard. He should have a father's name and a mother's name."

And she walked out of the marriage.

"I could not live a moment longer as Mrs Bhattacharya."

Reclaiming her birthright, her identity and her dignity, Sudeshna now needed a roof over her head. She quickly discovered how difficult it was for a single woman on a teacher's salary to rent a house in Kolkata.

One landlord asked, "What time will you leave and what time will you come back?"

Sudeshna replied," I can tell you when I will leave but I can't tell you when I'll come back!"

"My husband had such a big ego... He never thought that I will really leave him and go."

Another lady bluntly said to her, "Oh, you will stay alone… so, you are characterless."

After a lot of searching and convincing, Sudeshna managed to rent a house. But the day she was shifting out, Atanu staged another drama.

"He had taken an overdose of sleeping pills and written a letter saying, 'I am going off… world…. please forgive me.'"

Sudeshna dragged him into the bathroom and put him under the shower. When he became conscious, she gave him salt water so that he would vomit and empty out the poison. Then, she called the family doctor.

The doctor told her, "He is lying through his teeth. If he had really taken 25 Valiums he would be gone by now. I think he has taken maximum 3-4."

But why all this *naatak*?

"He wanted me to be there, he wanted her to be there…he wanted everybody."

Like a spoilt child, always used to having his way.

As I was leaving, he said, "If you go, who will cook for me, who will give me morning tea?"

Sudeshna burst out laughing.

"Your new wife is coming… she will nurture you! Be happy together, at least for the sake of the baby."

And thus Sudeshna began a new life. But a life of struggle and hardship and deprivation.

"My salary was a meagre ten thousand rupees a month. I could barely afford the advance and monthly rent."

There were days when she had no money to have dinner.

"I would buy a packet of wafers, take some water and go to sleep."

People said – go to your parents, go to your husband and ask for some financial support. Sudeshna refused. But help came from Prosenjit Dutta, a musician friend whom she knew from her theatre days.

"You take up a part-time job in my company, teaching AutoCAD software," he said.

Before marriage Sudeshna had briefly worked with an IT firm as a marketing person, and learnt AutoCAD on the job. Little did she know how useful that would prove.

"In April 2006, I joined on a salary of ₹ 3000 per month. Every day I would go after school and take my classes."

But, the company was in a bad shape. The two owners – a businessman and a mechanical engineer – were not putting in much effort.

"There was no one to do the marketing," recalls Sudeshna.

In June, Sudeshna lost her job. By July, there was talk of the company being shut down. It was then that Prosenjit came up with a bold idea.

"Let *us* take over this company."

Prosenjit believed Sudeshna would make a good business partner for two reasons – her persevering attitude and her complete honesty.

"I knew we would never face the kind of issues which are typical among business partners."

The duo convinced the owners to lease the equipment and let them take over the CAD franchise.

"Since Prosenjit was working in another company, he asked me to be the sole proprietor. We called the company Digitech HR."

Towards deposit and working capital requirement, Digitech HR needed ₹ 3 lakh. Prosenjit took a personal loan from ICICI bank, while Sudeshna sold half her ornaments. The other half she had sold the previous year, to make the down payment and pay stamp duty for a small flat of her own.

"What is jewellery for anyway. It is for a woman to use when she is in distress or trouble. I put my jewellery to good use!"

"I have always been an idealist, as a teacher I never had greed to earn more money from tuitions."

The work of Digitech HR now began in earnest. Although initially, both Sudeshna and Prosenjit continued in their jobs.

"We employed a boy called Jayjit. He was at that time just a commerce graduate looking for a job. He had lost his father in his childhood and I knew he was a very sincere person."

Jayjiit handled the admin and accounts, along with one more junior staff. The company's main focus continued to be AutoCAD and STAADPro training, but with more emphasis on marketing.

"In the first year (2006-7) we had turnover of ₹ 9 lakh," she recalls.

Enough to convince Sudeshna to quit her teaching job. A few months later, Prosenjit joined the company full-time as well. A new opportunity soon came their way.

"People who came to to take training from us said that they had lots of drawings which needed to be converted into 'soft copy'."

That's how Digitech HR started offering digitisation services.

"This was in 2008 and we had also picked up many good clients such as Stewards & Lloyds, BOC and Military Engineers."

A number of clients came in through Prosenjit's contacts in the industry. But they stayed on and gave additional business because they were satisfied with the quality of Digitech's work.

Meanwhile, there was an offer from a well-known businessman in Kolkata for a joint venture.

"We thought they are good people and willing to back us, so why not!"

A new company was formed, with an office in Salt Lake.

"His only condition was that 'my son will join the company'."

But that proved to be the undoing of the partnership.

"The son started playing games with me, insulting me in public. Basically he could not digest that a lady can be at par with him".

Sudeshna and Prosenjit decided it would be better to stay independent.

In March 2008, Sudeshna went to Raipur to conduct a training session which got an excellent response. After that Stewart & Lloyds asked Digitech to take up a 'detailed engineering' project for the company.

"That means plant layout drawings, equipment layout drawings, process flow diagram – everything."

Sudeshna quickly hired 7-8 detailers to execute this project. And she once again visited Raipur, which was booming at the time, to drum up more business.

"I got calls from Monet Ispat, Jindal Steel & Power and Hira Group of Industries to conduct training seminars."

There was one more call – from Kolkata Police. An FIR had been registered claiming that Sudeshna and Prosenjit had stolen ₹ 65 lakh from their joint venture partner.

Sudeshna rushed back from Raipur and went straight to the police station.

"Both of us, we sat with the police officer and said, 'You go and check the office room. This is the hardware and software you will find there. Nothing has been taken out by us."

Eventually, the case was dropped. And there were other positive developments. New clients like ACC Cement, Bhilai Engineering Corporation and B K Engineering came into the fold. Both for training and engineering services.

By March 2009 the company had 20 employees and a turnover of ₹ 27 lakh.

"Although profit margins are good in our business, salaries also are high because we employ qualified engineers."

Apart from AutoCAD Digitech also started Project Management training.

"Both Prosenjit and myself completed certification from Project Management Institute."

"We are working with technology but, no technology can do anything without human resources. That is most important asset of any company."

And then came a big breakthrough. Digitech had successfully conducted Primavera* project training at ACC's plants in Jamul and Sindri. The company was to now set up a clinker bulk loading plant in Himachal Pradesh.

"I met the MD – Mr Sumit Banerjee – in Mumbai. He was impressed by the excellent feedback to our training programs."

The MD said, "Can you take up a project management assignment at our new plant?"

Yes, yes, yes! This was the opportunity Sudeshna had been hoping and waiting for.

"We were already listed with Military Engineers. We had done engineering designs for bullet-proof bunkers and they have been implemented."

But working with ACC is like getting a break in a Yash Chopra film.

It *mean*s something.

"We had never done such a large project before but we were confident that we *can* do it."

Project management requires deployment of engineers onsite, based on the size of the plant. These engineers do the planning, tracking, the scheduling and monitoring.

"Of course, Prosenjit and myself were constantly travelling back and forth and monitoring the project."

The ACC project was of 5 months duration. The targeted date of completion was 15 November 2010. However, Digitech was able to complete it ten days early.

* A popular project management software.

"Since we performed so well, ACC asked us to handle additional projects at Kymore and Chandrapur."

But why should ACC employ an outside agency for this very important job? Because a third party casts an unbiased eye on the project and acts as a bridge between the contractor and the client.

"We systematically break down the project and force the contractor to do his job properly!"

What goes around, comes around.

"When we do training, we give more than is expected. Those who are coming for AutoCAD training, we are also teaching them industrial drawing. They need to know that also, on the job."

A good teacher completes the syllabus. A great teacher goes beyond, and uplifts the student.

"Same philosophy we have in our business. We always work harder and deliver more than asked for."

In 2011 Digitech not only became an authorised monitoring partner of ACC Cement, it also started working with Ambuja and L&T. The company turnover in March 2011 crossed ₹ 1 crore.

"In May 2011 have also converted to a private limited company and renamed it as PS Digitech HR. Where PS stands for Project Solutions."

While Prosenjit is the technical brain of Digitech, Sudeshna has been its heart and soul, handling the marketing and HR. As the 'face' of the company, her official designation is that of Managing Director and Chairperson while Prosenjit is Executive Director and CEO.

"We have recruited senior professionals like GM (Projects), GM (HR) and a head of design."

Digitech also put together an Advisory Board of experienced professionals from the engineering and project management field.

The year 2011 also saw Digitech make a foray abroad, bagging projects from Dubai and Australia. Most recently, the company bagged a project in Sri Lanka.

"I had gone there to find out the opportunity. I met the people, talked to them and we got a project from IRCON (Indian Railways

"My value system, power of adjustments and honesty – all I got from my parents and my younger brother."

Construction). It is for the railway line which was washed away during the tsunami 8 years ago but never got reconstructed..."

Sudeshna travels 15-20 days a month on work, and is comfortable anywhere and everywhere.

"I have travelled first class a/c where I am the only lady in the compartment and never faced any problem."

And similarly at training seminars, conferences and client visits, being a woman – often the only woman – has never been an issue. Like Arjuna, Sudeshna is focused only on the eye of the fish.

"I am completely dedicated to this company – to grow it and take it to new heights."

It's not about personal comfort, or material wealth. Even the profits earned so far have mostly been reinvested.

"First we have to *give* to the company, only then we can take... Even Prosenjit's wife Sheila understands and supports that. She is also my good friend."

Digitech HR crossed revenues of ₹ 1.5 crore in March 2012 with net profits of ₹ 25 lakh. And there are ambitious plans for the future.

"In 5 years I want to see my company with a turnover of ₹ 60 crore. And become a multinational as well!"

I wonder if, somewhere deep down, there is a desire to prove to her ex-husband – "See how far I have come!"

"He is nobody to me now, so why do I need to prove anything to him? He is married to that girl and we have no contact."

But yes, she admits that adversity has made her a stronger, more resilient, better human being. 'Alone' in the eyes of society but complete within herself.

"I hope... when I get some time... to start dancing again," says Sudeshna.

Already, her eyes are dancing.The spirit is swaying, to a cosmic beat.

She is the creator, the choreographer and the performer.

In a personal, primal *taandav nritya*.

ADVICE TO WOMEN ENTREPRENEURS

Everybody is capable of doing something on their own. Do not take 'no' for an answer.

When I left my school job and started this business, my relatives, my parents, my friends were against it. What if you fail?

I said, I will make sure that it succeeds. If one person can grow, I will be that person. So, the positive mind is the most important thing.

Every time I hit a problem I say no, I have to do it. I have to find a way to overcome. Struggle struggle and struggle... till now I'm not out of struggle. I am going on struggling.

But, I know one day I will win.

LADY IN BRONZE

Jasu Shilpi,
Sculptor

Jasu Shilpi entered her profession precisely because Michelangelo once said sculpture is not a 'woman's work'. Today, her larger-than-life statues of Mahatma Gandhi, Martin Luther King and Rana Pratap occupy pride of place – in India and across the world.

Her hands are wet with clay. Her brow, furrowed. Perched on a scaffold, next to a 24-foot high statue, she is oblivous to the world.

All around us are 'body parts'. A hand here, a head there. A full-size bronze statue of Mahatma Gandhi.

"*Yeh wala America jaa raha hai*," beams Jasu*ben* Shilpi. (That one is going to America.) "Air India people will come and pick it up from my doorstep."

Jasu Shilpi's farmhouse is very little farm, very little house. It is mostly occupied by her workshop and a museum of bronze sculpture, which is her legacy. Her tribute to the life she has spent, devoted to this art.

First, with husband Manharbhai, her soulmate and partner in life and work. Then, as a young widow with two children to raise. Now, beyond the roles and requirements of society.

Living on her own terms, for her own self. And for sculpture.

Since she broke away from the family in 2004, Jasu has blossomed further. The size and scale of her work had grown, nationally and internationally. And so has the sense of peace and inner joy.

"Pehle life ki jimmedari nibha rahi thi. Ab main sachmuch zindagi jee rahi hoon." (Earlier life was more about responsibility. Now, I am really enjoying my life.)

As much as I admire her sculpture, I admire this Declaration of Independence. This personal bill of rights.

The right to release the self from attachments.

To become that magnificent human being, glowing with inner light.

LADY IN BRONZE

Jasu Shilpi,
Sculptor

Jasumati Ashra was born in Ahmedabad, with enterprise in her blood.

"My family had a dyeing and printing business in Dani Limda. My mother managed the factory with 35 workers while my father went out for marketing."

Jasu grew up in Mandvi-ni-Pol and attended the RBMK Girls' High School.

When she was 13 years old, there was an exhibition at her school. Her drawing teacher said, 'Jasu, you draw well – why don't you paint something?"

Jasu put her whole and soul into it and created a 6-foot-long canvas which she called – 'Sita Charit'.

"That painting was liked so much that my school gave me a cash prize of ₹ 500. *Yeh pachaas saal pehle ki baat hai*!" (This was 50 years ago.)

It was a lot of money back then (the price of gold was ₹ 80 per 10 g). Jasu was overjoyed.

"*Maine socha ki chalo – art ka line le kar kuch aagey badoon*!" (I decided to take up art as a profession and move forward in life.)

As a student of the 'Drawing Teacher Certificate' course at CN Fine Arts college, Jasu went on a study tour. In Gwalior, she was fascinated by a statue of 'Rani of Jhansi.' The Rani was seated on a horse whose front legs were suspended in mid-air.

She wondered, "How did the artist make this statue? How does the horse bear the weight of the queen on top of it?"

Most of all, she wondered *who* might be the creator of the statue.

Can *I* do something similar?

That's when Jasu took a decision that would define her life forever.

"*Maine sculptor banne ka rannirnay kiya*." (I took the firm decision to become a sculptor.)

A most unusual choice, for a woman.

At the age of 18, Jasu began teaching painting at the Mahipatram Ashram in Ahmedabad. Here, she met Mohammedbhai, who was teaching the girls how to carve wooden toys and make artistic objects from metal.

They got casually acquainted.

Around this time there was a proposal from a boy in Bombay, who had studied at the prestigious J J School of Arts. Although both boy and girl liked each other, the wedding could not take place.

It was a huge shock and disappointment for Jasu.

Meanwhile, she remained in touch with Mohammedbhai. Their relationship had deepened into friendship. And one day Jasu realised – *this* is the man I want to spend the rest of my life with.

The thought had not even crossed Mohammedbhai's mind. He was a simple man, a shy man. Moreover, he was an orphan. How could he dream of proposing to a girl like Jasu?

Only she could make it happen.

Every day Mohammedbhai would cross Lakkadiya bridge – now known as Ellisbridge – on his way home from work. One evening, a voice called out from behind. He turned and saw it was his colleague, Jasu.

She simply said, "*Kya tu mere saath shaadi karega?*" (Will you marry me?)

It took her 15 days to convince him that indeed she would be happy in his humble abode. On 24 July 1970 Jasu eloped with Mohammedbhai and they married in Mehmadabad court.

At this time, Mohammed renounced the Muslim faith and became a Hindu – Manharbhai. They once again exchanged vows at the Arya Samaj temple in Ahmedabad.

Jasu's family was furious and did not attend any of the ceremonies. In fact, they disowned her.

"I started my married life in a one-room house in Ambawadi," smiles Jasu. "There was no honeymoon, but so much love!"

Jasu and Manhar adopted the surname 'Shilpi' (sculptor) and that's exactly what Manhar did. He started a small workshop in his home. Jasu assisted him but also worked as a drawing teacher in an English medium school.

"*Us time paise ki bahut tangi thi.*" (Money was very tight those days.)

Jasu's wedding sari doubled up as a blanket. Even a movie outing was rare. But the young couple was too lost in each other to care.

In August 1971, Dhruv was born. Followed by his sister Dhara, 18 months later. Managing home and work became a challenge. Manharbhai would babysit Dhruv while Jasu went to school.

But, Jasu had bigger dreams and ambitions.

"*Hamara accha bada studio aur sculpture workshop hove, bade scale par kaam karein…aisa main chahti thi.*" (We should have a big studio and sculpture workshop, work on a grand scale – that's what I wanted.)

On New Year's Day, 1974, Jasu visited her parents, along with her children. Initially they were cordial but then a quarrel started over

"When I was 16, I read a book on Michelangelo which said, 'Sculpture is not a woman's work.' "I decided right then, this is what I want to do in life."

> ***"Koi baat nahi, main bhi kamaungi, shaadi karenge toh dono saath kaam karenge. Zindagi ban jayegi."***
>
> **(Don't worry, we will get married and work together, earn together. We will make our own life.)**

some trivial matter. Jasu was humilated and vowed never to visit her *maaika* (parents' place).

"That day I realised our society gives respect only to those who have money. I vowed – I will one day become a rich woman."

Jasu quit her job and started scouting for more and bigger work for Manhar. She would scour newspapers for government advertisements and tenders. Following up every small lead, getting some small orders.

In 1975, the municipal corporation of Rajkot floated a tender for a statue. The day she came to know about it, Jasu jumped onto her Bajaj scooter and headed out.

"I used to go everywhere by scooter – all over Gujarat," she shrugs.

Wearing a jacket, cap and muffler – she would pass off as a man.

"I was careful on the highway but of course, that time we didn't have as much traffic as today."

In Rajkot, she met the mayor – Arvindbhai Maniyar.

"*Aap itni door scooter par chal kar aayi*?" he asked. (You have come all this way on scooter?)

Jasu had no track record. But, impressed by her daring, the corporators decided to give her the contract. A full-size statue of Babasaheb Ambedkar was commissioned for the princely sum of ₹ 25,000.

Now came the big question – how would they *make* such a large statue? Manharbhai made only small pieces whereas Jasu had studied sculpture but never actually created one.

"I had no practical knowledge. We had to run around and learn everything from scratch!"

A Baroda-based sculptor by the name Kolhatkar who made bust-sized statues was of some help. But another well-known artist refused to even meet the couple.

"We only wanted to see his workshop, get some guidance. *Unhone baahar se hi bhagaa diya*." (He did not let us even enter his home.)

When the bravehearted and clearsighted encounter a rock, God sends a chisel. Hamiddujman, an artist from Bangladesh, arrived at Jasu's house. He was an expert in bronze sculptures and in one week, he taught them everything.

How to first work with clay, then wax – right down to casting and welding.

"*Is tarah hum naye kaam mein master ho gaye*." (With his help we mastered this new kind of work.)

Technique is important, but a true sculptor is one who works from the heart. A good statue is one which captures a person's physical attributes. A great one reflects the personality as well.

"Our first statue was very much appreciated and installed on the main road of Rajkot city."

From then on, there was no dearth of work. Orders started coming in from Shibpur, Himmatnagar and soon, from all over Gujarat. The only problem was that Jasu and Manhar did not have a proper workshop. Welding and casting had to be done outside and this was a big bother.

"Even after making advance payment, sometimes we could not get our work done on time," she recalls.

There were times when Jasu had to ferry her work around on a handcart from workshop to workshop. And on one occasion, she even carried around an open gas cylinder.

> **"*Jahan bhi kaam milega main apna scooter utha kar pahunch jaati thi.* Even as far as Rajkot and Somnath."**
>
> **(Wherever we smelt work I would hop on to my scooter and reach the place.)**

"Scooter lekar ghoom rahi hai, matlab uske andar ek himmat hai, toh bhale woh abhi pehla pehla kaam hai, lekin hamein usko ek chance dena chahiye."

(She has the courage to come so far on scooter, that is admirable. Even though she has no experience, let us give her a chance.)

Ultimately, they took a small place on rent in Raipur, which was at some distance. But transporting the moulds back and forth was hard work. And, who would take care of the children in their absence?

Jasu once again decided to take a bold step.

"*Maine thodi himmat ki aur Vastrapur mein zameen khareed li.*" (I worked up some courage and bought some land in Vastrapur.)

To do this the couple borrowed from friends, as well as the bank. They first constructed one room and kitchen with a temporary roof.

"We built the house with our own hands. Even the children helped by filling sand and passing bricks."

Slowly, the dream was becoming a reality. A workshop and furnace was built in the backyard. Some workers were hired. But a lean period followed, with very little work coming in.

"The loan amount was ₹ 1.65 lakh and we couldn't pay the installment for 3 months."

The bank sent a letter, threatening to attach the plot. Jasu went to meet the bank manager and requested a grace period of 6 months.

It was a tough and desperate period for the family. Since sculpture work was not bringing in enough, Jasu also took up a painting assignment. The contract was to make murals at Kevadia colony and Ukai dam site in central Gujarat.

"The work was fetching a good price but travelling so far on scooter was a problem."

The couple decided to buy a second-hand Ambassador car for ₹ 25,000. This way Jasu could easily carry her raw materials to the dam site. She would work all day, returning late at night.

"My husband would wash my feet with warm water, children would massge them. Then we would all cook food together."

Three months went by like this, with hard labour and little rest. The loan was paid in full, the land was finally safe.

"That was the last time I took a loan in my entire life," says Jasu.

Life became a little more relaxed, more comfortable. The family constructed a proper house with three more rooms. Jasu planted a small vegetable garden. When her friend Urmi came to visit, the two would be engrossed for hours. On such days, the children would pluck fresh veggies and cook the evening meal.

"I trained both my children to be very confident and independent."

The story goes that as a child, Dhara was terrified of jumping off the diving board. When Jasu heard about this she climbed up the 16 ft ladder with her daughter and threw her into the water.

"You have to be tough in life!" she exclaims.

And certainly that toughness has helped Jasu at every bend in the road. Just as life was looking good, perhaps even perfect, a tragedy struck the family. Manharbhai was diagnosed with cancer. Life went topsy turvy once again.

Jasu had to take over the business, as well as take care of her husband. Despite every effort, Manharbhai passed away in 1989.

"*Dhakka toh bahut laga. Phir kya kare…* " she says. (It was a big blow, but what could we do…)

A day before his death Manharbhai said to her, "Stop spending on me, you have to bring up two school-going children."

He added, "Don't live like a widow. Wear your bangles and lead your life normally."

"Kisi ne thodi si disha batayi, phir maine apni soch aur magaj se kaam kiya aur uske andar doob gayi."

(Someone gave me a little direction, then I applied my mind and immersed myself in the work.)

"The table that served as a base for making sculptures also doubled up as our dining table. But there was fun in that also."

Three days after her husband's death, Jasu re-entered the workshop. Because, the show must go on. But it wasn't easy. Jasu missed the presence of her husband both at home and at work.

"I had to do everything now, from mixing the clay to paying the *karigars* on time."

Worst of all, there was no one to leave the children with when she had to be away. Jasu would lock them in the house with the promise of returning in two hours. But meetings with government officials would often get delayed.

"I used to feel terrible as a mother but I had no choice."

Jasu's perseverance paid off. Shortly after Manhar's death, she bagged a dream project – a 10-foot-high, 14-foot-long bronze statue of Shivaji Maharaj. No woman sculptor had ever made a statue of this size.

"I was very excited but I knew I have to prepare myself."

Jasu pored over history books and covered her studio with photographs of Shivaji. She even visited a few places where such statues already existed. But more than the man, she was worried about the horse he was to be shown riding.

"I could not get a sense of how to mould the horse from photographs."

Jasu decided to solve the problem by using a live specimen. She telephoned the chief of police, who happened to be an acquaintance.

"Sir, I need to borrow one of your horses for 15 days."

And that's how the 3.25-ton bronze statue finally came to life. It was installed on Racecourse Road of Rajkot city with pomp and fanfare.

But the journey of life is never smooth for too long. In 1994, Jasu and her daughter met with a bad accident. Her right knee and left shoulder were both fractured. While the leg became functional quickly, the shoulder required insertion of a plate.

"You must not work for some time," the doctor advised.

Naturally, Jasu did not listen and she had to bear with pain. And undergo multiple operations. She had an order for an 11-foot-high Maharana Pratap statue. How could she let that go?

"I had to work with one hand, somehow climb the scaffold, but I completed the statue," she smiles.

Ultimately, on the advice of a well-wisher, she consulted a renowned orthopedic surgeon in Bombay, Dr K T Dholakia. With proper treatment and rest, Jasu finally made a full recovery.

"I believe in Goddess Amba. She is my mother, friend, guru and guide."

Jasu makes it a point to visit the Chotila temple whenever she bags a big order.

"I have climbed the 800 steps to the temple even with plastered hand and limping leg," she recalls.

One fine morning Jasu opened a letter from the Rajkot municipality and started dancing with joy. She was being asked to make a statue of the Rani of Jhansi. The very same rani who had inspired her to become a sculptor.

Another long-held dream was soon to come true. Jasu travelled to the United States, to receive an award. She spent 25 days in the US, enjoying hospitality and recognition from the Gujarati community across America.

"I assign my work or burden to different deities. One God looks after my orders while another looks after my health. That way I am relaxed and comfortable!"

"I worked so hard to buy my property but when that property became a source of tension I thought, better to give it up."

"*Mujhe itna pyaar aur samman mila, bahut accha laga*." (I got so much love and respect, it felt very good.)

Meanwhile, both Dhruv and Dhara had grown up, got married, settled down. Now Jasu could have retired peacefully, but living with the extended family did not suit her temperament.

"I used to do my work of course but there was always *khich khich* and tension in the house."

There was also the issue of male ego.

"*Chhokre ki jaat hain na... apni behan hogi, ma hogi, toh woh agey nikaal jayegi na? Woh sehen nahi kar patey. Mere bete ke saath yehi hua*". (The male species cannot tolerate if the women of the house – sister or mother – become more successful. That's what happened with my son.)

Jasu was suffering mentally, and emotionally. The home atmosphere was such, she could hardly focus on her work. At this point, she took a radical decision.

"In 2004, I divided my property, jewellery and money between son and daughter. Then I shifted outside the city, to Tarapur."

On a large plot of land, Jasu set up a new home and workshop from scratch. Here, she says, she is finally 'enjoying life'.

"I feel like I have been reborn since I shifted to my farmhouse. And I am now 10 times more productive, even my workmanship is 10 times more."

Jasu enjoys the fresh air and natural surroundings. Her day begins at 6.30 am and ends only at 10 pm. At any given time, 10-12 statues can be seen in the workshop, in various stages of completion.

The most important aspect of any sculpture is capturing the appropriate facial expression. This, Jasu handles herself, working with mud and then wax. The metalwork – including casting and finishing – is handled completely by her staff.

"I have a staff of 15. I work for myself and I work for them also. *Mera kaam art bhi hai aur business bhi*." (My work is both art and business.)

Since the move, business has flourished. Orders for 'Gandhi statues' started coming in from America. What's more, at the time of installation, the Americans would insist that the sculptor should be present.

"They give a lot of respect to the artist. My name is written there, that 'this sculpture is by Jasu Shilpi'. *India mein kahin nahin likhte*." (In India, the sculptor's name is not mentioned.)

Which is a crying shame. It is for this reason that Jasu is setting up an entire museum dedicated to bronze sculpture. Featuring personalities ranging from Abraham Lincoln to Amitabh Bachchan.

"All will be smiling, I prefer to make smiling pose only."

And she laughs heartily.

The bigger the statue, the bigger her smile. Jasu relates a recent truimph – the making of a 28.5-foot-high statue of *panchmukhi* Hanuman (Hanuman with five faces).

"I had never done a project of such a size before, it took a whole year to complete."

The statue had to be transported to Rajasthan by road, in several parts. Where it was finally soldered and welded into one giant piece.

"*Bahut mazaa aaya, bahut sabne appreciate kiya*." (I enjoyed doing it and everyone appreciated my work as well.)

And of course, Jasu was paid a handsome amount. The price of a statue can range from ₹ 16 lakh (for an 8-foot-high Martin Luther King) to ₹ 1.2 crore (for the Hanuman). The major input cost being bronze metal, and the rest artistic skill and physical labour.

"Kuch karne ke liye kuch sehan bhi karna padta hai."

(To achieve something, you give up some things.)

"When my mother had an accident it was me and not my brothers who did *seva. Stree aisi hi hoti hain, jimmedari wahi nibhaati hain.*"

(A woman never shirks her duties.)

Years ago, Jasu discarded saris in favour of dungarees and cut her hair really really short. Which makes her look far younger than her 65 years.

"*Kaam jitna karti hoon aur jawan lagti hoon* (*laughs*)." (The harder I work, the younger I become.)

Jasu no longer needs glasses and says even her bones are much stronger. She eats organic vegetables, drinks cow's milk, enjoys fresh air. And the love and support of her staff.

"Mere workers mere bachche jaise hain." (My workers are like my children.)

Yes, there is one small regret. Her '*jigar jaan*' friend, her husband Manhar, is not here to enjoy all this.

"When he was alive, we never sent a single statue outside Gujarat. And today – I am travelling all over the world!"

But, in spirit, he is still with her.

"Hamare 19 saal ke vivahit jeevan mein, kabhi ek time bhi jhagra nahi hua. Itna pyaar tha. Toh woh pyaar ki wajah se main ji rahi hoon…" (In 19 years of married life we never fought even once. There was so much love between us, that love is still keeping me alive.)

There has never been and there never be another man in Jasu's life. Her 'second marriage' is to her work.

"Jeevan mein kabhi maine haar nahi maani. Zindagi jeene ka naam hai, jeeti rahi, jeeti rahi, jeeti rahi."

Life is a collection of experiences.

To experience each moment fully and accept it is an art.

The art of living gracefully and never growing 'old'.

EPILOGUE

I met Jasu Shilpi in November 2012 at Tarapurgam – her farmhouse-cum-workshop off the Sarkhej-Gandhinagar highway. We shared a simple, home-cooked meal and then she showed me around the sculpture museum under construction – her pet project.

Jasu was excited – full of life and plans for the future. And in the pink of health.

Two days before this book went to print, I received the shocking news that Jasu was no more. She passed away on 14 January 2013 (Makar Sankranti)*, due to sudden cardiac arrest.*

She was 64.

I am printing her story, without altering a single word, because that is how she wanted it.

My heart is heavy but I know she will live on and continue to inspire – through her life, through her work, through her art.

ADVICE TO WOMEN ENTREPRENEURS

Ek disha lekar baith jana chahiye. Phir planning karna chahiye. Uske upar pura pura dhyan dena chahiye.

(Choose one direction. Then plan how to go on that path. Give it your full attention.)

Fir usme zara sa gadbad ho gaya, to haar nahin manana chahiye. Pehle pehle jab main casting karti thina, toh kabhi kabhi mera casting fail ho jata tha. Koi baat nahin, maine phir se kiya, aur seekh liya.

(If you fail or goof up initially, do not give up. Initially my casting used to fail. I did not take it to heart, I kept trying and mastered it.)

Apne husband ko batana padega ki maine koi kaam karna hain. Aap mujhe isme madad karo. Matlab dono saath mein baith kar, saath mein chale, anand se chale – toh gaadi bohot achhi chalti hai aur agey jaldi se pick up hota hai.

(You will have to tell your husband that you wish to do your own business and need his help. If both of you sit down and discuss together, agree to support each other, then your work will be smooth and life will be happy. Your work will also pick up quickly.)

Jab kuch karna hai aurat ko, toh routine life ko chhod dena padta hai. Lekin abhi kya hai, ladkiyan sochti hain, bas, paisa wạla chokra hain, bank balance hai, gaadi hai,bangla hain – kar lo shaadi. Aisa maine socha hota toh main aaj kahaan hoti?

(When a woman has to achieve something, she has to sacrifice the routine life. Nowadays, girls think – boy has money, car and bungalow – ok, I will marry him. If I had thought that way, where would I be today?)

Courtesy: *Entrepreneur India Magazine*

GOING SOLO

Dipali Sikand, Les Concierges

Dipali dabbled with politics and corporate life before bouncing back from personal tragedy, to become an entrepreneur. Rakesh Jhunjhunwala is an investor in her company Les Concierges, a unique and highly profitable business.

Dipali Sikand says her life is 'like a soap opera'.

I beg to differ.

Our soap operas are about women who suffer in silence, women who 'accept' their fate.

Dipali is different.

She walked out of a bad marriage to start a new life. Then, single and single-handedly, she raised both a young baby and a young business.

"I owed it to myself and my child – I didn't want to be a financial burden on my parents," she says.

With passion and determination she turned a small idea into a big business. A business which not only makes money but makes people happy.

Goodness comes out of sadness.

Strength comes out of difficult situations.

So yes, her life is like a soap opera.

But one yet to be telecast.

Perhaps they are afraid. If they show women like Dipali on television, fewer women will simply 'accept their fate'. More women will be strong and determined and 'do something' to improve their lives.

Because they will realise 'I am a person in my own right'.

Capable, of *anything*.

GOING SOLO

Dipali Sikand,
Les Concierges

Dipali grew up in Calcutta, a city with its own charm.

"Life was much less complicated, happy go lucky, there was no TV, no mobile phone."

Dipali attended La Martiniere Girls' School and invariably got into trouble for her naughty antics.

"I was always very outgoing, very noisy and extroverted."

Kolkata city allowed Dipali to grow and experience a lot, at a young age.

"The Bengali tradition is always to protect women, so our parents felt safe and allowed us to be independent."

Dipali's father was the Managing Director of a shipping company while her mother was a housewife, but also worked for UNICEF. Both parents encouraged Dipali to be daring and unorthodox. So an entire summer holiday – after class 9 – Dipali worked at a travel agency and learnt all about the travel business.

"My dad made it sound like a fun thing – just go and see what it's all about."

In the same spirit he packed Dipali off to climb the Everest Base camp, right after class 10. At the Himalayan Mountaineering Institute, she actually trained under the legendary Tenzing Norgay.

"I probably had a lot more confidence because of all this exposure while growing up!" she admits.

The year that Dipali completed class 12, Calcutta University delayed its admissions. While most of her friends applied to study abroad, Dipali was not keen to leave the country. Instead, she joined St Xavier's College in Bombay.

"I studied at Xavier's from 1983 to 1986, and I stayed at the infamous Savitribai Phule hostel on Marine Drive. We did some really crazy things!"

One memorable incident involved the girls *gheraoing* a minister – to protest the awful quality of the hostel food.

"My picture appeared on the front page of *Midday*," chuckles Dipali.

In her final year of college Dipali was elected to the Student Union, which was affiliated to NSUI at the time. After graduating, she decided to get a taste of active politics, by working with the Youth Congress in Delhi.

"Mom and Dad encouraged me – live your dream! So, that's what I did."

Dipali worked under Anand Sharma, Youth Congress President on a host of issues. There was energy and optimism in the air with a new and young Prime Minister – Rajiv Gandhi.

"It was a voluntary job as far as money was concerned but it gave me a lot of confidence, a lot of understanding of our society at grassroots level."

But society does not change in a day. Along with the optimists and the idealists, there were the usual *neta* types. One such politician – a Bihari gentleman – tried to act fresh with Dipali and another female party worker.

"I turned around and slapped him in public."

Two Black Cat commandos were assigned to be with Dipali, wherever she went. But the incident forced her to introspect.

"I used to think I am an 'equal' but reality is different. How many *netas* will I try to change, how many will I slap?"

Disillusioned with politics, Dipali returned to Bombay, where she bumped into a friend who was working with Essar Industries. The company had an opening in Human Resources – would she be interested?

"I was not a qualified HR person but, I think HR is all about how you engage with people, so I applied."

Dipali got selected and joined the recruitment department in 1989. She rose rapidly up the ranks and was soon working in the chairman's office. This opened a whole new window of opportunity.

"Everyone thinks HR is about manuals and personnel policies but I was working on Greenfield projects – new areas where Essar was expanding."

For example, Mobile Telephony. Back then, nobody knew which people to recruit, what were the competencies required. That was the challenge – and the excitement. Another project involved setting up a textile mill in Mauritius.

Although technically part of the HR team, these assignments gave Dipali an overall understanding of business. And what makes it tick.

But even as she excelled on the professional front, her personal life was in shambles. In 1992, Dipali had married a man whom she knew for many years, now she was expecting a baby. But things deteriorated to such an extent that she decided to move on.

"I shifted to Bangalore, as my parents were living there. I decided I would live there, work there, raise my baby."

Aditya was born in January 1996, by an emergency C-section. But worse was to follow.

"When I came out of the operation theatre I learnt I had lost all I had earned, from my joint account. I had nothing left, except my dog, myself and my baby."

"Unless you sit on the shop floor, you can never understand the customer and you can never scale up."

"Till today we don't have a marketing department. Business comes in only through referral."

This was a moment of inner awakening. Dipali knew she had to fight back – for herself and her baby.

"I cannot be a financial burden on anyone," she vowed.

Ten days after the delivery, Dipali was back in office. In Bangalore, she helped to set up JTM mobile network. It was a much smaller job profile, which made it easier to manage work and motherhood. But soon enough Dipali was bored.

"I had been in HR for 9 years, I needed to do something different."

When an assignment to work with a Chinese telecom network came her way, Dipali grabbed it. However the job was based in Singapore. Dipali uprooted her mother to come there and live with her. Yet, life was tough.

"It was really difficult to manage everything – buying groceries, paying the electricity bill, washing your own dishes after dinner."

In India, there had always been someone, 'taking care of things'. That's when Dipali realised, there must be a million other employees suffering just like her. That's when the germ of an idea entered her head. Could someone take care of all the 'small stuff' and grow it into a big business?

"That's how Les Concierges was born."

Once you have the seed of an idea, you need fertile soil to plant it. On her annual vacation in India, Dipali bumped into a gentleman in her building who happened to be a senior person at iGate*. She casually mentioned the concept, likening it to a 'concierge' in a hotel.

"I like it," he said. "Can you start it at our company?"

The gentleman introduced Dipali to his admin head, Mr Joseph. He too was very enthusiastic. And that's how the first ever Les

* iGate was then known as Mascot Systems.

Concierge desk came into being. And it was staffed by Dipali herself, with the watchman from her building society agreeing to do the running around.

The response was amazing. One month whizzed by and Dipali decided *this* was what she wanted to do.

"My father thought I was crazy to quit a high-paying job but I loved what I was doing!"

Especially the joy it brought in people's lives. Employees were thrilled to see a bill paid, or drycleaning picked up. It made a real difference to their quality of life.

The IT revolution had just started. Companies jostled with each other to offer the best benefits. That meant whatever one company would start, the other would copy. And that benefited Les Concierges tremendously.

"My second customer was Wipro and they wanted 14 'Life Care' desks at one shot. So, I had to look for 14 people at one time and quickly train them."

Growth happened quickly and purely by word of mouth. By the end of the first year the company had 140 employees.

"I had done large-scale recruitment at Essar, so I was never worried about hiring of people."

Dipali knew she would never get a readymade concierge. The cardinal rule is that the word 'no' does not exist in the concierge dictionary. As long as a request is legal, it must be fulfilled. So you need to employ people who are customer-centric, who will go the extra mile.

"Basically I was looking for 'nice' people. Because I can't train you to be nice, I can train you to be a concierge."

This was an area where Dipali was fully confident. But that wasn't the case with other aspects of the business, such as finance.

"My constant worry was that I have 5000 bucks in the bank – how the hell am I going to make my payroll at month-end!" she recalls.

Luckily, she signed on some large clients like IBM who actually paid 3 months' retainer in advance. A great help to a young business, back in 1998. Balance sheets, statutory requirements and income tax remained a headache. But Dipali's father stepped in to handle it.

> **"I tell my staff that their job is to just say yes and find solutions. 'No' is never an alternative."**

A startup is like a newborn baby – it keeps you on your toes at all times.

"There was so much to do, so much to learn, I don't remember sleeping through a single night."

With new and different requests coming in every single day, there could be no set process. Someone wants a passport, someone wants tennis lessons, someone wants their mother-in-law picked up from the airport. You simply had to go out there and find a supplier.

"Initially, it was all pen, paper and telephone. Over time, of course, we got organised and started using technology to make it easier."

In the early years, clients could not even pronounce the company's name correctly. They would say 'Less' Concierges and Dipali would politely remind them – "we are more, not less!" And that, literally, is the story of this enterprise.

A client would sign on in Bangalore and then ask for more locations. By the year 2000, Les Concierges was operating in Mumbai and Chennai. Cities like Delhi, Kolkata, Pune, Hyderabad and Ahmedabad quickly followed.

"We also realised that there were more ways in which we could serve the same companies."

Some of the early add-on services included a product to help companies 'Reward and Recognise' employees. As well as a Customer Loyalty Program for companies like Hindustan Lever and Standard Chartered Bank. However, the 'bread and butter' of the company remained its 'Life Care' desks.

"We charged companies about ₹ 20,000 to ₹ 25,000 per month to deploy a concierge within their premises. Some services were also billed separately to employees."

By its fourth year of operation, Les Concierges had opened its 200th 'Life Care' desk. And it might have continued to grow in this organic fashion when in 2004, there was a gamechanger. Rakesh Jhunjhunwala stepped in, as an investor.

"I don't know how he found me but, I believe someone from Standard Chartered Bank told him about me. That there is this unique business with a very niche customer base."

At the time Les Concierges was operating around 200 desks and had annual revenues of ₹ 3 crore. Rakesh believed the company had far greater potential.

"The greatest thing was that I could stop worrying about where next month's salaries are coming from. Be more creative and productive."

At that time, Dipali was clueless about term sheets, performance clauses and venture capital in general. So this investment was a small miracle.

"I must admit, Mr Jhunjhunwala is the sweetest investor and sharpest investor who is a rock and at the same time he is not there in your face."

With investors* on board, growth took on a more rapid and systematic face. Les Concierges developed a proprietary CRM technology to improve its service levels. The company also introduced a new 'product' called Ms Moneypenny – the perfect receptionist.

The basic 'deliverable' was a pleasant and efficient person but Ms Moneypenny went a step further.

"We specify everything from what she will wear to how many rings before the phone is picked. And in case of an absence, another Ms Moneypenny will be sent to temporarily fill in."

Today, Les Concierges has over 300 'Moneypennys' deployed across India.

A third business which grew out of the original is Les Concierges 'Live'. On the one hand, the company had a crème de la crème database of customers. On the other, brands were keen to reach this target audience. Say, Cadbury's wants to conduct an activity where employees can 'earn their Bournville'.

* In 2008, US-based Acacia Redwood Partners also took a 13.7% stake in Les Concierges.

"Last year we filed 3,00,000 income tax returns – it's hard to believe at times, how far we've come!"

"We make it happen for the brand and it's fun for employees."

In 2008, Les Concierges made its international foray with the acquisition of 'Club Concierge' in Dubai. This service goes beyond running errands, it's about the needs of high net worth individuals – travel, dining and all kinds of unusual requests.

"Someone wants an ostrich feather bag, another wants to play polo with a Maharaja. We've even arranged for a pair of ducks for a marriage proposal!"

These services do not happen through a 'physical' desk, but through a call centres. In fact, Les Concierges now manages a multi-million dollar yearly contract to play concierge for the leading name in payments across the Middle East and Africa.

Combined with 1,300 concierge desks across India, the company has chalked up revenues of ₹ 56 crore in FY 2010-11 (as per industry estimates, profit figures remain undisclosed).

"We keep reinvesting the money we make to grow the business further."

40-45% of Les Concierges business still comes from IT companies with Bangalore continuing to lead in the number of desks. But services are being rolled out in Aurangabad, Jaipur, Nasik and even the port town of Mundhra in Gujarat.

Expansion is completely led by demand from clients. The brick and mortar part of the business is the person actually sitting inside the company, dealing with employees and their needs. But there is also a strong back-end with 'specialists' who know exactly how to deliver.

"We have RTO specialist, passport specialist, flowers and entertainment specialist, live shows specialist... you name it!"

Les Concierges is 1,700-employee strong – and growing.

"The attrition level is relatively low," says Dipali. "Because your work is directly helping so many people, there is a lot of job satisfaction."

75% of Les Concierges staff is female so the workplace is very family-friendly. Flexible hours are available – to both men and women. Because you need to be happy in life, to be great at work.

And no matter how dark the storm you are caught in, eventually, the sun comes out.

"I lost my father under very strange circumstances", recalls Dipali. "He only had a cough but he was very uncomfortable, so I decided to take him to hospital."

That day the whole of Bangalore had shut down due to the kidnapping of actor Rajkumar. The only hospital close by was severely understaffed. Dipali left her father in the waiting area while she completed the registration procedure.

"When I came back he was gone… I mean he had passed away."

The nurse had given him an injection meant for someone taking a CAT scan. There was a fatal allergic reaction.

"It was one of the most difficult moments in my life… which I will never forget. You just want to cry out loud and break everything in the damn place. You want to scream 'how dare you'!"

But then you are humbled by the fact that absolutely nothing can be done. When you have to go… you have to go.

The police came, there was paperwork to take care of. By the time Dipali reached home, the news had reached her mother. And she was in shock.

"My son Aditya was hardly 4 years old at that time and he didn't know any father other than his grandpa. He had no idea how to cope."

"Never underestimate the power of what a meeting with another human being can do for you."

"I've been told I am the 'fittest fat person' in the world. How relaxed you are or how happy you are is all in the mind."

When Dipali returned home Aditya was nowhere to be seen. After a frantic search she found him, sitting with a stranger in the park.

"Who are you? What are you doing with my son?" she asked the man.

"This child looked upset. I asked him where are his parents, but he won't say anything," came the reply.

That's how Dipali met Rajeev. They became friends. What's more, Aditya got very attached to this 'nice man'.

"I hadn't thought about getting married again… it just happened."

In 2006, Dipali gave birth to a daughter – Diya. This was another small miracle, at the age of 41.

"People around me were zapped – I was overweight, overstretched. But my doctor had confidence that I would pull through and I did!"

There are people who go with the flow and there are people who decide the course of the river can be changed. Dipali is one of those 'yes, we can' types.

In August 2008, live music performances were banned in Bangalore city.

"There was so much talent around and no outlet for it. Rajeev being a musician, we decided *something* had to be done."

To circumvent the ban, Dipali came up with a unique solution – a 'theatre-cum-fine-dine restaurant'. To make this happen, she went to Singapore and procured an 'Asia Pacific license' for theatre. Armed with this license, Dipali procured a liquor license from the local police.

Ultimately Bangaloreans got what they had been craving – musicians performing live, every night.

"It was a long and tedious process but the idea was to support music and musicians. And it made Rajeev and his friends so happy!"

Kyra opened its doors in Indiranagar on October 2008. In fact, Dipali even managed to convince the Commissioner of Police to come on the first day and sing karaoke.

Inspired by the success of Kyra*, Dipali set up a second venture called Gigbox. This company represents artists and organises monthly 'familiar' music concerts in Bangalore and across India.

"We bring the best tribute bands from around the world, for example Pink Floyd, and we actually recreate the magic of their concerts."

Down to details like paper butterflies fluttering into the audience with Coldplay numbers and a giant pig balloon floating in the air during the Pink Floyd concert.

Dipali's 16-year-old son thinks it's a very cool business to be in.

"I'm the only kid in class who goes to rock and roll concerts with my mom," he jokes.

Aditya also likes to help out backstage, especially with the sound.

So, how *does* Dipali manage to do all this? And how is it possible, for every woman?

"I have a wonderful support system – my mother is truly my anchor," admits Dipali.

At 74, Mira Sikand not only plays the role of *naani* to perfection but manages her own business, taking care of corporate guesthouses.

"My business is not such a big one, I just like to keep busy," says Mira.

Both her mother and grandmother live next door, so the children always have someone to be with. And the same home help has been with Dipali for over 20 years now so, no complaints on that front!

* Estimated monthly turnover of Kyra is ₹ 45 lakh (source: *Entrepreneur Magazine*, March 2010).

"People leave their jobs because of a bad boss, it's the same with home help. So, always treat everyone well."

"But look, I don't have unrealistic goals like I want to be the perfect wife and the perfect mother and the perfect business woman."

The day starts early – around 6 am – with Dipali waking up the kids and readying them for school. She drops them at 7:15 am and proceeds to office, where the day will stretch up to 6:30 pm. During exams or projects the kids drop by, sit and study with Dipali.

"It is only a question of keeping an eye or answering their queries."

Dipali believes that the more confidence you have in your kids' ability, the better they perform. So no nagging about '*kitna padha*?' or 'when is the next exam?'

But it's not all work and no play for this family. Which, by the way, also includes 2 alsatians, 2 labradors, a Siberian husky and a litter of pugs. 'Chillout' is spending Saturdays on the farm on the outskirts of Bangalore. Where they work, rest and play together – in the company of more animals!

"Devices are not switched off. You never switch off but... you are at peace."

But too much peace can be too much of a good thing. Just when things were looking settled, somewhat predictable, Dipali decided it was time for a new adventure. In January 2012, while on holiday in Egypt, she took a radical decision.

"I decided to reinvent myself."

Leaving India operations in the competent hands of her colleagues, in May 2012 Dipali shifted to Cairo. To set up Les Concierges Egypt.

"Cairo is exactly Bangalore 14 years ago – the streets smell the same, the people are the same, the opportunities to do are so much!"

The goal is to draw on experience and build in 24 months, what took 14 years in India. The family has stayed back in Bangalore, meeting daily on Skype and during vacations. Giving each other time and space and the support for a big new dream.

"I needed to push myself and see if I have it in me to start all over again. With no name, no contacts, no credentials."

To stretch yourself more than you have to. To dive into the deep end because, you *can* swim. Through still water, muddy water and extreme turbulence.

That is what it takes, to rock with it, roll with it, stand tall, above it all.

And feel truly *alive* from within.

ADVICE TO WOMEN ENTREPRENEURS

I think there are only two rules that are important.

Firstly, whatever you are doing, make sure you are passionate about it.

The second thing is, don't be driven by money. Making money is important, but it should not consume you. You should be driven by the idea of creating an enterprise or creating something that leads to the creation of wealth, by default.

This is in general for anyone, but for women in particular.

I believe that women have a great advantage at being in a business because they can sell, they can convince, they can open doors to places where many men can't get in. Lots of people like to buy from women because we are are far more passionate and transparent in our dealings.

Just don't be defenceless *ki mai yeh nahin kar sakti.* Be confident. That's the main thing and the other thing is – keep your sense of humour. That is one of the sureshot ways to always be successful.

Even in the worst and stressed of times I keep telling myself – this cannot last forever. I have learnt to be self-reliant and non-judgmental with people and situations.

You have to be proud of what you are and whatever you do, do it fully, don't give up half-way. You absolutely owe it to yourself.

DIL SE

Paru Jaykrishna,
Asahi Songwon

When her family's textile empire collapsed, Paru Jaykrishna started a new business, to secure a future for her two sons. The ₹ 230 crore Asahi Songwon company is a testament to the power of a mother's love.

I am waiting in Paru Jaykrishna's home office. There is something sacred and very serene about the place.

Money can buy almost anything but this is not one of those cold interior-decorated wonders. There is something personal and warm and dignified about it. Just like Paru herself.

Dressed in a plain dark-blue *salwar kameez*, she appears much younger than her 68 years. She is vibrant and vivacious. There is *masti* and mischief in her eyes.

Most girls dream of marrying into a higher status family. But Paru's dreams were different. Destiny propelled her into the home of Jaykrishna Harivallabhdas, an icon of Ahmedabad city. But Paru was always determined to create an identity of her own.

Early on, she chose to do a small business – a travel agency. But it was at the age of 46, that crisis pushed her into truly coming into her own.

With the Shree Ambica Mills textile business collapsing, Paru sensed a bleak future for her two teenage sons. Surely they would have money, but was money ever enough? Young minds needs a vocation, a purpose, a passion in life.

Paru decided to create a new business, a large business, to secure their future. A business built on the bedrock of principles. Principles which have guided her throughout life.

The success of Asahi Songwon Colors is proof that you don't know need to know the *hows* of a business. If you know what you stand for, and where you want to go, you *will* find a way.

And whether it be business or family life, it's not about 'I' or 'me'. If you understand the economics of emotion and live with others, *for* others, what you want happens without apparent effort.

Magic is all around us, and most of all in a mother's heart.

DIL SE

Paru Jaykrishna,
Asahi Songwon

Paru was born in Ahmedabad, to a family of modest means.

"My father was a teacher, and he also did some business. But unfortunately, I lost him when I was six."

Life became difficult.

"My mother looked after us – five brothers and sisters. Although we never had much money and luxury she made sure we all studied a lot."

But the most important thing Paru's mother gave the children was a value system. Rooted in the principles of Jainism.

"My mother used to run an '*ayambil shala*' – a special place for fasting. So from a very young age, I used to keep *upvaas* (fast). Like in Jainism we have *attham* (3-day fast) and *atthais* (8-day fast)."

Practices which built discipline, focus and mental strength. To cope with anything and everything in life.

"My mother passed away when I was just 16. My whole life changed…"

In school, Paru was an excellent student, always taking part in sports and debates. Winning awards and certificates by the dozen. She had always wanted to become a doctor, because it was 'benevolent work' – to save somebody's life…

"But when my mother expired, I had to give up my ambition because the entire responsibility of the house and my four siblings came on me."

So Paru switched from Science to Arts, majoring in Philosophy and Sanskrit. But that was not the only change.

"The death of my mother was a big shock. From that day onwards I started wearing white, white and only white."

For the next eight years, Paru stuck to a standard pattern white *salwar kameez* – whether it was to college or to a wedding function.

Call it *zid*, call it determination, or just a personal principle. Once Paru sets her mind to something, she makes it happen.

"You know I had always studied in Gujarati medium up to graduation. One day I realised I cannot speak even a single sentence of English correctly... I felt ashamed!"

Paru decided to learn English. And not to just learn it, but *master* it.

"I learnt to speak well, write well, express well. I decided that I will do my MA with English literature. And I did!"

After completing her master's with distinction, Paru started teaching English literature to third year students. It was her first job, with a salary of just ₹ 600.

"I remember, with my first salary I bought four small gifts for all four family members. Of course it was nothing, but I felt so proud."

And then, at age 24, Paru fell in love. And not just with anybody, but the son of a multi-millionaire.

"Mrugesh and I were working together for six years, at an organisation called Junior Chamber. My brother Dhanpalbhai was also very active there, and a friend of Mrugesh."

One fine day, things just 'clicked'.

"We knew each other so well. We thought, why not get married?"

But Jaykrishna Harivallabhdas was one of the leading industrialists of Ahmedabad. Would such an affluent family accept a simple girl like Paru?

"I was not so beautiful or sophisticated. I used to wear only white clothes – no makeup, no style. I was a studious person, a sportsperson, very ordinary kind of person."

Another small problem was that Mrugesh came from a Patel family, while Paru was Jain. But then sometimes, love conquers all.

"My parents-in-law were very positive, very modern thinking. They accepted me immediately."

Paru and Mrugesh were married on 7 December 1967. And Paru quickly adjusted to her new way of life.

"My father-in-law was an MLA, as well as mayor of the city. Morarji Desai and Indira Gandhi used to come to our house... The atmosphere was very different!"

But despite the many privileges she enjoyed as a daughter-in-law in this household, Paru always wanted to *do* something. Something more.

Even as she was expecting her first baby, Paru enrolled for another degree.

"It was my brother who told me, 'Paru, *zindagi mein*, if you don't do law, life is not complete. Law makes your mind analytical and you can really see the world correctly.'"

So, law it was.

"I was married, I was expecting a baby, but I did the course, and I did very well. However, it was not possible for me to practice."

It was a large joint family, running a large joint business – the Shree Ambica group of textile mills. What was the need for a *bahu* of such a family to work?

"All my sisters-in-law were enjoying life, and I could have done that also. But I could not just sit at home, I *had* to do something."

Her second child was just a few months old, but Paru could wait no longer. She requested her father-in-law for permission to start a small business; he agreed.

"I decided to set up a travel agency. Not that I knew anything about the travel business, but *dheere dheere seekh liya*..." (slowly, I learnt everything.)

Operating from a small office with a manager and two staff members, Paru built the business slowly.

"I had the advantage of Papa's contacts – political contacts, social contacts, business contacts. While I did not *use* them as such, but naturally it did help."

Paru admits it was more of a 'hobby' than a business.

"I have always been a fighter in life, at every stage, in whatever I do."

"It was never a big earning proposition... we made a nominal profit. The advantage was that I could travel free abroad and so, we could travel every year with children – twice, thrice."

Over time, Paru became more savvy and the business grew to a bigger level.

"Between 1975 and 1980 it was at the peak. Skyjet was one of the very good travel agencies in Ahmedabad city."

Not that the family owning Shree Ambica Mills considered it to be 'big'.

"Nobody ever came to that office, even saw that office. It was too small to talk about even (laughs). But I enjoyed every moment."

And what about the children?

"The advantage was that we were living in a joint family, everybody is around. So, even if you go out for 2 hours, 5 hours in the day, children will be taken care of."

So it was with complete confidence that Paru could go out into the world and take on new challenges. And in worlds quite removed from her own – in the area of cricket!

It happened like this.

"My father-in-law was President of the Gujarat Cricket Association and my husband was Vice President of BCCI. They were keen that international-level cricket matches should be played in Gujarat but at that time we didn't have a stadium of international standard in the state."

BCCI said, "Build a stadium, we will give you a match."

So the Gujarat Cricket Association decided to build a stadium. But this decision was taken in January 1983 – the match was to be played in November 1983.

But was it possible to construct an entire stadium – pitch, ground et al – in less than ten months?

It was at this time that Paru said to her father-in-law, “Don’t worry. Just give me the project and it will be done.”

That meant everything from raising the money, to buying land and physically supervising construction.

“I was working 18 hours a day. I didn’t know cricket, I didn’t know architecture, but I handled everything. It was tough, so tough but we did it!”

In November 1983, the first ever international cricket match was hosted in Gujarat at the newly-completed stadium. And soon after, Paru took on another challenge.

She decided to start a new business.

“Ahmedabad city used to be the Manchester of India. But in 1985, due to changes in government policy, almost all the mills in the city shut down.”

This included the six textile mills owned by Shree Ambica group. The family remained multimillionaires, but without a running business.

“At the time, my sons Gokul and Munjal were 16 and 17 years old. I wondered, what is their future now?”

When an industrial unit is declared sick, the case is referred to BIFR. Court cases, bank cases and *mazdoor* cases become the norm.

“I thought *ki* if my children get entangled in this mess, this negative life, they will be affected badly. So we sent both of them abroad for studies.”

In the meantime, Paru decided *she* would do something. Something that would draw them back.

“You see, wealth is not enough. We had enough wealth to last four generations. But if your children have only money and no right path, they will smoke, drink, gamble or get into drugs. I could *not* let that happen!”

The need of the hour was to create a new business, a new direction. But for the Jaykrishna family, which had once employed 10,000 people, thinking small and from scratch was impossible.

Paru’s father-in-law agreed to let her try, but with one condition.

"I have strong empathy for joint family. Though you have to adjust, accommodate a lot, but there are many many advantages. One should always live in joint family."

He said, "You can do business if you like, no problem, but you will not be able to get a single rupee from the family."

Paru accepted the challenge. Now came the difficult decision of *what* exactly to get into. The criterion was simple: the project must be a 'big' one.

"I knew the project had to be in manufacturing, which will be long term, which can grow in size. Also, I was very clear that we would go only for 100% export-oriented unit."

Ahmedabad city had always been known as a hub for textiles. But it was now also a hub for the chemical industry. Hence, chemicals became a natural choice.

"I decided to get into 'dye intermediates', because at that time most of the manufacturers in the West were closing down plants, due to stringent environmental norms. They were instead sourcing the product from India."

Thus in the year 1989, Paru set up Aksharchem. Dye intermediates were a commodity, the technology was freely available. But starting a project – any project – is like taming a wild elephant.

It takes every ounce of your strength.

"The major issue for me was raising finance."

Paru borrowed approximately ₹ 21 lakh from friends. As a woman entrepreneur she also received a cash subsidy of ₹ 5 lakh from the Gujarat government. But what about working capital?

"I approached Bank of India as I thought *ki chalo wahi bank main jate hain jahan apna Ambica ja business chalta tha.* They know us all very well."

The bank was positive, and agreed to finance the project. But a couple of days before the money was to be disbursed, an officer called and asked for an additional meeting.

To Paru's surprise he told her, "We have instructions from the head office. There are disputes pending with Ambica mills, so we won't be able to lend to you."

So Paru went to State Bank of India and told them, "Look, I won't be able to give any collateral, but I need money. I have a very good project!"

Somehow, she convinced them. But there were other hurdles.

The raw material for input was ethylene oxide, which was produced only by IPCL in Baroda. The project requirement was very small – just one tanker in a month. Yet it was impossible to get.

"There was a big racket in procurement and I refused to pay bribe. Neither did I have the money to spare and nor was I mentally prepared to give it."

Paru then used her family connections to meet the chairman of IPCL. Although he wanted to help, he was actually helpless.

"It's better you go through some of the agents," he suggested.

Paru remained adamant.

"You see the entire industry, wherever you are supplying, is there any woman entrepreneur?" she countered.

The chairman admitted, her case was unique.

"See, I am the only woman entrepreneur in this business and that's why I am facing all these challenges. So, you make an exception for me. Arrange for me, just one tanker!"

This argument finally melted the systemic ice. Paru got her tanker of methylene oxide without greasing anyone's palms. And thus, production started.

Now came the issue of marketing. Starting as an export-oriented unit is all very well, but how do you connect with buyers overseas? You pick up the telephone and start calling.

"I used to talk to purchase managers of multinational companies, say I am so and so. My company is so and so. This is the product I wish to sell to you."

"Being the daughter-in-law of a big family with a big name was a hurdle rather than a support to me at times."

They would invariably reply, "Madam, we already have very good suppliers.Please don't bother us!"

But Paru was persistent.

"I will telephone again and I will telephone again. Then I will request, please at least test my sample."

With lots of persuasion, after a year or so, a couple of companies agreed to test the sample. But the samples were promptly rejected.

"It is absolutely useless. Don't come to us again", they would say.

And yet Paru persisted. She realised, just speaking on the phone would not be enough. It was important to physically meet clients to convince them. But getting an appointment was not easy.

"Many times it happened that I go there and come back without meeting. So that way the first three... four... five years were really very very very tough."

Paru's first export order came in 1996 from a Taiwanese company called Everlight Chemicals*.

"My first customer," she beams. "And still my best customer."

So how did they get convinced?

"Well, I realised our product was not good enough, so we put a lot of work into improving the quality. But once I got a chance I established a relationship. My *entire* business is running on that relationship right now."

It is a commodity market, there are many suppliers. So why buy from a small company based in Ahmedabad run by a woman with hardly any experience?

* Everlight is currently the second largest manufacturer of dyestuff in the world.

"I think the strength I have is that I speak the truth. That is the biggest strength. They trusted me as a lady."

And Paru upheld that trust. In fact, she had her own brand of ethics and principles, which made her stand out.

Being a cyclic product, prices of product fluctuate – and quite wildly. Most suppliers take advantage of these fluctuations by entering into a 1-year contract for supply, but only 3-month contracts for price.

"So, what happens, when the price goes up they will make some excuse *ki hamare plant mein kuch gadbad hai, aapka maal thoda late hoga.* Actually, they will divert the supply to someone else willing to pay a little more on spot rates."

Paru never ever did that. She recalls an incident which occurred with Everlight.

"We finalised a contract in March for April, May and June. But in the month of April, the price shot up, shot up like mad."

From $2.4 per kg it shot up to $4.2 per kg.

The purchase manager telephoned Paru and said, "Let us revise the contract or supply to someone else."

Without any hesitation Paru replied, "I don't know whom you are talking to but I will not change the contract. I will supply in time – at the same price – however high the price may be right now."

Thus Aksharchem fulfilled the entire order at a very low price, with perfect timing. Everlight made a handsome profit. The chairman of Everlight called Paru personally, to thank her.

"And they became my loyal customers for life!"

In fact Everlight designated Paru's company as a 'prime supplier'.

"We will give you 5 cents more than anybody else always," was the chairman's promise.

A promise that has been kept.

Working with both Everlight and Kyungin* also proved to be a great learning experience.

* 50% of material produced at Aksharchem is supplied to these two companies even today.

"I was very small and I wanted to grow. When you want to grow, you have to step forward. You don't have money, so you have to get public money. So, IPO was the only method."

"Both these companies taught me everything, I am obliged to them for that. Even their lab people supported us very well."

Aksharchem thus took rapid strides on all fronts.

"We improved in quality, in packaging, in despatches... on all fronts!"

With all these learnings and experiences, Paru embarked on a second project. In 1993, she set up Asahi – a colour pigmentation unit in Mehsana town of Gujarat. Again, starting small, with production of just 5 metric tons*.

"One good thing was my sons Gokul and Munjal came back to India that year. And they joined the business... they had no choice (laughing)."

But they were young and inexperienced and the new business was equally challenging.

"Although it is also chemical industry, colour pigmentation clientele is completely different!"

Even as the pigment business was going through teething problems, Paru decided to raise money for the dyechem project, which was relatively settled. At the time, Aksharchem was producing 60 metric tons per month and had a turnover of approximately ₹ 10 crore.

When Paru approached Nimish Kampani of JM Financial – a family friend – he was taken aback.

"It was a very small public issue, only about ₹ 4 crore. Nimishbhai joked, *'Chaar crore ma to tumney issue nou basic kharcho pan nahi posay*?' You know the merchant banker services are expensive."

* In 2010-11 Asahi Songwon production was 1500 metric tons.

Paru replied, "Whatever it is, you have to do this for me."

And thus Aksharchem went to the market in 1995, touting its long list of multinational clients including Hoechst, BASF and Clariant. The issue was a huge success.

In 1996, the colour pigmentation business received a boost when there was an offer for collaboration from a Korean company – Songwon. The company was scouting around for an Indian partner; one of the many promoters they contacted was Paru.

"That time my pigment company was, you know, just one and a half years old. So they came home. We talked and then I went to Korea and met the chairman."

With felicity and grace, it all worked out.

One small but significant factor was the strong cultural rapport. Since her father-in-law was founder chairman of Gujarat State Fertiliser Corporation, the family had strong ties with the Far East.

"I do have a lot of understanding of Oriental culture. Perhaps that is one reason so many of my clients are from Japan, Korea and Taiwan," muses Paru.

Thus was born Asahi Songwon Colors Ltd, a joint venture with both technology collaboration and a buy-back Agreement for 'CPC Green Crude'. The agreement with the Korean principals was signed in April 1996.

"Once Songwon had invested in the company, the same year we went for a public issue and raised ₹ 10 crore."

The business grew quickly.

"When Gokul and Munjal came back, the business was not very big, but it was there. So, they could come and see it and work with me. And then, they learned and then they blossomed and so did the company."

In 2004, Asahi Songwon had a second public issue where the company raised ₹ 40 crore.

"We worked with JM Financial every time. Because whoever I start with, I work with them for life!"

The Japanese company DIC (Dainippon Inks and Chemicals) also invested money into Asahi Songwon. In January 2000, the

"Family life can be very smooth and simple. It's only when you make small things into an ego issue, there are endless problems."

company won the award of outstanding export performance for the Government of Gujarat.

"We diversifed the product range and also set up a new plant in Baroda for 'CPC Blue.'"

Even as both Asahi Songwon and Aksharchem were growing, Paru took up a completely new challenge. She became the first elected lady member of the Gujarat Chamber of Commerce and Industry (GCCI). An apex body with more than 8000 members across the state.

"You see Pappa (Harikrishnan Vallabhdas) had once been President of the Gujarat Chamber of Commerce. But when we lost our textile mills, we lost our status in society as well."

Paru was determined to win that status back.

As the only lady on a 100-strong executive committee, she faced a lot of resistance.

People asked, "Why are you coming? What is there for you to do here?"

What they did not know was that once Paru starts climbing a mountain, her aim is to quietly and efficiently reach the very top.

"I remained an executive member for 8 years, and became the chairman for many different committees."

Finally, in the year 2007, Paru Jaykrishna was elected as President. The first ever woman to hold the post in 60 years.

"It was a very big challenge. Because our society is male dominated and men never like to take orders from a lady."

That too, a strong lady who makes her own decisions, not one who will be a puppet.

"But that was a great experience, I did lots of projects and it was very very successful. I was applauded from all the corners and I also enjoyed it."

Asahi Songwon continues to grow at a galloping pace. Company turnover crossed ₹ 230 crore in FY 2010-11, while profit after tax were a healthy ₹ 22.5 crore.

"I think in a few years we should be a ₹ 500 crore company, positively."

Apart from Korean and Japanese collaboration, there is now a German interest in Asahi Songwon. Clariant is investing ₹ 30 crore and bringing in both technology and a buyback agreement.

The dye intermediate business under Aksharchem banner is also well set, with ₹ 100 crore of annual revenues.

So what is the secret of all this success? Very simple.

"We have the best quality, best service and very very timely delivery. This ensures continuous support of our customers!"

And let us say there is a genuine problem, there will be a delay. Asahi Songwon culture decrees that the customer must be informed in advance.

"If you tell the truth, you face less problems. If the customer knows in advance he can change his production schedule accordingly. Otherwise he will suffer a loss!"

Interestingly, even the very first business Paru started – the travel agency – is still running in a small way.

"Just for sentimental reasons," laughs Mrs Paru Jaykrishna.

And in all this, what is the role of *Mr* Jaykrishna?

"Most important role. My husband has been the motivator, he has been guide, he has been the visualiser, and he is the soul behind everything you see today."

In the early days Mrugesh would advise Paru on small-small but important aspects of doing business.

"He would say *ki* if you go to meet so and so, talk like this. This is what you can expect from them. And so on. Also he taught me about finance, where I was a complete novice."

In the early days Mrugesh never physically attended the office. But

"A woman should never try to equate herself with men by earning money. There is nothing wrong in it, but that shouldn't be your goal of life."

now Paru, Mrugesh, Gokul and Munjal leave for the plant every day, and come back together in the evening.

"Each one has different work to handle. We travel together, we eat together. So, we discuss everything – day in and day out."

But Mrugesh is not even on the board of directors...

"You are right, he is not on the board... he is not in the picture... not very visible."

Isn't that unusual for a man?

"Well, I think Jaykrishna family, we have a reputation in society. Anywhere we go, people know who we are. So Mrugesh does not need a designation to have social status."

But didn't Mrugesh – or any other family member – ever grumble about Paru neglecting her duties as a wife and mother?

"I never neglected my family, not even one minute," counters Paru. "My home has always been the first priority…"

It's not physical time or presence that matters as much as threads of emotional attachment, woven between hearts and minds. The Jaykrishnas continue to live as a large joint family.

"My mother-in-law Padmaben is 85. And my children are married and they have children but we all live together, we all eat together. Everybody knows everything that happens in every day!"

'Family Sunday Lunch' is a must – no matter how important other work may be. So is attendance at all key occasions – birthdays, anniversaries, *poojas*. What's more, all 11 travel together, twice a year. But does it get claustrophobic at times? Don't the younger members feel a need for 'space'?

"You are right, but you see fortunately we have money. We are 4 families living in 4 houses but emotionally and mentally, we are always together."

Two of the houses are adjacent to each other in Gandhinagar while two families reside in the old family home in Shahibaug. Children have their own rooms, daughters-in-law have their own interests, everyone is free to make personal choices. But, all accept one basic principle.

"Whoever is the head of the family, his or her word is final."

Whether you like it or not, you accept. No arguments.

"I am very proud that, I never exchanged one harsh word in 44 years with my parents-in-law. Never."

The fact is that families clash, not just over major life choices, but the smallest of matters.

"I remember when I was newly married, I once wore a yellow chiffon sari and thought I was looking great. But when my father-in-law saw me, he quietly remarked, 'Have you seen yourself in the mirror'?"

Paru didn't say a word, she went back to her room and changed.

"I came back smiling, not feeling angry or resentful. Because I knew that if Pappa has said something – and he spoke rarely – there has to be some logic. He is far wiser than me and he will always have my best interest at heart."

Later, Paru realised that the sari was indeed transparent and quite unsuitable for the gathering she was to attend. A joint family is a balancing act, and you need a single ringleader, to keep it all together.

"Take the matter of who will decide the menu. You like *karela*, I like *tindora*, she likes *bhindi* – so who will decide what is to be cooked? Only my mother-in-law."

"You should have goals, for this minute, for the day, for the week, for the month, for the life. How much you want to study? Travel? Sleep? Have all kinds of goals."

"My goal in life is 'peace of mind'. At the end of the day, I should be sleeping peacefully and quietly, without a single thought."

The *niyam* was that you have a choice of two vegetables – take the one you like. But, you cannot *leave* anything uneaten on the plate.

Words like obedience and discipline and truly *believing* that your elders know what's best are rarely found in the dictionary today. But these principles are the Fevicol that binds this family together. And influence even the manner in which the Jaykrishnas do business.

On a more practical level, there is a large staff, which keeps the home 'factory' running. A staff of 55 people including drivers, cooks, gardeners and caretakers keep the 35-acre family estate in good shape.

Apart from the human occupants, there is a menagerie of animals to look after – 4 horses, 7 dogs, 50 geese and a bunch of roosters.

"We have a big staff and big establishment, huge gardens also. So, it's lots of management and I have keen interest in everything. A single leaf can't be cut without my instruction, here, there or anywhere."

Paru is an avid gardener. The land which houses the beautiful gardens and greenery all around was once barren, undeveloped.

"We bought this land in 1980 and at that time there was no road, there was no electricity and there was no water. It used to take one and a half hours to reach here."

Armed with a thermos of cold coffee, Paru would come every week, and work on 'developing' the plot.

"One of the first things I did was plant a big forest of 5000 eucalyptus trees. Out of every 100 trees, 90 would die, because the soil here is sandy. But slowly, we made it green – like what you see today!"

The love of nature reflects in the landscaping of both the industrial units Paru has set up.

"Flowers, trees and gardens must be there!"

Beauty in everything, harmony with everyone. That is Paru's *mool mantra.*

"In my twenty years in business I have never had a single bad debt," she smiles.

Paru has, of course, chosen her partners carefully.

"I only deal with good people, multinationals who never haggle and always send the cheque on time!"

As for her own time, Paru now spends much less of it on the business. In another 2 years – as she turns 70 – she will withdraw even further.

"Last 3-4 years, Gokul and Munjal are handling everything so well. So in future, I see my role in more of an advisory capacity."

But Paru is engaged as ever – with yoga, reading, gardening. And, inspired by her mother-in-law, more and more into social work.

Paru makes juggling all kinds of balls in the air look so easy...

"When I was Chamber president, I was doing so many activities and still I was looking after business and still I was looking after home. And still I was attending dinners and parties and all that."

But it need not be exhausting.

"If you plan well, and you are emotionally well set with the family, everyone supports you automatically."

Life is fun.

Life is a pleasure.

"The minute, I stop enjoying, I will stop working."

ADVICE TO YOUNG ENTREPRENEURS

There is no need to be more aggressive or confrontational as a woman. I believe in the principle of '*Satyameva Jayate*'. If you speak truth, you have no issues, no problem. You can just go forward.

The second thing is, you must dream. Different kinds of dreams – today's dream, tomorrow's dream, one year's dream, 5 years' dream, the dream for life – what you want to do? If you dream, then only you will reach there.

Then, you must live in the present. Suppose, I am here with you right now, I am here with you. What must be happening in the office, doesn't matter. The minute you go, I will start all my work and all my calls and everything but not now.

As for balancing work and home, I feel that women should keep the family and children as their first priority. The minute children are independent – say by age 12-13 – you are free to do what you like.

Basically I feel that if you are not *required* to work, means your husband is earning well enough, then do not work for the sake of money. You do something great, something creative. You are a woman, you have a heart, your emotions, you create the family, you create the society, you create the world.

And if you decide you want career and reputation above all else then just forget about the rest. Never be unhappy that you are neglecting your children. And family and husband and *saasu*. Because that is bound to happen, unless you live in joint family.

Just remember, if you earn crores of rupees and if you are not happy, everything is worthless. This is what I say not just to women, but to men.

VISA POWER

Binapani Talukdar,
Pansy Exports

This gutsy entrepreneur from Guwahati travels all over the world with an array of Assam handicrafts. Overcoming the barriers of language, of safety and of opposition within the home, to carve out her niche as a 'lady exporter'.

Bina's cellphone is constantly 'switched off or outside coverage area'. I wonder if the number is correct, but keep trying.

Finally, we connect. She apologises. *"Abhi abhi Brazil se lauti hoon."* (I have just returned from Brazil.)

This is highly unusual, and intriguing.

We meet in Guwahati, on a Sunday afternoon. In between a family function. Bina is far younger and prettier than I imagined. Immaculately dressed in an Assam silk sari but that's just choice of dress. She is bold and outspoken.

"I am a lady and I am from Assam so it's not easy for me. But I still work hard and fight to get ahead."

She talks frankly and bluntly about other problems. Including lack of understanding from the family. For ambition can be a crown of thorns, for a woman.

Yet Bina wears her crown with grace.

And chooses to smell the roses.

VISA POWER

Binapani Talukdar,
Pansy Exports

Binapani was born and raised in Guwahati, the eldest among five brothers and sisters.

"*Mera bachpan bahut acche se guzra* (I had a very happy childhood). My father was a lecturer in the BEd college and he always encouraged me to study and make something of myself."

In fact, his dream was to see Bina become a doctor while her mother wanted her to become a lawyer. But she was more interested in painting, art and craft.

"Ghar mein sabne kaha art and craft karke kya fayda." (At home everyone said what's the point of studying art and craft?)

After completing her schooling from Gopal Boro high school in Assamese medium, Bina enrolled for a BA degree in Dispur College. But at the age of 18, while still a student, she got married to Sukumar Talukdar – nine years her senior.

"It was a love marriage."

Bina gave birth to a son in July 1998. That same year she gave 'birth' to another entity – m/s Pansy, a small-scale unit (SSI) under Directorate of Industries and Commerce (DIC) at Guwahati.

"I was guided for that by Mr Prafulla Saikiya, MD of DIC. Because I wanted to start a cottage industry."

Pansy started on a very small scale, with Bina herself making decoration items from bamboo, along with dry flowers. The reason for going into business was two-fold. Working with art and design made Bina happy. Secondly, at the time, there were some financial problems at home.

"By doing a business I thought – I can also help other women."

In October 2000 Bina registered the Assam Woman Welfare Society along with Smt Renu Chowdhury and Smt Chandrapava Talukdar. The NGO was formed to involve women from rural areas in collecting raw material and also manufacturing.

"My idea was that I will give the design and they make the product. I will buy the product and sell it through m/s Pansy."

The business continued on a very small scale, with very little support or encouragement from the family. However her husband had a positive attitude.

"Initially he encouraged me quite a bit. Because of that I went to NISIET Hyderabad for a certificate course in garment design."

Sukumar also gave her ₹ 1500, which she used as her seed capital. But that was the first and only time she took any money.

"After that I am only earning in the business and using that."

The art of dry flower arrangement is an ancient one in Assam. Flowers are collected from as far as Shillong, Mizoram and Nagaland. They are dried in the shade of the sun, then treated with natural and chemical ingredients.

"*Is tarah preserve karte hain toh flower jaisa hi dikhta hai lekin long life hai*." (This way we preserve the beauty of the flowers but give them a long life.)

A delicate process done by hand, and hence the scale of the business usually remains small. In 2004, Bina had a chance to attend a course at the Indian Institute of Entrepreneurship (IIE) in Guwahati and realised she could do much more. The course exposed her to 'management' and 'marketing'.

"Dr Sunil Saikia Sir at IIE encouraged me a lot. The course gave me confidence to grow my business."

That same year, Bina opened an art and craft school by the name of 'Awaaz'. She took classes for beginner and advanced levels – both drawing and painting. The school was run from a building owned by her husband's family in Ganeshguri area of Guwahati.

"We lived on the top floor and the school was on the floor below."

The school was a big success. There were more than 150 students, keeping Bina busy all day. Initially, she taught all 3 batches. After her daughter was born in October 2005, Bina employed some of her own very bright students as assistant teachers. And somehow they managed it all.

"*Bachche ko side mein bithake main class leti thi, painting bhi karti thi. Kabhi kabhi ye bahut roti thi tab students sambhalte the*." (My daughter would sit beside me while I took classes or did my painting. When she was crying too much my students would take care of her.)

Bina's unconventional style of parenting did not bring any harm to the child. But it certainly harmed her relationship with her husband.

"He felt that I am neglecting my duties, neglecting my child. *Unko mera kaam se problem hone laga*." (He started having problems with my working.)

To maintain the peace, Bina shut down the school. At that time, she had 5 employees and was earning ₹ 25-30,000 per month as a profit – a tidy sum in Guwahati. However Bina treated the school more like a hobby than a business.

"We used to give some donation to the orphanage and other NGOs. The rest I used for my personal expenses, so I did not have to depend on anyone."

Bina shut down the school, but she did not shut herself down. She thought of taking her cottage industry – which was operating since 1998 – to a higher level.

"I thought why can't I export my products."

Exporting dry flowers was difficult. So Bina turned to silk. Assam is famous for its Muga and Eri silk which have unique colour and texture. Using her designing skills, Bina created handbags and stoles from Eri silk. Through NSIC – National Small Industries Corporation – Bina got an opportunity to attend an exhibition abroad.

> **"In Brazil everyone wears jeans so I look odd in a sari. Still, I wear my saris and get a very good response."**

"The director of NSIC was J K Mahanta and they liked my work. So he sent me for a B2B exhibition in Brazil."

It was Bina's first trip abroad and was to become the first of many. At the exhibition, there was a buyer from South Africa who liked the silk handbag – he had never seen anything like it. The buyer placed an order for 10,000 pieces.

"*Yeh meri zindagi ka pehla order tha*." (This was my very first export order.)

To make 10,000 pieces Bina required working capital. With the letter of credit from the South African buyer in hand, she approached the bank for a loan, and secured it. However, as the amount was large (a crore of rupees), she had to mortgage the family property.

Fulfilling the order wasn't easy. Every piece involves stitching by hand and Bina did not have trained manpower to turn to.

"I involved 10-12 of my old students in this work and it became easier to handle."

The order was eventually completed in one year. Blood and sweat went into the work but sadly it did not yield a profit.

"I had quoted a very low rate. I had no idea about all the formalities involved in export, the cost of packing and shipping."

But she shrugs it off as a learning experience – a small 'fail' in an examination set by the School of Life. Many other such tests, she had passed with flying colours.

"*Main Assamese medium se padhi hoon. Mujhe English itni acchi tarah se nahi aata hai. Phir bhi abroad mein kuch problem nahin hua*." (I have studied in Assamese medium, I don't speak good English. But I had no problems when I travelled abroad.)

Before leaving for Sao Paolo, Bina did a very smart thing. She bought a book and learnt some important words and phrases in

Portuguese – the official language of Brazil. Similarly, she picked up some Spanish and Russian.

"*Mujhe bhaasa seekhne ka shauk hai aur isiliye mujhe shayad business mein thodasa mujhe kamyabi aayi.*" (I am fond of learning foreign languages and perhaps that is why I got success in export business.)

Your words may be wrong, your pronounciation funny, but the fact that you are *trying*, creates a bridge. But that is Bina's only concession to the foreign country. Wherever she goes, she prefers Indian dress.

"Seeing me in the traditional Assam silk sari, with *bindi* and jewellery people are surprised. I think it makes them curious to see my stall also."

But the 'lady in a sari' is also a cross to bear.

"Initially I did not feel but now as a woman I find there is discrimination. Many times, I don't get invited by Export Promotion Council to important exhibitions."

On complaining, Bina was told that taking a lady entrepreneur in an all-male delegation was a '*museebat*' (headache). And it doesn't stop there.

"*Aadmi log samajhte hain ki paise ke liye aayi hai toh hum paise deke isko bhi khareed sakte hain.*" (Men think she has come for selling goods so she herself is also on sale.)

The indecent proposals have been many. Bina recalls one buyer who bluntly asked, "How much money do you want?"

"Are you placing an order?" asked Bina.

The buyer smirked, prompting her to lash out.

"You can buy a piece of flesh in the local bazaar for $10. But you will not get an Indian lady… not for $10… not for a million dollars."

In this fiery Kali-*roop*, Bina added one parting shot.

"World is full of 'Made in China' that's why our handmade products stand out."

> ***"Jitna labh karti hoon, utna nuksaan ho jata hai... phir bhi main ladh rahi hoon."***
>
> **(I make profit, then I make loss... but still I am fighting to keep my dream alive.)**

"*Agar meri iccha hai toh main direct aap ko bolungi. Ab jao yahaan se*!" (If I desire you, I will come to you. Now, get lost!)

I am shocked and fascinated by her boldness. And the confession itself. Bina is talking about a reality which exists but which we rarely talk about. Because somewhere, it's always implied that a woman brings such situations onto herself.

"*Ghar mein kitna samajhtein samjhta hai ye nahi pata mujhe. Ye ek museebat hai hum ladies ke liye.*" (I don't know to what extent my family members understand this… this is a problem for us ladies.)

In the modern era, Ram may not demand an *agni-pareeksha* of his Sita but he can make life difficult in other ways.

"*Mera husband thoda naraaz rehta hai. Kabhi lagta hai yeh sab chhod doon…*" (My husband is cross with me. Sometimes I think I should leave all this.)

Bina has a distant look in her eyes – there is no easy solution. Perhaps she has revealed too much. She brushes the topic aside.

"Videsh mein agar patni rahe aur desh mein husband rahe to thoda bahut naraazgi to rahegi hi. Chhodo in baaton ko…" (If the wife stays abroad a lot the husband will miss her and feel bad at times. Let's talk about something else.)

Bina keeps experimenting and creating new products. Inspired by a fashion show in Germany, she made a jacket made of Moga silk. The natural shade and texture found a discerning buyer in Italy.

Over time, Bina has learnt to handle the paperwork associated with exports. But quality control remains a challenge. Even small variations in weight or design are not tolerated and she has had to learn this the hard way.

"My entire consignment was rejected twice. I had to suffer a loss."

One such shipment got stuck in Kazhakastan and Bina had to go and take care of the matter. The goods had to be disposed off in the retail market at a heavy discount.

Due to these kinds of goof-ups, the turnover and profit figures of the company fluctuate wildly. This year she expects it will be close to ₹ 33 lakh. In a previous year, with good number of orders, it touched ₹ 70 lakh.

The profit margin is 30-40%, however one bad shipment and the entire profit for the year can get wiped out. But Bina handles it all within herself.

"Kisi ko nahi batati thi ki maine ye kiya, vo kiya. Mera itna nuksaan hua… main kabhi rotee bhi nahi." (I don't tell anyone 'this happened' or 'that happened'. I have suffered so much of a loss… You will never see me crying.)

On one such occasion, Bina simply took out her jewellery from the locker and went to the bank. The outstanding loan was quietly settled.

"Nuksaan hi to hai, kabhi laabh bhi to hoga. Agar bhagwan ka marzi hoga to zaroor hoga." (It's only a loss, surely I will earn a profit. God willing, I will definitely earn it all back.)

Bina believes that God has been with her, every step of the way. That is how she has made it, so far.

"Let me tell you the biggest *haadasa* (worst incident) of my life."

Travelling back from an exhibition in Sri Lanka, Bina landed at Indira Gandhi International Airport at 1 am. She decided to spend the night at a budget hotel in Paharganj, where she had stayed on an earlier occasion.

This time, it appeared deserted but Bina was exhausted from the journey and didn't think much. All she wanted to do, was sleep.

"Main apne aap ko duniya ke samne produce karna chahti hoon… mera bhi kuch naam ho."

(I want to have my own identity.)

"Ghar mein tension laane se kya fayda? Main bahut jolly rehti hoon hamesha."

(What's the point of bringing tensions home? I am always jolly at home.)

Around 3:30 am, there was a knock on the door.

"I woke up with a start – who will knock at this time?"

She refused to open.

The knocking became more insistent. Soon, it was more like kicking and banging on the door. And not one person, but two or three.

"I called the reception and the manager simply laughed."

That's when Bina realised she was in grave danger.

"Mera dimaag kaam nahi kar raha tha... Main itna dar gayi thi." (I was so scared I could not think straight.)

Bina dialled her husband in Guwahati and he advised her to immediately dial the police helpline – 100. Luckily for her, they responded swiftly and arrived on the scene within minutes. Just before the door gave way.

The culprits were some students from Haryana who were also staying at the hotel. They were arrested and booked for 'attempt to rape and murder' but subsequently let off on bail.

"I travel all over the world alone. I can walk on the streets of Paris at 2 am – no problem. But Delhi *(shudders)...* in Delhi I don't feel safe."

A sentiment echoed by millions of women.

There is safety in numbers – whether on the street or in the world of business.

"I have faced many problems… simply because there are very few ladies in my field. If there were more of us, we would be a group, we would be a bigger force."

Bina believes more women want to join 'export line' but hold back because it's not easy.

"Maine dekha hai zyaadatar ladies ka hai ki husband aur wife saath mein kaam karte hain aur travelling part gents dekhte hain." (Mostly I have seen that if there is a lady exporter husband and wife will work together and the man will do all the travelling.)

So how does Bina manage? Her kids are older and son Kumar is in boarding school to get a better quality of education. There is a maid who prepares meals so Bina enters the kitchen only when she is 'in the mood'.

Husband and daughter Debahuti are now used to Bina's business trips. Employees manage the showroom in her absence. Handicraft work continues in the village while stitching takes place in a small unit in Guwahati.

Bina's dream is to open a showroom in Europe, with handicrafts from every Indian state. It's a tall order but she says if it happens, '*mazaa aa jayega'* (it will be so wonderful).

It is not so wonderful when relatives pass snide remarks or label her as '*ghumnewaali'* (one who is always outside the home).

"I don't take these remarks to heart. They simply don't know how tough it is."

Since Bina is a vegetarian, food becomes a major issue. Especially in countries like Brazil where beef is the staple diet. One time Bina recalls surviving only on fruits and juice for 9 days.

"Even water is very expensive!"

Bina has no assistants or helpers at the exhibition venue – she must carry the heavy cartons herself. What she doesn't carry around is guilt.

"Jab mein baahar rehti hoon ghar ke baare mein nahin sochti hoon. Aur na hi baahar ka tension ghar mein laati hoon." (When I am outside I don't worry about home. And when I am home I do not carry the tensions of the outside world.)

Such a simple philosophy but so hard for most.

Be where you are, in that present moment.

Be all that you can be, and more.

ADVICE TO WOMEN ENTREPRENEURS

Lagan se har ek kaam ko positively liya jaye... jo bhi design banaya jaaye... job bhi karna chahte hai, mere hisaab se lagan se karne se sab kuch mil sakta hai.

(Anything you take up, do it with passion and positive attitude... whatever your design... or even if you do a job, I feel you should be devoted to it, then you will get every success.)

Business mein ladies ko accounts rakhna aana chahiye. Thoda mushkil padta hai par main sab kuch dekh leti hoon. Jab baahar jaati hoon to ek ek kharcha Excel sheet mein daal kar rakhti hoon. Phir aakar CA ke saath discuss karti hoon kaise kya karna hai.

(In business, ladies should know how to keep their accounts properly. It is a bit tough but I manage it. When I travel I keep noting every expense in an Excel sheet. When I return I sit with my CA and we do the accounting.)

Hamesha sober rehna chahiye. Travelling mein jeans pehenti hoon magar chunni ke saath. Sab se main friendly rehti hoon par kabhi galat impression nahin deti.

(We should dress and behave modestly. When travelling I wear jeans but also drape a *chunni*. I am friendly with all but not over-friendly.)

Husband-wife mein accha understanding hona chahiye. Shuru shuru mein mera bahut problem aaya tha. Usne mana bhi kiya, lekin maine thoda himmat rakhke kar liya. Ab sab samajh gaye hain ki main kuch serious hoon.

(Husband and wife must have good understanding. In the beginning we had problems, he did not want me to do business but I stood my ground and I went ahead. Now everyone has understood I am capable and serious.)

Husband log aur thoda samajh jaaye to ladies bahut aagey badh sakti hain.

(If husbands are more understanding, women can move very far ahead and achieve anything.)

SOUL SISTER

Ela Bhatt,
SEWA

Defying caste and curfew, Ela*ben* fought for the rights of her worker-sisters – the vegetable vendors, rag-pickers and midwives. 40 years on, SEWA is 1.7 million women strong; keeping Gandhian values alive in a hyper-capitalist world.

As a student of IIM Ahmedabad I often visited a shop called 'Banascraft' at CG Road. It has the most amazing embroidered bedspreads, cushion covers and wall-hangings. We bought them as gifts to take home.

I knew this to be the work of 'SEWA.' And I knew of Ela Bhatt. But I never went into it much more.

It was years and years later that I found myself in front of her, listening to her. In complete awe. Ela*ben* must be tired of telling and re-telling her story* but here she goes, once more.

"I am not an economist, I am not a social worker. I come from a trade union background and the struggle of SEWA has been to organise and empower the self-employed."

The bigger struggle has been to get people to recognise, that the *chindi* worker, the vegetable vendor, the rag-pickers should have any *adhikaar* (rights) in the first place.

The work of SEWA required Ela Bhatt and her worker-sisters to take head-on the textile mill owners, the municipal corporation and the state government. They led delegations and protests, defied curfew and practiced *dharna.* Fighting legal battles, where necessary.

I am leaning forward, straining to hear Ela*ben* speak, for she is so soft-spoken.

For the first time I understand the meaning of the word 'Gandhian.'

That hidden rod of steel within a frail body.

A resolve to work for nothing but the greater good.

For every suffering soul is my sister, my *ben*.

* *For an in-depth understanding of Elaben's work I recommend you read her book* We are Poor but so Many: The Story of Self-Employed Women in India *published by Oxford University Press in 2006.*

SOUL SISTER

Ela Bhatt,
SEWA

Ela Bhatt was born in Ahmedabad but grew up in Surat, where her father practiced law.

"My father, my cousins my uncles – they were all lawyers and we were three sisters, no brother."

Ela passed her matriculation at the age of 13, in the midst of the freedom struggle. In 1948, when she was in college, India had become newly independent. There was idealism in the air, there was a goal – to rebuild the nation.

"I had no confusion about my career because Gandhiji had shown the way."

After graduating from L A Shah Law College in Ahmedabad in 1954, Ela joined TLA (Textile Labour Association). TLA was formed by Mahatma Gandhi in 1917 and served as a role model for labour unions across the country. At the time Ela joined, TLA had the allegiance of 1.5 lakh textile workers.

"I worked in the legal department and took up small cases related to textile workers. Mainly the negotiations for wage-rise, for bonus and so on."

Ela was the only woman on the TLA staff. And it was often the same situation outside. Her early days in the labour court were tense.

"The slightest comment about my clothes or my short height would upset me, and I would begin to stammer. There were hardly any women in court…"

Ela also caused a stir at the TLA office because she did not cover her head. It was the custom in Ahmedabad but not in south Gujarat, where Ela grew up.

"The complaint went to Anusuya*ben* Sarabhai, who was the president of TLA. Although Anusuya*ben* always covered her head, she did not force me to do so."

This was, perhaps, Ela's very first, very gentle form of rebellion. When she believed in something, she stood firm.

In 1956, Ela married Ramesh Bhatt, though her parents were not keen on the match.

Ramesh was her classmate from college, a handsome man and a student leader.

"He gave me good books to read like J. C. Kumarappa *(smiles)*."

Ramesh also introduced Ela to completely new ideas and experiences. During the first census of independent India in 1951, Ramesh persuaded Ela to accompany him for data collection to Maynafalia slum in Surat. The plight of women there deeply moved her.

"Ramesh taught me so many things, he was a very big influence."

However, Ela was from a upper middle class Brahmin family while Ramesh was a textile worker's son. Hence her family was against the marriage.

"Parents always want to raise their status through the daughter's wedding. And also, genuinely they thought how I am going to live in, you know, a less well-off home."

They had to wait for 7 years but ultimately, the family relented. It was a simple '*shaadi in khadi*' after which the young couple began their life in the Gujarat Vidyapeeth campus, where Ramesh was teaching.

"The atmosphere at Gujarat Vidyapeeth as well as at TLA where I worked was so *bauddhik* (intellectual). I learnt so much, I 'grew up', you can say."

In 1958, Ela gave birth to her daughter Ami, quickly followed by son Mihir. During this period she worked part-time, resuming full-time work in 1961. This time, she took a position in the Labour Ministry of Gujarat as an Employment Officer. She was later put in charge of 'Occupation Information' by the Gujarat government.

"In this role I reviewed existing definitions of various occupations in the National Code of Occupation and framed definitions for new occupations."

In 1968, Ela rejoined TLA as head of its Women's Wing. At this time there was an invitation from Tel Aviv, Israel for a training program and Ela was nominated to go for it. This became a major turning point in her life.

"What I learnt there was really phenomenal. I saw how the whole country worked on the joint action of union and co-operatives."

Whether it was an airline, a bank or a farm, all the workers had full membership of the union and even the spouse had the right to vote. The idea was almost 'Gandhian'.

Ela returned after 3 months, with an international diploma of 'Labour and Cooperatives'. She knew she had to do something – exactly what she did not know. But the many years spent with TLA and the government had opened her eyes to one thing: a large number of economic activities were being undertaken in the informal sector.

These 'informal' workers had no union, no social security and no protection under labour laws.

"My background being that of an 'organiser', I thought that they should also be part of the Labour Movement."

But where does one begin? In the informal sector there is neither a specific contract nor an employer-employee relationship. In fact as per the census of 1971, self-employed women were not even recognised as workers*.

* In 1971, 89% of India's workforce was in the informal sector. Today, the figure is 93%.

"It was a struggle to register SEWA because our concept was so new. We questioned the very definition of work, of worker, and of trade union."

That same year a group of women who worked as head-loaders and handcart pullers in Ahmedabad's cloth market came to Ela*ben* with their grievances. She took up the cause and ultimately won a promise of higher wages from the cloth merchants.

In 1972, Ela and the *bens** working in the cloth market decided to form their own union called SEWA (Self-Employed Women's Association). In this effort they received support from TLA President Arvind Buch. SEWA thus functioned under the auspices of TLA's Women's Wing with Buch as President and Ela as the general secretary.

"According to me what is unique about SEWA is that we are rooted in Gandhian way of thinking. Meaning *apna adhikaar bhi maango* (speak up for your rights) but at the same time go beyond unionism and *naarebaazi* (sloganeering)."

Bring about change through constructive work.

The very first thing SEWA did was to survey the informal workers, sector by sector. Because you have to know what the problem is, before you can solve it.

The 'investigators' came from the same background as those being surveyed. So a *chindi* worker was recruited to ask her companion *chindi* workers – just ten simple questions. The findings varied from trade to trade, but were more or less clear.

"There were common two problems – one was shortage of capital and the other was presence of the middleman."

To put it very simply, these women paid 10% a day as interest to procure stocks/ raw material. 49% of vegetable vendors did not own their own pushcarts but rented them. With income ranging

* In Gujarat, it is the custom to address a woman as *ben* (sister).

from ₹ 50 to ₹ 350 per month, a majority were heavily in debt.

The survey served another important purpose. It gave SEWA an entry into the minds and hearts of women.

"We covered 700, 800, 1000 families, noting down details of their economic life and small-small problems. Then we went back and discussed the findings with them."

At one such meeting in December 1973, Chanda*ben* from Poori Bazar asked. "Ela*ben*, why can't we have our own bank?"

"Because we have no money," Ela explained. "You need a large amount of capital to start a bank!"

"Well, we may be poor, but we are so many," Chanda*ben* replied.

This was an extraordinary insight.

In 6 months' time, the necessary capital was collected, with a minimum investment of ₹ 10 per *ben*. 15 charter members of SEWA were then taught how to write their names. These shaky signatures were put on paper and in May 1974, after much convincing, the Gujarat government inaugurated the Shri Mahila SEWA Sahakari Bank Limited.

Popularly known as SEWA Bank.

With an initial capital of ₹ 71, 320, the bank could only extend very small loans*. But these made a big difference to the womens' lives.

"*Aaj somwar ko* take 50 rupees, on next Monday repay 51 rupees. And take another ₹ 50, ₹ 65, ₹ 100 – like that."

Ela Bhatt was the Chairperson and the bank operated on the simple principles of trust and '*swadharma*'. Within a year the bank enjoyed a working capital of ₹ 300,000 and it continued to grow. As did the membership of the union itself.

By 1975, SEWA had a membership base of 5258 women, each paying ₹ 5 as 'annual fee'.

That same year, Ela attended the world conference of the 'International Women's Year' in Mexico City. There, she met feminist leaders from all over the world. And discovered that

* SEWA Bank started 3 years before Mohammed Yunus started 'Grameen Bank' in Bangladesh.

"There were so many things but everything we cannot do, so which is the most pressing problem we can solve?"

women everywhere were facing pretty much the same issues.

"Esther Ocloo from Ghana shared her stories about the position of women in the markets of Accra. I could share my experiences with SEWA and SEWA Bank."

This sharing led to an important conclusion – there was a need to set up a global organisation to serve the needs of low-income women. This seed of an idea was to grow into Women's World Banking* (WWB), with Wall Street banker Michaela Walsh as its first President.

Meanwhile, the activities of SEWA continued to expand, in response to the needs of the members.

With the help of LD Engineering College and the National Occupational Health Institute, SEWA designed an improved *haathgadi* (handcart). This cart included extra space for carrying a baby underneath as well as a braking system.

A literacy program received poor response so SEWA turned its focus on welfare activities. A childcare centre was set up for vegetable vendors while the Mahila SEWA Trust made health, maternity, widowhood and death benefits available to members at a modest price.

"We did so many simple things like eye checkups and providing glasses to women."

One major problem which SEWA took head-on was harassment of vendors by the police and the municipal corporation staff. Hitting and kicking was common, apart from fines and daily bribes.

"When we first started organising the vendors, we studied the Police Act. The act perceives them to be criminals."

* Women's World Banking was officially incorporated in 1979 and today serves 24 million micro-entrepreneurs in 28 countries.

There were daily struggles with the Ahmedabad Municipal Corporation and the police. For more sensitive treatment and for licences.

"I remember that only 400 licences were given and all to men because the authorities didn't accept women as vendors in their own right."

SEWA distributed *patrikas* or fliers listing vendors' demands and held small *dharnas* (sit-in protests) all over the city. Ultimately, this led to the development of the famous Law Garden market. But on a day to day basis, it was a case of one step forward, two steps back.

"Sometimes the situation would improve. But as soon as a new police officer or corporation official was appointed, the situation went back to square one or became even worse."

Finally, Ela met Chief Minister Babubhai Patel and found support. It was agreed that SEWA's identity cards would be considered as good as licences.

For the first time these poor but enterprising women had a voice – loud enough to be *heard*.

In recognition of all these efforts – and many more – Ela Bhatt was conferred with the Magsaysay Award for Community Leadership in 1977.

At that time, SEWA had a part-time committed staff of 20. The union was governed by a 22-member executive committee and a 'board' made up of 153 elected leaders from seven different trades*. These included the *kapdewallis, doodhwaalis, sabjiwaalis, kabaadiwaalis, chindi workers, haathgadi waalis*** and miscellaneous workers.

Leaders of each group met every month and they knew the exact conditions under which their 'sisters' worked. This provided the vital link between the ground reality and the executive committee.

And this idea that each *ben* is important, no one 'bigger' or

* Garment makers, milk producers, vegetable vendors, junk-smiths, used garment dealers, handcart pullers.

** Loans worth ₹ 15 lakh were given by nationalised banks to SEWA borrowers from 1975 to 1976.

"I was young when I had my children. I had plenty of time to enjoy their growing up. By the time I was busy with SEWA, they were ready to leave home for further studies."

'smaller', is at the very heart of SEWA. What members want is what members get.

Take the decision of keeping SEWA an all-women organisation. Early on, Ela was open to men joining the SEWA movement. But the members emphatically refused.

They said, "We will feel inhibited with men around – they will try to dominate and create tensions."

So the men were kept out but you can't keep out tension. In 1976-77, SEWA Bank was hit by a major crisis. The country was under 'Emergency Rule' and there was a rumour that Indira Gandhi had announced a 'loan waiver'.

The women promptly stopped repaying.

The main issue was the loans for larger amounts which had gone to SEWA members* from banks like SBI. These banks had been directed by Mrs Gandhi to seek out 'small borrowers' and they did the needful.

"When the women defaulted SEWA was blamed… we went through a tough time."

The irony was that SEWA Bank was not affected. Because it had a typical 'woman's way' of dealing with money.

"Our slogan at that time, more or less same today also, was *bachat* (saving). We gave loans only to those who were regular savers and we rarely had any default!"

Meanwhile, there was an election and a new government and new

* Based on a petition by SEWA, the Supreme Court granted a stay on eviction of vendors and directed the administration to find a permanent solution for accommodating them.

set of corporators came into power. The spirit of co-operation gave way to renewed struggles.

The most memorable was the 'Manek Chowk' conflict in January 1981. The new corporators wanted to evict vendors and create a 'disciplined market'. Matters came to a head when a minor scuffle over parking a scooter led to a brawl. Curfew was imposed for more than 10 days, affecting the vendors' daily bread.

When discussions led nowhere, SEWA decided it was time to practise 'civil disobedience'. The vendors would set up the market – *aage ka dekha jayega* (we will see what happens).

"We arrived in the market at eight in the morning. Four police vans were already in position, as if they feared violence."

The police approached Ela and said, ""You don't seem to be concerned… about breaking the curfew. What if there is trouble?"

"We will make sure there is no trouble," Ela replied calmly.

The market was already buzzing with customers and the hum of business. The police withdrew and the vendors continued to sell in Manek Chowk for five days.

"For those five days, all of us managed the traffic. Business thrived till late at night. And the vendors were able to enjoy full sales – no cuts to anyone, no confiscation of goods."

Subsequently an agreement was reached with the authorities and vendor harassment ceased*.

But, a bigger storm was brewing. So far, SEWA had been operating under the umbrella of TLA, which Ela was part of. But relations had become strained.

"When I got the Magsaysay Award in 1977, the leadership felt that it is all TLA's work – why is she getting the recognition?"

But the matter actually boiled over in 1981. Riots had broken out in Ahmedabad city on the issue of reservations for *dalits* in medical colleges. SEWA held a *prarthana sabha* and appealed for peace. The resolution also condemned attacks on lower castes.

* In 1986 the working capital of SEWA Bank crossed ₹ 1 crore.

"Poverty is ongoing violence, it is not God given. It is through the consent of the society."

After all, a third of SEWA members were *dalits*. Being self-employed, they were suffering due to frequent curfews. But TLA did not support reservation and was annoyed that SEWA had issued its own 'press statement'.

Two days later, Chief Minister Madhavsinh Solanki held a meeting with eminent persons and Ela spoke strongly in favour of reservations.

"I was totally unaware that there was a TV camera, there was radio… so it all came out whatever I said. I became hugely popular with dalits and hugely unpopular with everybody else."

Ela's modest home in Usmanpura was pelted with stones every night. The family had to shift elsewhere until tempers cooled. Even later, the 'boycott' continued.

"The sweepers, the grocers, everybody boycotted us. Even my relatives did not like me to visit their homes."

TLA took a tough stand. They said, "You are an employee and you broke the discipline."

On 1 May 1981, Ela was expelled from TLA and SEWA was booted out as well.

"We were more or less on the footpath. They withdrew our bank deposit… they tried to kill us. I felt hurt and betrayed."

Ela had never conceived of SEWA without the TLA. How would it survive?

Ramesh gently said to Ela, "Consider this a blessing."

And that is exactly what it was.

In 1981, SEWA had an office building, a rural centre, one vehicle, and a few typewriters. But what could not be taken away was its organising ability. Its ten-year history of uniting women from different trades, tribes and religions under one banner.

"Thanks to the solidarity of the members – the women's courage – we survived."

In fact, TLA hardly understood the rationale behind SEWA. There was an unspoken understanding between mill-owners and unions that women were better off as 'home makers'. The irony was that these women were working precisely because, due to modernisation, their men no longer had textile mill jobs.

"Every time a textile mill shut down, it was the women who came out on the street to sell goods or started a stitching business at home – to support the family."

Unfettered by TLA, SEWA could now chart its own course. For maximum benefit and maximum *adhikaar* (rights).

The 'new' SEWA took up a campaign for higher rates to *chindi* workers. The small-time businessmen and contractors who gave them jobwork did not agree. Instead they stopped dealing with the most vocal agitators.

"We became conscious that these women have no bargaining power. So how do we gain bargaining power, how do we generate that?"

Thus in July 1982, SEWA started its own production unit – Sabina Co-operative.

"We created our own *khol* (patchwork quilt) from *chindi* (pieces of cloth) and pushed it in the market from our own shop. So that gave us power, gave us a 'lever'."

Women now had an option – do jobwork or join SEWA. Shortage of labour forced the greedy contractor to raise his wages so ultimately, it was a win-win situation for the workers.

Of course, the co-operative offered benefits beyond wages, such as banking, childcare and social security. Additionally the profits were shared with members in the form of dividend. All this created pride and a sense of ownership.

"All these *Musalmaan* (Muslim) women, (they) learnt how to conduct a meeting, how to manage their affairs. It's a very empowering process."

And the effect was felt in every aspect of their lives. An old lady called Bismillah, whom everyone called 'Khala' used to conduct

> **"I don't think too much. But, I am clear that I want to do it the right way, from the beginning."**

chindi business while her husband took a nap. When he discovered this, she was severely beaten. But as soon as she recovered, she was back at the Sabina Co-operative shop.

Eventually, the women at the co-op offered her a job at the weighing machine for a salary of ₹ 500 per month. No one was sure how she convinced her husband, but she made it work each morning. With fear in her eyes but a smile on her lips.

"After a few months there was a strange sight – Khala's husband began coming to the shop at noon every day, carrying a hot tiffin lunch for his wife!"

Running a co-operative is not easy and there were some early setbacks. The rag-pickers' co-operative failed when the woman leading it became greedy. She and her husband began acting as 'middlemen' and even withdrew money from the group bank account. Dissolving the co-operative became a bitter and messy affair.

"But this failure was one of SEWA's major learning experiences."

With proper checks and balances in place, SEWA continued its work. And over time, the model of union combined with co-operatives did work wonders. It became a '*sidhant*', a directive operating principle. One by one, SEWA registered co-operatives for every economic activity its members were engaged in.

Land co-operatives, dairy co-operatives, artisan co-operatives and 'service' co-operatives in healthcare, childcare, video production.

Along the way, there was resistance.

"Our co-operatives were suspect because they did not manufacture any products; the midwives' co-operative was asked why delivering babies should be considered an economic activity; the video producers' co-operative was denied registration because the directors, the producers and the sound and camera technicians were illiterate..."

But SEWA persevered, and got its way. Recognition for the movement came in the form of the Padma Shri award in 1985 and Padma Bhushan in 1986. Ela was nominated by the President of India to be a member of the Rajya Sabha. As an MP, she drew the attention of Parliament to the struggles of informal workers and street vendors.

When you are visible, you have a say. When you have that say, it can impact policy.

On one occasion SEWA was invited by the Handicraft Board for a workshop in Delhi. Each of the members was asked: "If you were the police commissioner or municipal commissioner of Ahmedabad, what policies would you make?"

The deputy chairman of the Planning Commission MS Swaminathan and the chairman of the All India Handicrafts Board Laxmi Jain attended the session and listened carefully. From their notes of the session they wrote an entire chapter in the Planning Commission's report titled 'A Fair Deal to the Self-Employed' or *Do Tokri Ki Jagah* ('Two Baskets Worth of Space').

For years, SEWA had been demanding a 'National Commission for the Self-Employed'. In 1987, this commission came into being and Prime Minister Rajiv Gandhi appointed Ela Bhatt as its first chairperson with five members, all non-political.

"We travelled across the country to understand the problems of self-employed women, and what are the possible solutions."

In 1988, the commission submitted its landmark 400-page report titled 'Shramshakti'. The report and its recommendations were used by the central government, state governments and various women's organisations to develop programs for self-employed women.

It was these earthy, hardworking women who were Ela's closest allies, friends and 'work sisters'. Chanda*ben* – who bartered used clothes for stainless steel utensils, Soopa Goba – who carried bales of cloth on her head and Lakshmi Teta – a 'grand-looking' vegetable vendor at Manek Chowk.

"Chanda*ben* and Lakshmi*ben* were natural leaders."

But a movement like SEWA needs many skills, many allies. Ela*ben's* work also attracted bright, well-educated professionals.

"SEWA is not like an edifice. SEWA is like a tree, so if wind comes from this side, the tree can move this way or that way, but the roots are strong so it will not break down."

The first of them was Renana Jhabvala, who arrived in a clumsily tied *khadi* sari, with degrees from both Harvard and Yale. She came in 1977, to conduct field work for one year. But she never left.

"Renana was a careful observer and a fast learner."

She was also a powerful organiser and was instrumental in forming the first SEWA co-operative. In 1981, she was elected Secretary of the SEWA trade union, a post she held till 1995.

In 1984, Harvard-educated Mirai Chatterjee joined SEWA while Reema Nanavaty quit the IAS to do the same. In 1986, chartered accountant Jayashree Vyas gave up her job at Central Bank of India to work for SEWA Bank and take it to the next level.

"They have all come purely out of *sevabhav* (spirit of service)."

However, the 'white blouse' women – as Ela*ben* calls them – are working *for* the 'blue blouse' women. That is to say, the professionals are here to serve the self-employed, not dominate or rule over them.

"When we set up SEWA we followed the TLA constitution, which was written by Gandhiji. The objective he laid out was '*sampatti no sadupyog*' and '*samay no sadupyog*' (proper use of wealth and time)."

Under this constitution, there is a provision for 'honorary members' ie, members who are not workers but willing to dedicate their life to the cause of the workers.

"The maximum number of honorary members in SEWA is only 25 and they have the same rights as every other member."

SEWA operates on the Gandhian principle of 'decentralisation'. Every co-operative is autonomous and yet part of a 'whole'. Because every worker is a member of the SEWA union.

"So organisational structure we see, as the banyan tree. You have a banyan tree and it has its *shaakhas* (vines) which take root and then it sprawls and it sprawls."

The vines become trunks themselves and then a day comes, when the original is no more identifiable. They are *vad ka ek van* – a sprawling forest within the same, ever-expanding tree.

"The beauty that I see in the SEWA model, is that you can't destroy it, you can't. If you cut one branch it will not die, because it will suck the sap from other branches, from other trees."

Because we are all connected.

It is like that with Ela herself. In 1997, she retired from SEWA, handing over the reins to the next generation.

"I stopped going to the office completely because if I went people would keep coming to me..."

For new leaders can take their place in the sun, only when there is no shadow.

15 years later, the 'forest' is bigger and stronger than ever. SEWA, as a trade union, has 1.7 million members in 8 states. Also under the SEWA umbrella are 110 co-operatives*, 15 economic federations and 3 producer companies**. And what kind of economic might does all this represent?

"*Dekho na,* working capital of SEWA bank is about ₹ 170.4 crore and plus I am told another ₹ 200 crore is generated by the co-operatives."

Over the years, SEWA has started new co-operatives such as VimoSEWA, to provide micro-insurance and pension to members, and Mahila Housing SEWA Trust. But no matter how large SEWA grows the culture of trust and of being 'one family' remains.

SEWA offices are spartan, the table-chair jobs are filled from within the community and the language of communication is always Gujarati.

"SEWA Bank is run by professionals but the Board of the bank

* Of 110 co-operatives, 3 are defunct. The rest are all making surplus.

** SEWA Trade Facilitation Centre is a company with 15,000 artisan shareholders who are also suppliers and producers for the company.

"Whichever city of the world I have been to, I have made a point to visit its downtown vegetable market. Everywhere, the situation of vendors was the same."

is totally working class, elected from the membership, tradewise."

In fact, today even the General Secretary of SEWA – the single most powerful woman in the organisation – is from the working class. Jyoti Macwan comes from a family of agricultural workers in Kheda district and was originally a tobacco worker.

From 'white blouse' to 'blue blouse', the circle is complete.

SEWA celebrated its 40th anniversary in April 2012. Looking back, it happened because, it had to happen. There was no 'plan' or 'goal'.

What had to be done, was simply done.

"I was young, I had all the energy and idealism…"

And so did her life partner.

"Ramesh was never the typical husband who wants *garam garam khaana* and wants to be served. *Hamara ghar bhi bahut simple tha.* We never had servants, *bachche bhi apne apne kapde dhote the.*" (Our home was very simple; even the children washed their own clothes.)

The Bhatts rarely attended social events like weddings. As Gandhians, they were pained by display of wealth and status. And they didn't care much about 'what will people think'.

Or how much we have 'achieved'.

In SEWA, "We never forget to celebrate little success, to boost up our spirits. We do not detest failure, because we've never tasted success in the true sense… But what we have learnt from failures propelled our journey further."

Floods and riots, earthquakes and lawsuits – SEWA has seen it all. And survived and strengthened.

At 80, Ela is active both mentally and physically. Lobbying for new legislation which can help the working class. And a more decentralised way of living.

"People are so resourceful. My faith always goes back to the people, to the local capacity, to the local economy. And to the women, to my sisters everywhere."

We are all not poor, but we are so many.

Each with our own intimate struggle.

To find a voice, to raise our face; to be seen and heard.

ADVICE TO WOMEN ENTREPRENEURS

Simplify your life, particularly housework. Your home has to be clean, liveable and healthy, that's all. Women, you know, get consumed by housework. You need to put infrastructure for the family, that's enough.

I never spent too much time in cooking and cleaning. I do the minimum and I have more time for other things.

Don't have too many gadgets – even gadgets create more work. In the homes of our *bens* there are few vessels, they cook wholesome meals but just one or two dishes.

It is ideal for children when the mother is working. Children are always keen to do something or the other. I think housework is the best model of what you call multi-tasking. The children join you, and that is how they learn, you work together, and finish off the work.

Keep enough space in your mind to think, otherwise *tumhaare mind me jagah kahaan hai*? So much encroached by TV and books and fashions and food and all kinds of things. *Thodi jagah khaali rakh do*, have space.

Think in a correlated way. Think that when I drink a cup of tea or take a spoonful of sugar whatever activity I do, how it is related to myself, how it is related to the society, the community, and how it is related to the universe.

Improve your own lot and contribute to the welfare of the society, a peaceful constructive society where women are leaders.

LOVE ACTUALLY

Shona McDonald,
Shonaquip

When her daughter was born severely disabled, doctors advised Shona to put the baby in an institution. Instead, this South African mother vowed to give Shelly a better quality of life, and in doing so, helped thousands like her.

Raising a special child is an extreme test set by the Divine Examiner.

A test nobody is ever prepared for, or encouraged to take.

The doctors advised – "Put her in an institution."

Well-wishers advised– "Just have another baby."

But, said Shona McDonald, "This *is* my baby."

A living, breathing human being with a beautiful soul, in a twisted body.

Thus began a long, long battle for a young South African mother. And her daughter Shelly.

It started as an anguished effort, to improve quality of life for one little girl. A wheelchair to hold up her tiny body; teaching aids to help her communicate.

That effort is now a movement, speaking on behalf of disabled people, everywhere. A social enterprise which makes their life more comfortable. And meets their need.

The need to be treated as a human being.

The need to be a part of society.

To remind us all, perfection is not the answer.

All you need is love*.

* *This interview was conducted in Washington DC by Shefali Srivastava, to whom I am deeply grateful for a job well done.*

LOVE ACTUALLY

Shona McDonald,
Shonaquip

Shona was born and brought up in Cape Town and never ever thought of getting into business.

"From a very young age I was always passionate about making things better."

When she was 9 years old, Shona remembers making trinkets on her hand-sewing machine and selling them to the neighbours. She wanted to raise money for the shelter for stray dogs. Shona was also one of the junior founders of the National Seabird Rescue Institute.

"One of my neighbours looking after a penguin that she found rescued on the beach after an oil spill and I got involved. I helped clean and feed it... and slowly that became an organisation.*"

However regular stuff like school was a challenge. As a dyslexic, she couldn't spell or handle mathematics very well.

"I completed school but didn't get a chance to go to university. So I started working."

* SANCOBB (Southern African Foundation for the Conservation of Coastal Birds) is a well-known NGO in South Africa even today.

But Shona also enrolled in night college, where she studied art and sculpture.

Meanwhile, personal life took centrestage. While in school, Shona had started dating Mike – they quickly got engaged and married soon after. Shona had her first child at the age of 20 and her second two years later.

This was a turning point in her life.

"Shelly was born in 1982, severely disabled. She was quadriplegic and suffering from cerebral palsy, she could neither walk nor talk."

It was a devastating blow for the young family. Shona ran from pillar to post, begging for information. The doctors had just one piece of advice: "This child will be a burden on you. Put her in a home and think about having another baby."

Shona was horrified. Shelly was just 5 months old and the doctors had written her off.

"I wanted to prove the doctors wrong. I could not accept that my child is 'damaged goods' and giving up on her was the *only* option."

Thus began the long daily battle, handling one 'normal' child and one with special needs. Shelly could not sit, or speak, or even roll over. She had trouble swallowing and eating and she couldn't see in sunlight. In addition, she was 90% hearing impaired.

"I was left with no choice but to try and do things on my own, so that's what I did. I started finding solutions to make Shelly's life better."

Shona gave up her job and made the comfort and care of her daugher the sole focus. Luckily her husband was running his own business and was very supportive. But it wasn't easy. Something as basic as a made-to-order wheelchair was not available in South Africa. Neither could it be imported as the country had been economically and politically boycotted, for its policy of apartheid.

"Internet did not exist back then so I asked my cousins in the UK to send me anything with information on disability."

Shona saw a picture of a special electric wheelchair in a Swedish magazine. It seemed like the perfect seating solution for two-year-old Shelly. But how could it be replicated in South Africa?

Shona contacted the Bio-medical Engineering Department at the University of Cape Town, and found a kindred soul.

"I met an amazing person called Mr Price who could understand what I wanted and build a prototype."

Shelly loved her little electric wheelchair – it allowed her to sit up and see the world. She would ride backwards, round and round in circles, by pulling the joystick. Until one day her big sister Kim begged to try out the wheelchair. After much cajoling, Shona agreed.

"Shelly screeched with laughter as she saw her sister manoeuvre the chair. When she was put back into it, she was driving it just like her."

This was a big lesson for Shona. Kids with severe disabilities don't have an experiential system to guide them. Initially, they must learn by imitating others.

"Once she realised all the things the chair could do, she was downstairs and over the edges of curbs, on the road... it was absolutely a nutcrack keeping her safe!"

Now, Shelly was learning by experience, the way normal children do. Sometimes she would drive into the kitchen and put out her hand to touch the pots.

"I was very protective but I realised she needed to learn things, like any other child. If she burnt her finger once, she would know not to do it again."

Shona applied the very same principle to every area of Shelly's life. Even something like vocabulary.

"Words like 'up' and 'down' are meaningless to a child who doesn't move and can't speak. So, I would climb up the ladder, holding her in my arms. Speaking and showing her the words 'Shelly's going up.'"

An actual 'physical' learning which made the word come alive. But despite all the progress Shelly made, she was not eligible to join a school. It was simply against the law.

"Children with disabilities were not allowed to go to mainstream schools. They had to go to special schools. But, they wouldn't take her in either because they couldn't prove she was clever enough."

"I just really take it one day at a time. Because if I think too much I would become too scared and stop doing what I do."

The only option was a daycare centre which Shona vehemently opposed.

"I wanted my daughter to have an education, a *future*. So, I started teaching her at home."

A mother with a mission can move mountains. Combining her own ingenuity with remedial teaching and professional therapy, Shona taught Shelly to read. The child was intelligent but she needed as much stimulation as possible.

"It was then that I started looking at ways to change government policies so that she could go to school. And have equal rights, like other children did."

Shona started an activist organisation to fight for these rights. Over time, she raised her voice not only for disabled children but for an overall inclusive education policy – across religious and race divides.

"We were lucky, as the entire political system was going through an upheaval. We fought for change and we made it happen."

Shelly was finally able to join a mainstream school, with an assistant. Meanwhile Shona realised there was much more work to be done. There were hundreds of parents in her situation – wth disabled children. And they could all help and support each other.

"With a therapist and some friends, I started another non-profit organisation called 'Interface'. That grew into a national movement."

Initially, Shona held training workshops for parents to share all the techniques she'd used with Shelly. She also experimented with all kinds of little devices to help children communicate more easily – using switches, adapting toys.

"I wanted kids to be able to 'play', even if they didn't have good use of their hands."

In the process, Shona realised that if kids aren't sitting properly, they can't communicate properly.

"If they can't hold their heads up, they can't look at you properly, they can't balance their bodies. How will they free their arms to indicate or point or whatever?"

Many parents asked Shona if she could make custom-made wheelchairs for their kids. And that's how Shonaquip was born in 1992. An enterprise whose reason to exist was simply to help others.

"We didn't have capital, or any business plan. It started with one chair, and then we made the next chair."

The entire operation was run out of the family garage. The babysitter doubled up as an admin assistant in the evenings. But unlike her previous efforts, this was registered as a company.

"I had done a lot of fundraising for my non-profits – through Lions' Club, cake sales, Art events. But I was finding it very hard to do it on a sustained basis."

Due to a change in government policy donations from abroad went to a centralised state coffer, and not directly to any organisation. In addition, many donors were embracing new and more fashionable causes.

"HIV/ AIDS started getting the lion's share funding in Africa... many non-profits had to discontinue their programs because money had dried up."

This was not acceptable.

"I decided I would rather be making things I could be fully responsible for and if things failed it was *my* fault. Rather than putting blame on lack of funding."

"For centuries wheelchairs have been built for the person that's doing the pushing and not for the person that sits in the chair. I want to see that change in my lifetime."

"65 million people around the world need a wheelchair but 80% of them are designed to American or European standards."

But, there were some doubts in Shona's mind. Was it ethical to look at disability as a 'market' and make a profit out of it? Shona decided that she would charge but only to cover costs and create a self-sustained organisation.

At a more basic level, there was the issue of how to run a business.

"I struggled because I didn't know *anything* about business – cashflows, costing, all that stuff. "

What Shona did know and focused all her energy on, was the technical stuff. How to stop scoliosis. Maintaining biochemical alignment of the spine. Dealing with pressure sores and contractures.

"The things that fascinated me were how to make life better for these children."

And what kept her going through all the challenges was the huge impact the work was having on the quality of life for these families.

Children who had spent their whole life just lying on a mattress on the floor could move around on their own.

Children classified as 'ineducable' were learning to read.

As demand grew, so did Shonaquip.

"I had no idea where it was going except that I had to keep doing it."

Over time, Shonaquip started making a little bit of profit on sale. That money was used to subsidise kids who couldn't afford equipment and thus it became a 'social' business.

"I didn't know I was a social entrepreneur though," says Shona. "Only years later when I got an award and then I said 'oh'!"

Shonaquip's flagship product is the 'Madiba' buggy – very similar to the first wheelchair Shona had designed for Shelly. This adjustable modular seating system is designed for cerebral palsy users in a range of sizes – from infant to adult.

"We named the buggy 'Madiba' in honour of Nelson Mandela, as Madiba is his traditional name."

Other devices like the 'Shonabuggy', 'Snoekie' and 'Standing Frame' followed. All designed by Shona herself, keeping the requirement of the user in mind.

"I think my training in sculpture helps. I have this obsession of fixing things three dimensionally!"

But it was always creativity with a purpose.

"Where they already had the right pieces of equipment, I didn't bother to make stuff. But, where there was nothing, we would look at the problem and how to solve it."

In addition, every user is unique and hence equipment must be adapted, modified, customised. This takes a great deal of time and patience, as does training the users and their families. But Shonaquip is committed and passionate about every aspect.

"Somebody who works in an office with spinal injuries needs a very different wheelchair from a child that lives in a remote rural village who cannot sit up right and yet… this is usually overlooked."

In fact, disabled people as a whole are overlooked by society. And the less visible but equally important work Shona has done – over three decades – is addressing this issue. Working with hospitals, community workers and government, her work has led to policy change at the national level.

"You know, I get on the aeroplane in the morning to go on a business meeting and there are still only 20 of us (women) and 200 men on the bus."

"The challenge has been to grow but also retain that very precious part of the company driven by passion, not profit."

"The right kind of chairs are now procured by the government through tenders, therapists are trained to help users maintain proper posture."

Government support further accelerated demand. In 2004, Shona set up a factory in Wynberg, near Cape Town to manufacture, assemble and adapt various devices. Many of the workers at this facility happen to be wheelchair users themselves.

As Shonaquip rapidly scaled up, Shona realised she was out of her depth. She had to find people who knew more about running a business with 65% year-on-year growth*.

"I was also under pressure from many people – such as bank managers – to bring in professionals."

Shona took their advice and brought in 'real business people' in 2010. But that's when things started going terribly, terribly wrong. The people who came in had business skills but no understanding of the purpose or mission of the company.

"They ended up retrenching all the people who had a passion to help and serve. Staff strength dropped from 70 to 40 in just one year."

It was a really difficult time for Shona, in other ways as well.

"I had a bit of a personal calamity, I ended up getting divorced after 30 years and it rocked my confidence significantly. I let other people take control because I was battling myself…"

Eventually, Shona pulled up her socks and took charge of things herself. Recovery was painful and slow and made her realise that 'people' are the single most important asset a company can have.

"Now I personally interview everybody who applies to work for us. I am looking for what makes people get out of bed in the morning…"

* Shonaquip's annual revenues were USD 3 million in the year 2010, of which half the income was generated from government business.

People who *want* to make a difference. Yes they need to have skills – accounting, early childhood development or community work. But Shona believes skills can be learnt on the job. What you can't inculcate is attitude.

"My job now is to make sure everyone fits together and helps each other, like pieces in a puzzle. That is my main focus."

There's been another big change at the company recently. After 19 years of operating from home, Shonaquip moved into a dedicated office building.

"It used to be chaotic," she admits. "There were wheelchairs everywhere and people sharing your kitchen and your fridge, your stove and your bathrooms..."

Shona herself continues to work from home – from a desk under the staircase. That's because there are committed people who handle much of the day-to-day operational work.

"I don't do training myself any more because my colleague in the Department of Health has taken over and she does it far more professionally."

Over the last two decades, Shonaquip has benefitted over 65,000 people but that's still just a drop in the ocean. Now, the World Health Organisation is taking the programs global.

Shona herself is preoccupied with Uhumbo – the foundation she set up two years ago to raise money for research and advocacy.

"I want to actually prove the economic benefits of proper seating and wheelchair services by collecting stories from parents and caretakers."

The other aspect of this work is about going back to the roots, to see how parents and teachers can truly include the child in their family. Instead of remaining an object of pity or a mute spectator. Apart from that, designing new devices and teaching aids remains a passion for Shona.

"I have my studio with the most wonderfully talented young designers and engineers. We have redesigned a lot of our earlier devices to look smarter and also bring down the cost of manufacturing."

"I had friends who were scared to come visit us, in case they caught what Shelly had... those people just dropped out of my life."

In fact, the parts are now shipped to remote areas in Zimbabwe and Namibia where the company has trained people to assemble them. Which, Shona believes, will gradually create jobs for people with disabilities, around the world.

A woman feels responsible for everyone and everything. At home, at work, she is always 'on call'.

"You realise that as a working woman, you actually need a 'wife'," jokes Shona.

Shelly continues to be a wonderful inspiration but also a life-long responsibility. At age 30, she is an integral part of the business and the family but she will never be completely accepted by society.

"When Shelly was in school, a teenager, she saw other girls going out with boys and things like that. It did hurt her to see the things she can't have in life."

In a candid moment Shona admits, she does worry about Shelly's future. Because there is still a lot of social pressure to institutionalise those with special needs. But won't we *all* be in that situation at some point?

Shona's mother – who is 90 years old now – needs to be taken care of. It's a responsibility Shona accepts even though her parents have not been supportive.

"My mother wanted this perfect life for us and thought having a disabled child was like a sign that it wasn't a perfect life. But, in the end... I mean, it's all just worked out."

Shona's daughters – one younger and one older – were extremely supportive. So was her husband – initially. But over the years, as the business grew bigger and Shona started travelling a lot, things fell apart.

"I couldn't be this amazing sexy wife and run a business and be involved in policy and travel and look after the kids..."

Although going through the divorce was difficult, Shona has healed and moved on. To start a new phase in her life.

"I think we're far too scared of change," she smiles. "I feel quite liberated, free to take on many things I haven't done before."

More travel, more study, more 'me' time.

More desire, more fire, aiming higher.

Seeking to be. For all humanity.

ADVICE TO WOMEN ENTREPRENEURS

I think you just need to believe in yourself and be confident. You know…just get up there. Women can do far more than they think they can and they need the confidence to do it.

The problem is, society is not built in a way that applauds women for success. Instead it fosters a sense of guilt… that to achieve you must have sacrificed something to do with your motherly duties or wifely duties.

People never look at a man and say, "Oh, you've neglected your child but you work and travel along". It's, "Oh, you're a successful businessman."

Do what feels right and don't hesitate by worrying and dissecting too much. The next day you can change what you are doing, evolve it into the next phase of what you're doing. We need to constantly evolve to address the needs of people around us… on an hourly, minute basis.

It's the choices you make that construct your future. You can choose to become a victim or you can choose to make decisions that empower you.

Surround yourself with people who support your vision so you can keep your focus, and your energy!

SARASWATI

Armed with a professional education, these women are carving out an identity through entrepreneurship. They enjoy an unusual amount of freedom to be who they wish to be, beyond traditional roles.

PEACE, LOVE, BUSINESS

Nina Lekhi,
Baggit

Nina started making and selling canvas bags – just for fun – while she was a student at Sophia Polytechnic. 29 years later, her company Baggit is a national retail brand with ₹ 34 crore in annual sales.

Narayan Udyog Bhavan is not a pretty place.

Unlike the fancy stores where its pretty products sell, Baggit's head office is a mangled mass of cutting, stitching, inspecting and packing, spread across many small galas.

Nina Lekhi walks into her office, wearing a simple blue and black plaid shirt, and a broad smile.

"Give me ten minutes, will you!" she says.

And sits down on the floor just behind her desk, to meditate.

Ten minutes later, she is ready to take on the world.

The story of Baggit is actually quite similar. It may appear chaotic, but a certain quiet stillness – a central core of clarity and purpose – holds it all together.

Nina started the enterprise as a college student, just for fun. 25 years later, it is definitely a business to be proud of – in terms of size and scale. But, at the end of the day, it's *still* about fun.

Of experimenting and creating a new reality.

Not just with cloth and synthetic leather, but the very fabric of *your* life.

Because that is the greatest design experiment of all.

PEACE, LOVE, BUSINESS

Nina Lekhi,
Baggit

Nina Lekhi was born and brought up in Bombay, in a well-to-do family.

"I had a beautiful childhood. We lived at Worli Seaface and I went to one of the best schools – Greenlawns High School."

Nina's father was a businessman, manufacturing gears and machinery parts. And while her mother was a housewife, she wasn't at home that much. As a devotee of Mata Braj Deviji, she travelled around the country to be with her guru.

"From the time I was 12, I remember pretty much looking after the house, my brother, my father – and *padhai* – on my own."

But, somehow the house was 'blessed'.

Nina was a good student in school, a top ranker, and head girl as well. But then, she entered college and the freedom went to her head.

"It was like, now I'm into FYJC (first year junior college), what the hell! I want to watch every movie. Try out every new thing, whether it's drugs, alcohol, early boyfriends…"

Not surprisingly, she flunked her 'Foundation' course, a mandatory requirement for anyone wanting to study Commercial Art.

"It was the first time I ever failed – it hit me hard."

Nina would walk from Sophia Polytechnic at Peddar Road to her home in Worli every day, rain or sun, often in tears. This went on for about 3-4 months.

"I wanted to do Commercial Art because I love drawing and painting."

But that door was now shut. Nina now had the option of taking up either screen printing or interior designing at Sophia Polytechnic.

"They were part-time courses, so I took up both!" she says.

Screen printing sessions were from 9 am till noon, while the interior designing class was in the evening, for an hour and a half. That left the whole day free, and Nina was not one to waste it.

"What was the point of going home?" she says. "I decided to take up a part-time job."

Nina joined 'Shyam Ahuja', famous for its designer dhurries (rugs). The store was conveniently located opposite the Mahalaxmi temple, a short walk from Sophia college.

"I worked as a sales girl. I learnt stock-keeping, billing and how to talk to customers."

The salary was just ₹ 500 a month, and she didn't really need the money.

"I spent most of it on taking cabs!" laughs Nina. "But it felt good, to be working at 18, like kids do in other countries."

Earn a bit, learn a bit. Do it, just for the fun of it. Which is how Nina started this entire business of bags in the year 1984, at age 18.

"My best friend Mona and I, we got this idea. Like you have T-shirts with simple slogans, why not bags?"

Bags with attitude.

In the shower cubicle, after a swim, Nina and Mona quickly came up with the name – 'Baggit'.

"Inspired by Michael Jackson's 'Beat It'," she adds.

The bags were made of simple canvas. Mostly, on Sundays. A liftman helped with the cutting, while a 'zip repair' guy doubled up as *darzi* (tailor).

"Luckily I had done a tailoring class in my school holidays," says Nina.

And that's how Baggit started.

Nina scoured the bylanes of Bombay – places like Abdul Rehman Street – in search of canvas material. By that time she was working at another store – Mike Kirpalani – which sold trendy clothing.

Nina went up to the owner and said, 'Please stock my bags. If it sells, you pay me my share!"

Around this time, Nina met Manoj – or Manjo, as Nina prefers to call him. He was the brother of a close friend.

"Manjo was in the clothing business and they used to hold an exhibition-cum-sale. He liked my bags and put them up for sale."

Soon after, a shop at the Oberoi shopping arcade offered some counter space. *Sab kuch mila kar* (all put together) in that first year, Nina managed to sell about 30 bags a month.

"The bags cost about ₹ 25 to make, and we sold them for 60 bucks. So it wasn't big money or anything! We made around a thousand bucks a month."

Meanwhile, Nina managed to pass the Foundation exam but didn't have the 'guts' to do Commercial Art. Besides, by this time she was into making bags and textile design seemed like a good idea.

"I enjoyed it and also did very well. In fact, I won a State Award in Textile Design."

This, despite juggling college, practicals and a growing business. With shops like Amarsons stocking Baggit, production had to be increased.

"I used to be in college from 9 to 5. Then 7 o clock the tailors would come – I had two of them now. And of course we continued to work on Sundays."

The family watched on, with a touch of disbelief. No woman in the Punjabi household had done something like this before. *Magar kisi ne roka toka nahin* (But no one tried to stop her).

"In fact, my mom encouraged me a lot. Others found it amusing."

But slowly it became more than pocket money – this was cold hard

"In college, I sold bags just for fun. Even today it's just for fun... All these years, it's never been so profit-oriented. It's all been about how happy we are."

cash. Not only did Nina enjoy *udaoing* it in typical teenage fashion, she would pick up small things for the house. Like curtains.

"I started supporting the family, the house, because Dad's business started dwindling..."

By this time her partner Mona had quit – she went off to the US. But that never bothered Nina. By 1987 – three years into the business – Baggit was selling 300 bags a month. And not just canvas, but using new material like synthetic leather.

"Actually, I did try working with leather. I went and picked up a cow hide and coloured it in my verandah."

The stink overpowered the entire house.

Working with dead animal skin did not *fee*l good.

So, Nina decided to work with synthetic leather. She treated the material, using many different methods. Finally, she achieved the right finish – the look of *real* leather.

"Another advantage of using synthetic leather is you can sell at lower MRP."

'Use and throw' fashion, trendy and inspired. That's what Baggit quickly came to stand for.

Unlike most designers, Nina refused to simply copy styles from international catalogues. She had focused on small, original touches. Which made each bag more special to its user.

"For example, you go to the gym in track pants. If you have a little pockets inside the track pants, in the band, where you can put in couple of notes... it's user-friendly right?"

That's the kind of intuitive thinking Nina would put into every bag she designed. And customers loved it. By 1989, Baggit was a *serious* business, with an annual turnover of ₹ 30 lakh.

And Nina was, technically, still a student.

"Along with my textile design course I had completed 12th standard by correspondence. After Sophia, I enrolled for a BCom at Elphinstone."

Work hard by day, party hard by night continued to be Nina's motto. And it did not go down well at home.

"My mom used to get damn pissed off because I used to go out in the nights," Nina recalls.

Manjo was a part of the gang of friends. A guy Nina had known since her schooldays.

"One night we were at a pub and he just proposed to me."

Nina was dumbfounded.

"Oh God, I don't want to marry, I don't want to hurry this…I'm just 23," she was thinking to herself.

But the next time Nina stumbled home in the wee hours, she got yet another tongue-lashing.

"I blurted out the first thing that came to mind, to 'save my skin'. I told Mom that Manjo had proposed to me!"

By next morning, mothers on both sides had exchanged notes and fixed a wedding date.

"Before I knew it, I was engaged… a couple of months later we were married," she grins.

And it was actually the best thing that could have happened, to Nina.

"Manjo's sister Rita was my best friend, I was so used to their house and his family. It was absolutely, totally beautiful…"

There were no 'rules', no expectations or demands. Even though it was a large, joint family.

"I mean, my mother-in-law was better than my mother also…" says Nina. "I was always kept very comfortably, like a queen!"

Working, continuing the business, was not an issue at all. Manjo's family was in the garment business, both manufacturing as well as retail.

"Manjo had a couple of small galas in a building in Parel. Initially I worked out of the loft area in one of these galas."

"I guess it's the zeal, the love for what you are doing...for me time flies. I can be here all the time, it's just like that."

Nina spent her weekdays – 10 am to 8 pm – at the 'factory'. At this point, she had 20 people working with her, including a production manager.

"Apart from production he also managed the accounts, advance to the *karigars* (workers) – everything."

There was no 'business plan' as such, but Baggit was growing. And things kept flowing. Within a couple of years, the business outgrew its borrowed space. So Nina took up a gala owned by her father in an industrial estate.

"Then each time I needed more space I would just rent out another gala in the same building!"

However, Nina wasn't comfortable working out of rented premises. The normal Indian way of thinking is, might as well buy it. *Investment bhi ho jayega aur paise ki bhi bachat ho jayegi*. (It will be an investment also and you won't be paying rent.)

"Beg, borrow, steal... but buy your own place was my way of thinking," says Nina.

In fact, Nina and her brother Mukesh had just done that, to buy a shop at Kemp's Corner.

"We had just ₹ 2 lakh between us, but we borrowed from family and friends and bought the shop for ₹ 18 lakh."

This became Nina's Baggit's first 'exclusive' retail outlet – INXS. A store which showcased the entire range, and became an go-to place for young, trendy shoppers.

"It was owned and managed by my brother."

What Nina is passionate about, is great design. That's the reason she went into business. But to *stay* in business, you have to take care of the practical stuff. Like raising working capital.

"I started an account with Dena Bank – the closest bank. Manjo's company also had an account there, which helped."

While Nina was never focused on the bottomline, the company was growing 30% year on year. And that was enough for the bank to lend its support.

"They understand, I guess they know that designers are always going to be a little eccentric!"

An eccentric is actually just a person who is not 'like everyone else'. Who takes decisions true to her heart. In life, as in business, there are different paths. Only *you* can choose the path you want to walk.

"I got many offers to make bags and sell them under somebody else's brand name. It would have brought in large volume of business. But I was clear, that's not the path I want to pursue."

Thus when Regal – a well-known chain of shoestores – approached Nina, she agreed to stock her products. But only if the bags were sold with *her* label – 'Baggit'.

"I insisted on the same terms when Shopper's Stop came to us."

Building a name is the natural instinct of a designer. But it also makes sound business sense. As more and more retailers set up shop, Baggit found new shelf space and new markets. Both Lifestyle and Pantaloon set up a small exclusive area – a Baggit 'shop in shop'.

By 2006-7, Baggit was a respectable-sized company, with a ₹ 7 crore turnover. 50 full-time staff and 450 jobworkers. And then, for the first time, *ambition* awoke inside Nina.

"I attended a program called 'Pi', conducted by Manjo. And in this program I learnt a lot about creating a vision, working with tangible goals."

Nina decided to start her own stores. To make the brand 'Baggit' more visible, more known.

"We are growing through the franchise mode."

Not by diluting equity, but getting investment from the franchisees. And with bank loans.

Growth means change – in mindset, in strategy.

"I don't think of buying properties now," admits Nina. "We lease all our stores. That's what you need to do, to grow!"

"I take my designers with me for trips abroad to expose them to what's happening worldwide."

Baggit also hired retail consultants, and now works with an annual business plan and KRAs (Key Result Areas).

"We try to maintain that culture of working out of love for what you do. But KRAs keep reminding us of the bigger picture, the goals we have set for ourselves."

It's all the more important as the company grows in size. With 220 employees and 500 jobworkers it can't be as informal or 'personal'. Systems and processes *are* needed.

While production is decentralised to a string of smaller, company-owned units across Mumbai, the heart of the operation still beats at Narayan Udyog Bhavan in Lalbaug.

"We create all the new designs and samples here. I am fully and personally involved with that aspect."

In the fashion industry, production planning happens a year in advance. But the concept of spring-summer and autumn-winter doesn't really work in India.

"I do follow international trends to a certain extent but in India bright colours do well all year round. We wear yellows and reds and kurtis even in winter. So, you have to design keeping your customer in mind!"

The Baggit loyalist is the metro woman – both the young and the young at heart. She is style-conscious, wants to stand out in the crowd but also demands value for her rupee. A tough cookie to please.

"Every design has to pass a stringent test of usability before it can get into bulk production."

Nina still visits stores herself, once a week, to observe and understand her customer. Get new ideas and inspiration.

"You know, we're the ones who started selling mobile pouches. They became so popular, now everybody's copied the idea!" Nina exclaims.

All ideas need not be as radical. It could be just an extra compartment, for make-up and jewellery. Or a small eyelid so your earphone wire can sneak out.

"We hate doing things that are existing in the market – the fun of doing it is only in doing something new!" she admits.

If you're having fun and so are your customers, you *will* see bigger, fatter sales figures. Baggit closed the year ending March 2012 with revenues of ₹ 34 crore.

"We now produce 500,000 pieces a year which includes handbags, belts, wallets, mobile pouches... In fact, accessories are 50% of our turnover," says Nina.

What is most amazing is that even as Baggit has scaled up, the time Nina spends at Baggit has scaled down.

"I come to work only 3 days a week now," she says. A practice she started around 8 years ago, when daughter Veduci was born.

Was it a conscious decision, to have a baby at the age of 36?

"Well, initially I used the loop and later when we wanted a baby... It took its own time!"

And that brought with it, the unique challenge of motherhood.

"Having a baby kept me quite a bit away from work. So... it was very stressful for many years. There are days you are dying to go to work but you are homebound, which I guess every working mom goes through."

Luckier than most, Nina worked out her own means and methods of balancing out life and work. The close-knit, family-like atmosphere at Baggit allows the luxury of physical absence.

Because, in spirit, you are *always* there.

"Everybody has their own way of working and handling people and mine was to give my people a feeling of belonging."

The proof of that sweet pudding is the fact that many who began working for Baggit in its early years – as far back as 1989 – are still there. Heading various departments, handling new and complex functions.

"It's a passion – not work – and that's what I also try to keep in the spirit of the whole team."

"Meditation gives me time to introspect, to decide where I want to go, don't want to go, how fast I want to go. Most people just keep running, running, running...."

When Nina senses an employee is saturated, or bored, she changes their profile.

"I see what kind of person they are – right-brained or left-brained. And I give people new challenges, things they haven't tried out."

Last year, Baggit's design head was shifted to the marketing department. And she's done a fantastic job, says Nina.

Unorthodox methods, but they work!

Equally unorthodox was Nina's decision to shift her residence to Khatar Kadak, a tiny hamlet near Pune. Where husband Manjo has recently started an experimental school.

"Earlier my husband was with the family business. Now he works, but not for money. He works with our Guru Rishi Prabhakarji, setting up various projects."

One such project was Rishikul Vidyalala, a 'holistic' school set up on the MET campus in the year 2002. The Khatar Kadak school is the next step in that journey of discovery.

"We wanted our daughter – and other kids – to grow up in a more natural atmosphere. Mountains, fresh air, no TV, no google, no *kachrapatti of* Bombay..."

60 children from age 5 to 14 are currently enrolled in this school 'in the middle of nowhere'. And that's also where Nina spends part of her week.

"I go to Khatar Kadak on Saturday afternoons and drive back into work on Wednesday afternoon," she says.

Though work does continue. Mondays and Tuesdays Nina goes over reports, and gets time to *think*. Which is something one rarely has time for in office.

"I also observe a day of silence once in a week… that day is very important, very sacred to me."

A journey of the spirit which began with a meditation program Nina attended with Manjo soon after marriage. Where both found their guru, and a higher calling.

"I guess in my own way I followed the path my mom chose – of the inner search. The most important things in life for me are peace and joy – not the pursuit of money."

A view of life husband Manjo fully supports and endorses. As he supports Baggit – at an emotional level.

"Manjo's main contribution is telling me to chill! Don't get anxious, don't get obsessed with KRAs. Be in love, enjoy, laugh a lot – that's what he's taught me."

A good life is like a good meal – don't put too much on your plate. Only as much as you *can* eat, and what you enjoy.

"Like, I've never obsessed about cooking," says Nina. "I supervise it. I do it sometimes when there is nobody. But then I don't feel I *have* to do pack my daughter's tiffin with my own hands."

Similarly, Nina rarely shops for herself. If she has to buy anything, even for her daughter, she sends an assistant to pick it up.

"Time is so precious!" she laughs. "I only shop when I travel abroad. Because then I visit so many stores to see what are the trends, get some inspiration…"

Including the idea of taking Baggit international, with its own franchise stores. And even moving the brand beyond bags and accessories.

"Recently I realised you don't get good track pants in India. And immediately I thought – let's start a sportswear line!"

Many streams gurgle.

Many paths beckon.

The traveller shall rest a moment, consult her inner compass.

Before deciding which one to walk on…

ADVICE TO WOMEN ENTREPRENEURS

Do what you love to do. I think that's the most important thing. If you love doing something there is no feeling of 'working'. It's not time-bound then, there is no stress.

For women, it's a great big balancing act especially when you are running the kids, home and a million other things that come along with it. So it's true that many drop out, give up on their dreams.

But when you are passionate about something, you have that zeal 'I want to do this', then you won't leave because you can't just sit and *not* do anything. There's a fire within you.

BORN

THIS WAY

Sangeeta Patni,
Extensio Software

This BITS Pilani graduate worked with Hindustan Lever and Eicher before teaming up with her brother, to start her own software company. Her life is a living example of how to manage a career, along with motherhood.

The phone rings insistently.

"Excuse me a minute, I'll take this call," says Sangeeta.

"Hello… *bas beta* I'm just having my lunch. I'll be home in a little while."

There is a long pause.

"*Raat mein neend nahi aayi thi na aapko….hmm. Maa hoon tumhari, mujhe sab pata hai tumhare bare mein, so jao.*" Ok, bye.

It's a peculiar but true fact – the men I interview never get phone calls from their kids in the middle of a working day. The women invariably do.

That's motherhood for you. Being 'on call', and emotionally available, wherever you are.

Sangeeta puts it into sharper perspective.

"As a woman, motherhood is the toughest part. Being an entrepreneur is much easier!"

Well, at least easier than being a corporate slave, feels Sangeeta.

For a woman, entrepreneurship is an opportunity to be her authentic self. Taking up a challenge and show the world – it *can* be done.

"Status, power or money are not enough to motivate women," declares Sangeeta. "We have a tougher job being phonies than men!"

We dip into somewhat phony 5-star food and discuss the difficulty of finding a good maid.

An authentic problem we hope some woman out there will solve for us.

Because, it will bring joy to the world.

BORN THIS WAY

Sangeeta Patni,
Extensio Software

Sangeeta Patni is a Nagpur girl.

"My father was a mining engineer in the Railways – I grew up and went to school in Nagpur."

The only girl in the family – with one older brother and one younger – Sangeeta grew up in a fairly traditional home.

"In Marwari families there is this feeling the role of a woman is – *ghar raho, khana banao, bacche dekho* (keep house, cook food, raise kids)."

Luckily, Sangeeta's dad had studied at ISM (Indian School of Mines) at Dhanbad so he was very passionate about education, very open-minded and all that. And yet, when she got into BITS Pilani, they were reluctant to let her join.

"My elder brother had already enrolled for his BTech from Pilani. I insisted, they had to treat me alike."

Thus, in 1981 Sangeeta joined BITS Pilani to pursue a degree in Electronics and Electrical Engineering. On completing the course in 1985, she came back to Nagpur. Because now, the family said, is the right time to get married.

Waiting for a suitable boy to come along, Sangeeta took up a job at a private engineering college.

"Those were initial days when the education business was just opening up. I'm talking about 1985."

This was also the time that PCs were just coming in, but no one quite knew what to do with them. Sangeeta had a few ideas, and 25k in her pocket – all that she had earned as a lecturer.

"My dad had friends who were senior Chartered Accountants. So, we started a company – the three of us. I was just a chit of a girl but I had one advantage – I knew computers."

The company was called Data Cell and took up data entry and payroll processing. But before it could find its feet, within six months, tragedy struck.

"My father met with an accident and passed away. He was just 50 years old."

The family moved to Udaipur, where it had roots and relatives. But, very few jobs.

"Only 2 companies in Udaipur actually offer any employment to engineers. So, I joined one of them," says Sangeeta stoically.

Rajasthan State Mines and Minerals was a PSU, but luckily the Managing Director at that time – Anil Vaish – was a very competent and open-minded IAS officer. And a fine boss and mentor as well.

He set up a challenge for 24-year-old Sangeeta.

"You set up the computer department."

This, in a company which hadn't *heard* about computers, let alone used them. Additionally, Sangeeta took charge of the control and instrumentation engineering part of a large project.

"I designed one plant and its process control system. I was given full responsibility and full freedom".

In the 5 years she spent there, Sangeeta created the EDP department from ground up. By the time she quit in 1991, the team had grown to 8 members.

"We had computerised the payroll and the mining profit management. All home-grown applications, built from scratch."

In between, in 1988, Sangeeta tied the knot with Sunil. An arranged marriage, Digamber Jain family. But a progressive one.

"My father-in-law is also a mining engineer. My husband worked with ONGC – 14 days offshore, 14 days onshore."

Hence Sangeeta continued to live and work in Udaipur, even after marriage. But eventually she got bored of the job, bored of the town.

"I decided that I needed to move out. So, I took up a job with Hindustan Lever as Assistant Manager in Bombay."

That was another exciting phase in Sangeeta's professional life. She handled the first ever ERP implementation in the country in 1991 using a shrink-wrapped US software product called 'MFG Pro'. Unlike the home-grown customised solutions Indian companies were used to.

"Working with Levers was a new experience. Very different from RSMM!"

Here was a large, process-oriented, multinational company. Effecting a change in their entire system – from manufacturing to exports to accounting – was a big challenge.

"We were a team of about 10 to 12 managers and it took us more than 36 months!"

Five years at Levers and it was once again time to move on. Sangeeta took up a job as Systems Head with Eicher Motors in Indore. She was 32 at the time, ready to start a family but unwilling to give up her career. So *who* would look after the baby?

"My in-laws lived in Indore and were supportive, so I decided to shift there. I took a substantial pay but the role was exciting – to lead the entire SAP implementation."

Again, a new company culture. Home-grown in one sense, but Japanese in another.

"At Eicher we worked on consensus basis. At Lever's it was much more hierarchical."

As a hardcore engineering company, all the action at Eicher was at the factory. And that's where Sangeeta worked from, with a view of the assembly line from her cabin.

"I was the only woman on the senior management team."

In the midst of all this, Sangeeta had a baby in 1997. And though she continued working – with her in-laws' support – the job was no long exciting.

"That's one of the problems that I have always had, I get bored quickly!"

"When I was leaving for BITS Pilani my grandmother said, "*Zyada padh likh kar ladka hi nahi milega!*"

(You won't find a good husband if you are too educated!)."

By this time, Sangeeta's brother Vipin had moved to the US. He was a hardcore techie and was toying with the idea of starting his own software company.

A bulb lit up in Sangeeta's head.

"As a technology person I felt very strongly that companies were not doing much for user interfaces. I remember when I was at Eicher, we had to literally force people to learn SAP… and it would take more than a week for them to get the hang of it!"

The idea of building software with elegance and beauty excited Sangeeta.

"While I was with Eicher we had started the prototyping work. My brother and I pooled in money and outsourced the project to a consulting firm in Nagpur."

Ultimately, for practical reasons, Sangeeta shifted bag, baggage and baby, to Nagpur.

"Those were the days of the dotcom boom – java engineers were bloody hard to find. We decided to buy off the 6 engineers who'd worked on the prototype and start our own development office.

That's how we started Extensio, which came into existence in February 2000."

Extensio is essentially a 'middleware' company – it provides information to users from enterprise sources. Simply put, SAP or PeopleSoft data with access through a GUI (Graphical User Interface). But the average user would much rather just see that data on a familiar interface – like Microsoft Excel.

"How can I use Excel and still interact with PeopleSoft? That's the problem Extensio solved for users."

In fact, the initial idea was that wherever you are, you do an Alt-click on a particular word and related information would come up in a bubble on-screen.

"At that time, the company itself was called 'My Bubble'. And our business was basically targeted to the consumer web portals."

But by mid-2000, when the first version of the software was ready for release, the market had crashed. And with it, went all offers of funding.

"Luckily we had a few customers at that time, so we kind of sustained," recalls Sangeeta.

But for how long? It was clear that the consumer market would not pick up any time soon.

"I said, let's change to the enterprise market."

A market Sangeeta was familiar with, and intimately understood.

"We had to retool the entire product, and the technology. We built 'enterprise' adapters to extract data and deliver it on multiple interfaces."

And all this with programmers or engineers who were good, not necessarily the 'rock star' variety.

"This is one thing I learnt at Eicher. You can take a 10th class pass, give the right inputs, encourage and motivate the person… and you will see magic."

The idea that people are 'limitless', that talent can be nurtured and grown, was put into practice at Extensio.

"I've hired people who couldn't finish school but were great geeks. I've had people who flunked in their BSc or quit studies because they fell in love…"

It helps, of course, that the person heading this team is a core technology person.

"My brother Vipin is the one who architected the entire solution. He's built products with 'half an engineer' and takes great pride in that!"

And that too, remotely. In the initial couple of years Vipin did work on product development 'full time'. But once the first version was out, he went back to a job.

"Vipin is passionate about developing products, he's also a guy who wants to do 20 things at a time."

While Vipin remains the guardian angel of Extensio, technically speaking, he has little role in its day-to-day operations.

"We wouldn't spend money unless and until we had to. That's ingrained in me, it's on every cell of my being... to keep our costs very very low."

"He oversees the engineering side of it, making sure that the architecture and the strategy is correct. Otherwise, the business is entirely run by me."

In the very initial phase, when the company was in the dotcom and content business, it did have 45-50 people. But in the enterprise model, you can stay lean and mean.

"In India you basically have service companies where people sell 'bodies', so they have a large number of employees. But if you create and sell intellectual property, you don't need too many people."

Thus Extensio's core engineering team consisted of just 7 people, all based in Nagpur.

"The first year and a half, we were just developing the product... You know, we had to abandon the initial model and redo the entire effort."

And even when your product is ready, selling it is a huge challenge.

"The sales cycle for an enterprise product is typically 6 to 12 months," says Sangeeta.

And then too, it's complicated.

"All my colleagues from Levers are CIOs (Chief Information Officers) somewhere or the other. But, CIO is never the primary decision-maker in any company."

The CIO work is to enable the marketing people, sales people, finance people. So you have to woo them *all*, to fall in love with your product.

"Our technology speaks for itself. So, we offer to do a pilot, an experimental kind of a sale."

You understand the business problem, build the solution and offer it on a trial basis.

"Use it for 2 months and if it works for you... then we will talk about sale."

This is the kind of 'investment' Extensio made to snag its first enterprise customer – J & J.

A long cycle, lot of effort. But once you get a foot in the door, it usually swings open.

"Typically, we give about 25 user licenses for evaluation. When one person starts using SAP on his Excel, the other one also wants to use it, right? The third guy also wants to use it, and so on."

Extensio aims to sell 'unlimited licenses', based on CPU socket.

"As soon as the number of applications on our product increases, the load on the CPU increases. And then they have to buy more licenses."

There's also an 18-20% additional mark-up for after-sales support. The typical deal size is $100,000-$250,000 (₹ 50 lakh – 1.4 crore). Naturally, then, Extensio targets only a certain size of company.

"We only sell to large enterprises – companies with revenues of ₹ 2000 crore and above."

To build credibility with such customers, Extensio acquired SAP, IBM and Microsoft certification. As well as filed for a patent.

"The market we are focused on right now is enterprise mobility."

The need for people on the field to access SAP, PeopleSoft or Oracle data on mobile devices. Take orders, track shipments, and so on.

"Our USP is that we provide information delivery through triple channels. We do it on MS-office interfaces, mobile phone interfaces and web interfaces."

For the first 5-6 years, Sangeeta typically spent 70% to 80% of her time on engineering. Now, the effort is more on business development.

"I give 10 to 15% of my time to see what my existing customers are doing, how I can get more business out of them. The rest of my time is spent working with partners."

'Partners' are small, entrepreneurial companies who are creating products on the Extensio framework and selling that IP (intellectual property). This opens up a window to new kinds of customers – insurance companies, retailers, small business.

"One of our partners in Chennai has built 7 solutions in the past

7 months. A vehicle-tracking solution, a remote money-collection system, a secondary sales management system."

Sangeeta's role is that of hand-holding and support. Not actually selling but helping *them* to sell. To do this more effectively, in 2009, she shifted to Bangalore.

"I had to do this, to take Extensio to the next level."

While the engineering team continues to function mainly from Nagpur, there is now a small sales and support team in Mumbai, Chennai and Bangalore. Including partners, the 'family' is now 25-strong.

"We are completely self-funded, so we are very careful about costs."

For example, support is not a major cost centre, as much of the troubleshooting is possible through diagnostics built into the software.

"We built in a technology in such a way that you would need less 'human' support."

Many companies spend a lot of money to build a name in the market. Instead, Sangeeta relied on PR and the strength of her product.

"What we have done is essentially build enterprise credibility by interacting with analysts such as Gartner, Forrester."

The trick lies in choosing your engagements wisely, for maximum impact.

"IBM does lot of things for their partners, so, I worked very aggressively with them. It made a big difference."

While Sangeeta is reluctant to share Extensio's revenue figures, with 20 odd enterprise clients over 10 years, it is clearly still in the small league*. And it will probably stay that way, out of choice.

"When you work with a small group of people, you have an emotional connect. The moment you grow too big there is politics. That is the one thing I completely hated about corporate life."

Emotional connect is the reason Sangeeta could shift to

* As per NASSCOM, Extensio is an 'emerging' company with revenues under ₹ 5 crore.

Bangalore, leaving behind her engineering team in Nagpur to manage themselves.

"Of course, I did have withdrawal symptoms, because I babysat them for such a long time," she laughs.

But she is not worried about work suffering in her absence.

"My team is with me because of two reasons. Firstly, they believe that nobody else will give them such quality of work. I gave them opportunities which people otherwise don't get, at that stage of their life and career."

Secondly, it's about bonding, at a deeper level.

"I always chose people who had an emotional reason for being in Nagpur. You give such a person good money, good work and affection and they will give you their undying loyalty."

Concepts like flexitiming have been in force at Extensio for years, although a bit of regulation has crept in over the years.

"Earlier people would come at 2 o'clock in the morning and work till 8 o'clock in the morning, go home and then come back at 2," she laughs. "Now we have some guidelines."

Nevertheless, it's always been a 10 to 12 hour workday for Sangeeta. Nagpur, or Bangalore, she gets in around 8:45 am. And there is not fixed time to leave as such.

So, how does she manage her home life, and more importantly, who looks after her daughter?

"When I was in Indore, working with Eicher, my in-laws were a big help. Later in Nagpur, I was fortunate to have very good household help."

It's another emotional investment.

"The secret is to get really close to them, take care of them, if they have a problem help them out. They have been like family for me."

Sangeeta also encourages her maids to educate their daughters.

"She feels like my elder sister and I'm actually very fond of her so...that's also the truth."

It's also an unusual household, with Sangeeta and daughter Nidhi based in Bangalore while husband Sunil lives and works in the Gulf.

"I would feel less of a mother if I didn't make fresh *poha* for my daughter."

"Sunil is on an oil platform in Qatar since the last 15 years. So, he works 28 days and then he is home for 28 days."

Does that make life easier, or more difficult?

"There are times in your life when you want to be with your husband all the time and there is a time in your life when you don't want your husband around at all times," admits Sangeeta.

"But, after being married for 22 years now, it's now part of my routine."

"It is very tough sometimes but when he is home, he takes care of a lot of stuff. He is a true homebody."

If you ask Sangeeta, where is the *toor ki dal* stored in her kitchen, she would have no idea.

"I don't even know where it is brought from. I don't know. If you ask me *kya bhav pe milti hai* (what is the price of dal), I have no idea. I don't know…."

Because Sunil takes care of all that.

"But yeah, when he's here, he soaks up all my time alright. But, he very appreciative of the work I'm doing and he understands that it's difficult."

And her in-laws have been equally supportive.

"When I lived in Indore, my mother-in-law would actually make excuses for me. She would say, if you think my daughter-in-law should come with me for these functions to *aap mujhe bhi maat bulao* (don't invite me either)!"

(Ekta Kapoor, kindly take note!)

Despite all this understanding and support, motherhood hasn't been easy. In fact, starting a family itself was a challenge for Sangeeta.

"Nidhi was conceived after 8 years of my marriage. I had some problems because of which I couldn't have a baby earlier."

For a couple of years Sangeeta even grappled with the issue of whether she wants to be a mother or not, *could* she be a mother or not.

"I've suffered by delaying my pregnancy – it was a really very heavy price for me to pay. I've gone through fertility treatment it is not half as easy as it is made out to be."

On the positive side though, there are no regrets. Being an entrepreneur did allow for more flexibility, more time for Nidhi.

"I don't remember a single function that I didn't go to because of work. I've never left her alone when she was ill. Being an entrepreneur you do have more choices."

And, a feeling of doing real, meaningful work.

"In corporate life 20% is really work you enjoy and 80% is reporting, bureaucracy and politics. You start feeling, this is just not worth it."

You stay away from a young child *and* don't enjoy your work. That's too high a price to pay for 'success'. But, so is not working at all.

"I worked not for money but because I needed intellectual stimulation. Just cooking and keeping house would have driven me nuts!"

Not that you can ever *escape* these aspects of life.

"I didn't have household help for 6 months, after I shifted to Bangalore. I actually kept a diary and calculated the time I spent cooking – it takes about 5 hours a day!"

And even when there is a cook, there's always that one item she cannot rustle up – *maa ke haath ka khana.*

"My daughter's school provides breakfast and lunch. But this year she insisted, you make my *dabba*. So I get up at 6:30 in the morning and cook for her."

Like any mother would.

Because mothers do, what they have to.

With a dash of love, a *tadka* of concern.

A whisper of a blessing, in every silence.

As they rock the cradle of the world.

ADVICE TO WOMEN ENTREPRENEURS

The first thing is figure what you really like to do. If there is no emotional attachment, you will never be able to sustain anything. Motherhood is all enveloping. But, if you really really love doing something, you will find your way away.

Secondly, as soon as you get married and start thinking of having a child, think about who is going to support this child if it's not going to be you. I think that women must invest from day one in relationships that can sustain their children. Bond with your mother and mother-in-law – you will need that support system.

Once you have that, don't delay starting a family. The risks of having a baby in your 30s are significantly higher. Regardless of what the fertility experts tell you.

I also believe that for girls who are getting into higher education, how to manage motherhood and career should be an essential part of curriculum. I didn't have a role model as my mother was not a working woman, so I didn't know what to do, what not to do, when to do it.

The way I look at it, a woman is a womb plus a man. There's no difference in terms of ability, or what she can achieve. But a woman does need to know how to take care of her need to nurture and raise a baby. *This* is the place many women falter in their careers.

If you can figure out what are you going to do with your womb first, everything else will fall in place.

ACID TEST

Satya Vadlamani,
Murli Krishna Pharma

Satya had no experience of manufucturing when she decided to set up an export-oriented, FDA-compliant pharmaceutical factory. Despite delay and difficulties she never lost sight of her goal – to set up a world-class company.

You may have a degree.

You may have the desire.

But if you are a woman, will you be able to work? Just about everybody in your life has an opinion on this. And can put a 'stop' signal in your tracks. Then – what exactly do you do?

As a young wife and mother Satya Vadlamani faced this issue, and decided she *had* to pursue a career.

"My father-in-law belonged to the old school of thought where women did not work. More so, not in the male-dominated pharma industry!"

Satya was determined, and she was lucky. With the unstinting support of her parents, she managed to juggle home and office.

Eventually, Satya opted out of the rat race. She started a small trading company, in order to live life on her own terms. But then, she grew ambitous. And decided to set up a factory of her own.

Over the next 7 years, Satya experienced the good, the bad and the ugly side of entrepreneurship. The struggle, the pain, the endless running around for licenses and approvals.

The day we meet in her tiny Mulund office, she is running horribly late. Kind of like a metaphor for her company where things went way behind schedule.

But as they say, *sabar ka phal meetha hota hai.* The story of M K Pharma is sweet, earthy and inspiring. Just like the lady behind it.

The call of the mountain beckons every soul.

To climb or not to climb, is the question.

Once you start climbing, never look back.

ACID TEST

Satya Vadlamani,
Murli Krishna Pharma

Satya was born in Vishakhapatnam and grew up on the sprawling IIT Bombay campus.

"My faher was a professor at IIT Bombay, my mother was a teacher. Like all the other IIT children, I too wanted to become an engineer!"

When she didn't make it to IIT or VJTI, Satya joined Andhra University College of Engineeing in Vishakhapatnam. Girls were scarce in the engineering stream in those days.

"The owner of the *dhaba* where we ate put up a curtain so we could eat without being stared at!" recalls Satya.

While in her second year of college, Satya got married.

"It was a love marriage, I got to know my husband Eshwar Rao while he was doing his MTech from IIT Bombay."

Eshwar was working with Mukund Iron and Steel company in Mumbai. After marriage, he took a transfer to Vizag. On 2 December 1986 – while in her final year of engineering – Satya gave birth to her elder son.

"I managed to complete my engineering somehow," she grins.

After graduating, Satya took a break – to spend time with her young son and enjoy married life. But in 1989, the family returned to Mumbai. It was then that she had the urge to go out and work.

"I felt that I was wasting my time. So, I took a call that I should take up some job and that's how I joined the computer industry, specifically in the marketing part of it."

The job paid only ₹ 1000 per month, but it was a start.

"The first company I joined was CNC Computers in Fort area. Then I joined another private company – I don't even recollect the name – in Sakinaka."

Her third job was with K C Group of Industries – as a sales engineer.

"My specialisation, I found along the way, was primarily marketing. I was extremely good at marketing!"

During that period Satya's father-in-law Vadlamani Subbarao – a veteran of the pharma industry – shifted to Mumbai. Leaving Ranbaxy, he joined Armour Pharmaceuticals as Executive Director. Through him, Satya met Dr Atma D Gupta* – founder of the company.

"We had a couple of interactions and he felt that I had the ability to do a lot more marketing than what I was doing."

On his suggestion Satya agreed to join the company. Her role was simple: to get UNICEF approval for one of the company's plants in Mandgriti (Madhya Pradesh). The approval was to come from Denmark.

The prospect was exciting enough, so Satya readily agreed. But her father-in-law was not very pleased.

"He belonged to the old school of thought – that women should not be working."

And even if they had to work, certainly not in the pharma industry! But, since it was a small and temporary assignment, he agreed. Satya completed the project successfully and Dr Gupta was so impressed he offered her a new and meatier role. That of 'international marketing manager'.

* Brother of D B Gupta of Lupin.

"It took a lot of persuasion for me to be allowed to take up this job. My parents helped a lot – they took care of my children!"

Luckily her father was still working in IIT, while Satya lived in Hiranandani complex next door.

"My elder son would go to school, spend some time with the babysitter, then my mother would take him home. I would pick up the kids on my way back."

By this time Satya had another baby. The younger one was in fact just a year old when she joined Armour.

"That complicated things a bit," she admits. But the call to pursue her career was so strong, she could not step back. Somehow, she managed it all. Home, office, kids, in-laws. And learning all she could about pharma.

"I had no idea about this industry – I learnt everything from Dr Gupta. My father-in-law – although he was against me working initially – later realised I was serious. And he too taught me a great deal."

Satya found she really enjoyed pharma, and more so APIs ie, the raw materials which go into making drugs.

"My job involved export of APIs. I started with Southeast Asian markets and later handled Europe as well."

In 1995-96, Armour was going through some problems, so Satya shifted to a company called Biochem Synergy. Around the same time, her father-in-law was diagnosed with secondary stage cancer. He passed away after a brief illness.

"He was a very brilliant, very straight man. He set up numerous projects but never made any money out of it. Despite our differences of opinion, I looked up to him greatly," she recalls.

As DGM (International Marketing) at Biochem Synergy Satya's life was even more hectic than before. She headed the Bombay office, while the plant was based in Pithampur near Indore.

"I was handling the marketing and logistics. There was a *lot* of travelling!"

By this time Satya had a handle on the industry, a network of contacts and, most importantly, confidence. While Armour specialised in semi-synthetic capsules, Biochem specialised in Cephalexin.

"It's easy to marry for love but you find that love walks out at some point in your life. Then, you start concentrating somewhere else. I concentrated very heavily on my profession."

"So I basically was very familiar with two of the major lines."

In 1996, Satya joined Ajanta Pharma as GM, International Marketing. She worked there only for a year, because things were getting complicated on the home front.

"My kids were very young, my mother-in-law had gone back to Delhi and my husband was posted in Ankleshwar with United Phosporus."

While her parents were taking good care of the children, life had become too hectic. The Ajanta office was in Kandivili, which meant Satya left home by 7 am.

"We officially closed at 6.30 pm but generally that's when the MD would call for a meeting of all the HODs."

That meeting would go on till 8-8:30 pm.

"By the time I reached home it used to be 10 o'clock. So even on the days when I was not travelling, I used to leave when my kids were sleeping and return when they were asleep".

Satya knew that somewhere, she was losing it. This job, this life and career was extracting too high a price. But, there was an alternative.

"I thought let me start a small trading company of my own. I'll do it on my terms and on my risk. And surely I would be able to provide more time to the children!"

Satya informed her boss that she was quitting, and starting her own company. She was very clear about one thing – not using any clients or contacts from the current job, for her new venture.

But they also sent me abroad during the period for the World Aid Conference and all.

"Whichever job I have left till now, even today I am on very good terms with the owners of the company. The reason has been that I have never taken anything from the company which was not mine."

Satya completed her three-month notice period, and in December 1997, set up M K Enterprises. A colleague from Biochem Synergy – Vipul K Gondhiya and Satya's mother Mrs Sita Mahalakshmi joined the firm as partners.

"It was an indenting company. We would get orders for foreign companies, give it to the manufacturer and earn a commission of 2-3%."

M K Enterprises also became the India representative for a German company called FerroGMBH Export. That brought in a fixed monthly retainer.

In 1998, Satya converted the company into a private limited company – Murli Krishna Exports Pvt. Ltd.

"I have 50% shareholding in that company. My mother has 25% and Vipul has 25%."

Over the next 5 years, M K Exports also entered trading, and one of Satya's Swiss buyers became a partner in the company.But in 2003, the company was experiencing some problems with a shipment. At that time a good friend – Dr Vijay K Shastri – made a suggestion.

"Why don't you go into manufacturing? After all, trading does not have a very long life!"

The idea was intriguing. It made even more sense because the market was shifting to more regulatory based business. However, Satya had no knowledge or experience of manufacturing. So, she did the next best thing – rope in an expert.

Dr Shastri was a technical whiz in the pharma field, with a number of patents to his name.

"You want me to start? Then you also become part of it!" Satya said to him.

Dr Shastri agreed, and thus in the year 2004, Murli Krishna Pharma Pvt. Ltd came into existence. Other shareholders in the company included Satya's husband, her mother, her brother-in-law Mohan Vadlamani, Swiss buyer Rhenochem AG and Hongkong-based Elcon investments.

"The idea, from the very start, was to put up a unit which will be

"I have never tried to steal technology or tried to start a business while having a job because I believe loyalty is important. My conscience must always be clean."

export-oriented and FDA-compliant. As I said, I've not been a formulations person at all. So, it has to be a bulk drug product."

Setting up an API unit – that too a regulatory kind – requires an investment of ₹ 20 to 30 crore.

"We didn't have that kind of money. That left us with the option of semi-finished formulations. Within semi-finished, we chose to specialise in pellets."

Pellets are ready-to-fill products. To put it in layman terms, they are the small 'beads' you see inside capsules. This formulation comes with one major advantage – a delayed release mechanism.

"For example, an antacid drug like Omez (Omezaprole) must be released in the small intestine in order to be effective."

However, pellets were not a natural choice. Solvents are easier – and faster – to manufacture. But the technical expert put his foot down.

"Vijay's contribution here is very, very important," acknowledges Satya.

Solvents are known to be carcinogenic, he pointed out. They are being phased out internationally. Why get into such a technology at all?

It was a wise but expensive decision.

"To become a solvent-free company, we had to do extensive R&D. Work out new methods to make our products."

And all this had to be done on a shoestring budget.

"We've not been people with... what you call as financial background. And to go out and raise money was a new thing for me."

Help came in the form of Saidas Malladi, a distant cousin who was also an industrialist from Bangalore. He Introduced Satya to Bank of Maharashtra and put in a good word. A loan of ₹ 1.2 crore was sanctioned. In addition ₹ 65 lakh came in from investors.

The loan was sanctioned in July 2004, while construction began in November 2004. Problems cropped up in the very first year, as Satya ran a small experiment.

"I was very confident about marketing but I needed to get a feel of manufacturing, and purchase of raw material. So I decided to take a 'loan license.'"

A loan license is basically an operational arrangement between two companies.

"Say you have a product, and a license to manufacture, but no factory of your own. You can provide raw material to another company and get it converted into a finished product."

Murli Krishna entered into such an arrangement with a company called Ocean Pharma in Hyderabad. While Ocean received a conversion fee, Murli Krishna marketed the product as its own.

It was a good strategy, but with unexpected side effects. Satya had not factored in the loan license operation when she raised money from the bank.

"Actually there was hardly any margin in the loan license arrangement. I was doing it more to gain experience."

Meanwhile, the bank saw money coming into the account and decided to start taking EMIs earlier than scheduled. The bank was a 'rural' branch, as the factory was coming up in Shirur taluka near Pune.

"The branch managers in these areas are used to dealing with farmers, who are erratic in repayment. So their policy is to take money whenever they see it coming into an account!"

What's more, the plant was to be commissioned in March 2005. However, by the time the company got all approvals it was September 2005.

"We learnt a few bitter truths during this period."

Like factory inspectors are interested in going to old plants where they can make money, rather than visiting a new plant to give an approval.

"We make good project reports, we give it to the bank and later on we try to make ends meet. Believe me, it is a very very tough job trying to do that!"

"I had never dealt with corruption before. I never realised that when you put up project money you have to set aside money to 'get work done'."

All these factors threw the project calculations into a mess.

"Even before the plant started, we were feeling the heat. In fact, we had to take an additional loan of ₹ 88 lakh to cover the last mile...!"

In anticipation of the plant getting completed, Satya gave up the 'loan license' arrangement. Employees were hired, sales were made.

But entrepreneurship is an uncharted course.

"It is like deep sea diving without knowing where the bottom is. You just don't know... you go in unprepared."

A new plant's capacity is built slowly, regular orders take their own time.

"The beauty of it was that the first shipment from MK Pharma – the 'validation batches' went to a company in Greece called Medi Pharm."

But, financially the company was going through a mess.

"Question was what to do with the little money we had – buy raw material, pay salaries or give interest to the bank!"

Under the circumstances the only party one could default on was the bank. And of course, they were not at all happy about it!

"We had to sit with them and explain the situation. I was not financially savvy back then, so this entire episode was a huge struggle!"

The real issue was regulatory approvals. In the 90s, you could expect to get an approval in about 9 months. But in the year 2005, the gestation period was a minimum of 2 years.

"Even after you have approval, there is a long-drawn-out process which must be followed."

First your prospective client will take lab scale samples, then 'validation scale' batches. Followed by 'first exhibit batches'.

"In the meantime they run stability tests on their own finished formulations. They run bio-studies. The process takes an average of 1 year to complete!"

After this, the company files for registration. That process can take another two years.

"I knew approvals would take time. What I didn't anticipate was that it would take 5 years to see my first commercial order!"

Nor did Satya know that to get into regulatory market you have to maintain your plant in a particular way.

"We had to break and rebuild the plant three times to instal some new machines, or arrange the work flow in the manner required by the client."

All these are necessary evils. The only other way to enter a regulatory market is by filing as a 'generic' which means, after a product is out of the patent period, you can apply to manufacture it.

"However you must be among the first ten companies to file, and clear multiple quality checks. It's something like winning a lottery – luck plays a big part!"

Murli Krishna instead went the process patent route. This means you manufacture a product using a method which does not infringe on the innovator in any way. In fact, you have possibly bettered the original product.

To do this, of course, you need intensive R&D, quality assurance people, analytical equipment. Add to that capital cost and running cost and it's no laughing matter.

Still, with Satya's ability to sell, the plant was getting healthy orders for 'validation batches'. In fact, M K Pharma's turnover went from ₹ 1 crore in 2005-06 to ₹ 6.75 crore in 2007-8. And in the first three years, the company managed to make nominal profits.

Trouble began in 2008. That was the year M K Pharma took a fresh loan from Bank of Maharashtra, in order to meet the requirement of a US-based company called Cogentus.

"I was not financially savvy but I was forced to learn how to read a balance sheet. I had to learn about actual financial management, something which was not my forte at all."

"Cogentus had signed a term sheet with us and were paying an absolute premium price for our omezaprole pellets. In fact, they had completed Phase 5 clinicals in US which means the order was practically confirmed."

In September 2008, Satya even visited the company headquarters in California.

Two months later, Cogentus filed for bankruptcy. One of its major investors had gone belly up in the recession.

"Everything we had worked for went down the drain. Three years of toil and sweat for nothing!"

Thus, in 2009-10 the interest owed to Bank of Maharashtra was ₹ 1.5 crore per year, while revenues were only ₹ 10.75 crore.

"Remove the bank interest and the fixed expenses of ₹ 6 crore – where is the money for raw material, and everything else?"

M K Pharma had literally reached rock bottom.

The one silver lining in this dark cloud was Mylan. The registration process with this international pharma giant had also begun in 2008. But how would M K Pharma sustain itself over the 2-3 years the approvals would take?

At this point, one of the options was to sell out. The most eager suitor was a company called Dexcel Pharma Technologies.

"In fact, we had a LOI – Letter of Intent and they were paying us a good premium for a 30% stake."

But some time in January 2010, Satya got a bad feeling about the deal.

"They were willing to pump in $3 million but I felt that once they took over, they would dictate terms. For example, we would not be able to supply to Mylan, as it is a competitor."

And that was not acceptable to Satya.

"It would be wrong for me to walk out at this stage when Mylan had already invested their time and money."

So, though M K Pharma needed the money very badly, Satya walked out of the deal. By September 2010, funds were once again very tight. This time, a UK-based company called Solex Pharma stepped forward. And this time, Satya accepted the investment.

"I admit that we sold our stake at a lower premium to this company and we gave higher percentage but, the plus point is that today I am working both with Dexcel and with Mylan and I have no problems."

Sometimes you pay a price to breathe freely. And it is worth every lungful of lightly glorious air.

"I have the field open as far as my market is concerned."

In January 2011, Murli Krishna finally turned a corner. With the Myelin supply agreement in place M K Pharma started making good profits.

"*Lekin* I tell you, *papad bahut bele* (I struggled a lot!)" laughs Satya.

In the process, there was a lot of learning, as well.

"I think setting up an industry first time is the toughest. After that you can set up as many as you want!"

And no management school can prepare you for the experience. It stretches you to the limit.

"Vijay's specialisation was technical – he could stick to that field. But though I was a marketing person I had to handle a lot of other areas where I was really not competent!"

So what was it that kept Satya going through these terribly tough times?

"There is a point of no return in any business. When it came, I did not turn back. Because once you start something, you cannot accept failure. And that's probably what kept me going!"

Along with the support of family and friends.

"I am grateful to Vijay, my parents and my investors in Murli Krishna

"In India the moratorium for repayment is very limited and in the process companies die. Especially in manufacturing, where it takes at least 3 years to make profit."

who had faith in me, who knew I would never cheat them. I think it's that faith that allowed me to carry on."

There were sacrifices and compromises on the family front as well. Even though the kids were older and didn't need her as much, Satya had not realised the project would consume her so completely.

"I invested everything I had earned up to that point in Murli Krishna Pharma. And not just money, my time, my passion, my entire life!" she says.

For the first two years Satya travelled up and down constantly, the factory being a three-hour drive from Mumbai.

"I had to visit not just the plant but the bank and also my buyers. So, I had to juggle a lot!"

In October 2005, Satya decided to shift base to Shirur, along with her parents and younger son Krishna. This meant relocating Krishna to a rural school.

"Trust me, it helped my son a lot. In Mumbai he was a 50% student, there he gradually went upto 80%-90% and now he is studying medicine!"

Elder son Arjun stayed back in Mumbai as he was in the second year at Atharva College of Engineering in Mumbai.

"He is highly independent," she observes.

Just like her husband, an engineer who specialises in setting up new projects.

"Normally he takes up a project for 6-7 months and stays on the site. Then he comes back to India, relaxes for 2-3 months and then takes up another project somewhere else."

Doesn't he regret that his family does not join him?

"We got married when we were very young, you know. We've grown up together, so we have a very good understanding!"

Ishwar has his work, Satya has hers. Ishwar only got involved with Murli Krishna Pharma briefly, while the plant was being set up.

"We are both very independent as far as our working is concerned. It's not that we don't like each other... but we don't have a very conventional married life."

For example, food has never been a fussy affair in the household.

"I always cooked myself, but it was mainly 'one dish' meals."

The end result of all the passion poured into Murli Krishna Pharma is a world-class manufacturing company. One of the few, worldwide, with both EU and WHO-GMP approvals in pellets.

"Today people appreciate our products, our quality, our plant – there is the satisfaction that we have done something. The idea was not only to make money but to make a mark."

The M K Pharma plant has 110 full-time employees and another 40 who work on contract basis. Turnover for the year ending March 2012 was ₹ 15.5 crore, with profits of ₹ 2.17 crore. Satya continues to handle the marketing singlehandedly, with some inputs from Vipul who continues to anchor M K Exports.

"That company is very small but profitable. I am grateful because during our tough years at M K Pharma that's where my salary came from!"

Now that things have eased up, Satya finally has some time to stop, catch a breath. Go on a short holiday.

"I recently took my first real break after 5 years. I went to spend some time with my younger son who's joined a medical college in Hungary. It was a wonderful, relaxing two weeks!"

At the end of the day, however, Satya is one of those people who cannot sit still.

Aur bhi sarhadein hain, bulandiyaan hain, faasle hain...

Lofty peaks of ambition remain to be conquered.

With inner strength and fortitude.

And a positive attitude, above all.

ADVICE TO WOMEN ENTREPRENEURS

I believe that every woman should have some kind of job, or vocation. You must try to use your talents and abilities, step beyond the four walls of your home.

In my view women can make better entrepreneurs than men because women have more patience and they have more ability to multitask. But remember to think with both your head, and your heart!

Whatever business you do you pick it up in a field which you have been working in for a long time. Never take up a field because someone else thinks you should do it because then you will never be able to succeed.

If you don't know finance, you are in great trouble. Learn to read the balance sheet!

While trust is the basis to work on, also read papers very carefully because intentions behind the words are often different.

Handling egos of staff and co-workers is not easy. I prefer a soft approach which carries people along with you. It takes a lot of energy but smoothens your life in the longer run.

Lastly, when you raise money for a project ask for twice as much as you need. Don't be stupid like me!

FAT CHANCE

Shikha Sharma,
Nutrihealth Systems

Dr Shikha Sharma could have migrated to the US, or worked with a big hospital – like any other qualified doctor. Instead, she put her medical expertise into the weight-loss business, bringing health and happiness to her clients.

It's 3 o'clock on a Sunday afternoon.

"Sorry for bringing you to office today," I apologise.

"Oh, I always take Saturdays off and work Sundays," replies Shikha. "No telephone calls, no routine work. I get time to think and plan!"

Hmm, now that's unusual. But then everything about Shikha is just that little bit different.

A qualified doctor, she chose to get into business. And be ambitious and driven about it, but not at the cost of ethics.

At Dr Shikha's clinics there are no machines, no pills. Only medically guided diet, exercise, and ayurvedic principles. And yet, with 2000 patients a year, Nutrihealth is probably India's largest chain of weight-loss clinics.

Because, honesty does pay.

"Touchwood, I feel that whatever money that has come in is *barkat* (God's grace). Not only me, but the peon who's been with me for 14 years, has built his house."

Health first, then happiness, then wealth.

If more of us lived by this principle, we would carry no extra burdens.

Size zero not just in body, but light and easy, in heart and mind.

FAT CHANCE

Shikha Sharma,
Nutrihealth Systems

Shikha Sharma is a *Dilliwali*, through and through.

"I studied at Modern School Vasant Vihar and then attended Maulana Azad Medical College, also in Delhi."

Shikha was a diligent student. Hardworking, too.

"I won't say I was naturally blessed with big brains, I had to study and put in that effort."

Shikha's father owned a petrol pump while her mother ran a small business of fabrics. Education was a priority in the family.

"I have one brother, and one sister. My brother is an engineer, my sister is an architect, while I became a doctor."

Actually, Shikha hardly had a say in the matter – it was practically decided, the family needs one doctor.

"The first year of medical college was tough, because I got ragged very badly."

Things got worse when she complained to the Dean.

"Everybody stopped talking to me, said I had created an unnecessary fuss."

But somehow she couldn't take it lightly and keep quiet.

"I said, it's just not acceptable to me because they are crossing their limits… I think in some way I was fearless. I didn't care about public opinion at any point of time."

Over time, all was forgiven and forgotten, and college became fun. As did the subjects of study.

"I never enjoyed Anatomy and Biology. But in the final year, when we were reading about diseases like diabetes and cholesterol, suddenly I said ok. Finally it seems like we are doing medicine!"

Shikha completed her MBBS and was keen to go abroad for further studies. She started preparing for the USMLE (US Medical Licensing Exam) but the family put its foot down.

"They said, we can't send you abroad alone. Get married first."

Shikha just didn't feel ready.

"I thought, God, before I start my life I'm stuck with somebody else... No way!"

"Well, no way you are going abroad then," they said.

The logical step then, was to do an MD. But, somehow that did not excite Shikha. What could she do, other than the obvious?

"Then, I started thinking of business. Or even doing an MBA."

By this time Shikha had completed the one year 'house job' posting at the ICU in G B Pant hospital. The experience affected her deeply.

"Every day I could see one person go… you know… it became so common that I started feeling that what is life!"

If you are lucky, you make it to a hospital in time. You get a good doctor, you survive. To save a dying man is noble, but can medicine do something to make *living* better?

"I realised that preventive healthcare, rehabilitation healthcare is absent… and there is a huge need for it!"

And so 24-year-old Shikha took the unusual step of joining a weight-loss clinic as a doctor. Not that the MBBS course had prepared her for such a role. So, Shikha decided to educate herself.

"I joined a course on nutrition in IGNOU but found that it was not at all practical. So I picked up books, read up and understood on my own. And then I would put it into practice, to see if it works!"

A year later, Shikha got an offer to manage a weight-loss clinic in Noida.

"That was my first experience of actually running a weight-loss centre. They gave me a lot of freedom but somehow we could not attract enough customers."

The venture shut down in 1996, and it hit Shikha hard.

"It was the first time I had ever failed at something."

Looking back, she realises what went wrong.

"At that time I hadn't started thinking, I wasn't very confident about what I was doing. Since someone else had invested the money, I was fearful of trying out new things."

The centre's closure also affected Shikha's personal life.

"My family didn't approve of me going to Noida and working, they said it's unsafe. So, finally I said, I'm going to stay there."

It was complete blasphemy. *Hamare hote hue, kiraye ke makaan mein rahogi? Akele?* (When your family is in the same city, how can you stay in a rented house, alone?)

Shikha still remembers the conversation she had with her mother.

"I said, listen I'm not running away with some weirdo, I'm trying to work and you have to give me the freedom to work!"

She said, "But, why? Why can't you get married to some nice guy in US and do medicine there? Why do you want to create problems for us?"

Suddenly, the 'good girl' had become a rebel. Astrologers were consulted and planets like *rahu, ketu* and *shani* blamed. But, Shikha had a new-found confidence and conviction in herself and actually shifted to Noida.

"When the centre shut down it was a double whammy. I had to shift back home and everyone was like – we told you so!"

Shikha tackled that problem by making sure she was at home as little as possible.

"I took up a job in the morning. Then I took one in the afternoon. Then I took a job at night. As a doctor you can do that and get away with it!"

The routine was, come home, take a nap, change, freshen up and quickly leave again.

"It was my way of being with myself, dealing with my own failure."

Although the extended family and relatives sniggered, Shikha's mother stood by her like a rock. Help also came in the form of an understanding senior.

"It's important for a women entrepreneur to be financially independent, not have to justify every penny you spend."

"At one of the clinics I was working, my boss was a doctor and an MBA from FMS. I found in him somebody with whom I could have a discussion. Understand what went wrong, ask questions."

Even though she didn't get all her answers, talking helped put things in perspective.

"I realised failure is not such a big thing. There is no need to blow it out of proportion and go into depression!"

The boss also kept encouraging Shikha to look at alternatives like MBA or MD in Radiology.

"You are a good student, you will do well," he would say.

But once bitten, forever smitten. Shikha decided to restart the weight-loss venture, this time on her own. In 1998, she took a chamber on rent and was back in business.

"The chamber was in a hospital which attracted lots of patients. I identified 5 upper strata patients and offered them a free weight-loss program for a month."

These patients were so happy that they referred their friends and family. These new patients were willing to pay ₹ 1500 per month for the program. So, what went *right* this time?

"I had already failed so there was no fear of failure now. I was just having fun. I was a lot more creative.

Paisa doob jaega to chalega... it's my money."

Shikha's breakthrough idea was putting her medical expertise into the weight-loss process. Making it more scientific.

For example, a lady would come in and say, "I'm doing everything you say but my weight is stuck, it's just not coming down."

Dr Shikha's first-cut diagnosis would be, "Your liver is weak, it's not digesting the food. So, obviously undigested food will turn into fat."

She would ask for a complete medical check-up to be done. In 5 out of 10 cases the liver would not be functioning very well. So, that kind of medical understanding of the problem added an edge.

"People realised that I am an all-round solution provider, rather than somebody who would just tell them to starve."

Shikha was also more process-oriented.

"Coming from a good college you learn these things by default. I made them fill out proper medical forms, checked blood pressure and so on."

These small things added that professional touch. Of the first 100 patients who enrolled, only 50% would have achieved the target weight loss. But, in terms of their expectation from the program, all of them were happy.

With business picking up, Shikha hired a nutritionist, to do the 'boring' job of writing diet plans.

"I would tell her, ok, do this, do that, this seems to be the issue. Increase the protein levels or decrease her protein level and so on."

Because, from day one, Shikha knew this could not be a one-woman show.

"My boss had given me one important piece of advice: if you work as a doctor, you will earn X. If you are able to hire more people, you will earn 5X. So, focus on building a team."

Leaving Shikha with some hands-free time to think. And explore new ideas. Like becoming a consultant for the health show on Home TV, a channel launched by *Hindustan Times*.

"I did it for fun, for experience and also made some money!"

By this time Shikha had also bought a second-hand car.

"I think that was a very important decision for me... I no longer had to depend on the family car. I felt confident and independent."

And it was a small luxury for a business that was doing pretty well, in its very first year. With 15 patients a month signed up, the clinic averaged ₹ 50,000 in revenues per month.

"I quit my medical practice completely and made it a full-time business."

Very soon, Shikha had to take on an additional chamber on rent, and another dietician. Then came an offer from a club in Panchsheel.

"We like what you are doing," they said. "Come and operate from our premises!"

"Buying a car gave me a lot of independence and confidence. I advise all women to do it as quickly as possible!"

The deal was simple: the club would take 25% of Shikha's earnings. No rent, but she would have to do up the interiors and infrastructure.

"I accepted, without any negotiation. I borrowed ₹ 72,000 from my mother – which I promised to return – and I just went there, set up the business."

Dr Shikha's weight-loss centre at the Panchsheel Club was inaugurated on 16 October 1998. The first three months were extremely slow.

"In the afternoon, after lunch, all of us would actually go to sleep on the treatment beds!" she laughs.

Come February, and all that changed. More and more patients started coming in, through word of mouth. In fact, there were days when Shikha barely had time to eat her lunch, or visit the washroom.

"Sometimes, I would put the phone off the cradle for a few minutes, to catch my breath."

Shikha quickly hired 3 nutritionists, trained them and kept improvising diets.

"We started using the Atkin's formula for weight loss and found it worked very well."

Shikha enjoyed the creative challenge, and meeting people. Especially the VIPs who frequented the club.

"Not because they were rich or powerful but very interesting people to talk to. Most were achievers in their own merit."

There were other learnings on the job. Like dealing with plumbers, electricians and carpenters.

"I enjoyed dealing with tiling, woodwork, all that stuff. I enjoy creating things and putting them together!"

Another, harder lesson, was dealing with people. As a doctor, your work depends on your own capabilities. As a leader, it's about bringing out the best in your people.

"People management definitely still remains one of my weak areas because I get too emotional," admits Shikha.

She recalls an incident – more than ten years ago – when the competition, across the road, poached several employees.

"What really hurt me was that one of my nutritionists said she was getting married and disappeared. The second one also gave some *goli*. Why did they lie to me?"

It troubled Shikha so much, she developed acidity.

"It took time for me to accept that some people will behave unprofessionally and I can't do anything about it!"

But, where she *could* do something, she certainly did. Even if meant a giant leap of faith.

"When I started the clinic, passive weight-loss machines were very popular. I too invested my hard-earned money in a few such machines."

But, a doubt remained in her medically trained mind. Do these machines really work?

"I realised these machines are a complete fraud. It's just the diet which you have to do alongside, which makes it work."

Shikha decided to get rid of the machines.

Friends and well-wishers advised her not to do it. What's the harm, if people get psychological satisfaction?

But Shikha stood firm. No more Electronic Muscle Stimulators at her clinic.

"I didn't want to sell them either, because that is just perpetuating the fraud. So, I dumped the machines in my store room."

The clinic did lose a few clients but very quickly, business actually picked up. Well-travelled, well-read clients appreciated Shikha's no-nonsense approach, and came in droves.

"It was almost like a sign from God – when you do the right thing, you reap the rewards. This was phase 2 in my personal growth."

Phase 3 came when, for the first time, Shikha had to make a tough business decision. Patients were paying ₹ 2200 per month, of which the club kept 25%.

But one fine day, the manager called her and said, "Now, we want 33%."

"If you are running a small business, you don't need advertising. You give good service, the word spreads."

It did not make any sense. Already, Shikha was parting with a hefty 25% from her ₹ 5 lakh a month turnover. It made sense to take your own property on rent, instead.

"That's exactly what I did. In mid-2000 I opened my own clinic in Vasant Vihar and started seeing clients there."

In a weird sort of way, getting out of the club in Panchsheel Enclave was the best thing that could have happened. The business moved out of its comfort zone, and picked up its own pace.

"Within a year, I set up a second clinic, in Panchsheel."

Each clinic averaged a business of ₹ 5-6 lakh per month. 3-4 dieticians handled a patient load of about 300 per location.

Meanwhile, Shikha's outlook on health and nutrition was also evolving. In 2002, she decided to embrace ayurvedic principles into her diet plans.

"We don't use any medicines, only natural metabolic stimulators such as *adrak ka paani* with *tulsi*, *amla*, aloe vera, *hing*, *ajvain* and so on."

In fact, each individual is prescribed a diet most suited to his or her body type – *vata*, *kapha* or *pitta*. An unconventional approach to standard weight-loss plans. And it just might be what got Shikha noticed. By a very special client.

"One morning I got a call saying there is someone very senior in the government who wants to meet you for weight loss."

The person would not disclose exactly *who* it was but said he would send a car to pick her up.

"So, I got little anxious. I told my mother that you have to follow me. If I get kidnapped you just inform the police!"

Even when she saw a car from the prime minister's office parked outside her house, Shikha was only half-convinced.

"It's when I entered the PM's house that I realised, this is for real. The Prime Minister of India is consulting a chit of a girl like me!"

For the first time, Shikha became aware of a Higher Power in her life.

"All along I thought that *I* am doing this business, but I realised I am only an instrument. Whatever is happening, is happening through me but, someone else is guiding it from up there."

What *you* need to do is work with the right intention, dedication and consistency. And that is what Shikha focused on continuously.

From 2001 to 2006, Dr Shikha's weight-loss clinics opened one new branch every year.

"I never had a 'business plan' as such. I would just see how many clients are coming in… and we never had problems with that."

Each clinic could easily accommodate about 400-500 patients. But, 25% of the clients would come from surrounding areas – a ready market to expand into. But in retrospect, rapid expansion may not have been a very wise idea.

"I started having administrative problems. Suddenly all my time was going in *bijli ka bill*, lease rentals, internal politics, municipal hassles, '*kharcha paani*'."

With multiple centres coming up, employee morale fell.

"I was no longer in close contact with my people. So, petty issues started coming up, small things which were never a problem before because I would counsel them, guide them."

In 2006, matters came to a head. With 1500 clients and 7 centres across Delhi, it was a decent ₹ 3 crore per annum business. But after year upon year growth of 100%, business was flat.

"When you are small, I think you are less visible and you have less problems, you have a smaller staff to manage. At that size the whole thing hit me."

Shikha hired a consultant and started addressing various thorny issues. Such as the problem of retaining staff, especially dieticians. Invariably, girls would join, work a couple of years, get married and quit permanently. Either because the in-laws wanted a stay-at-home *bahu*, or the girl herself was not serious about a career.

"I tried to balance that by taking ayurvedic doctors and training them. But even with then, the girls usually quit working after marriage."

"Many women are only fooling around, pretending to be entrepreneurs. There is no dedication or passion for their work,no commitment."

Then, there was a problem with the MCD (Municipal Corporation of Delhi).

Problems with the IT consultant who took an advance but refused to complete the work.

"I always paid my vendors upfront, because that's how I would want them to deal with me. I learnt the hard way, that you should not write out cheques so easily!"

Shikha decided to take matters into her own hands. The idea was to stop physical expansion and go virtual, with a dedicated call centre.

"I visited a couple of call centres, read some books and realised we can do it without any outside help."

It was a wise decision, which has borne fruit. The call centre has been growing 100% year on year, and now serves close to 600 clients. In fact, it is far more profitable than running a physical centre. What's more, 80% of the call centre clients are from outside Delhi.

In March 2011, Nutrihealth Systems – as the company is now called – clocked revenues of ₹ 6 crore and served close to 2000 clients. The company employs 90 people, including 15 at its dedicated call centre. So, what next?

There are many ways to grow, but Shikha is being choosy about it.

"I explored the franchisee system. But I realised that a service model would not work. We would need to create proprietary medicines or unnecessary diet products for them to prescribe."

That's fundamentally dishonest – so Shikha would rather not get into it. Similarly, she doesn't want to take in outside investors, unless they share her vision.

"I think the future lies in holistic, not cosmetic solutions. Clients know that weight loss is not permanent, you have to keep working at it."

And so must Shikha. With rare and touching honesty, she admits that despite visible 'success', the last year has once again been a tough one.

One centre, shut down by the municipal corporation. Employees quitting and starting copycat companies. Even an income tax inquiry.

"When all these problems came, one after another, it hit me, affected me physically."

Sometimes even the good doctor needs to be nursed, back to health. To do that, Shikha plans to relook the entire business, and the business model. As well as hire more professionals.

Unlike many women entrepreneurs, Shikha has no family members working with her. And, she remains single, out of choice.

"My family realised I am too headstrong and would need to choose somebody of my own liking. I've had some relationships but, they are all 5th, 6th, 7th priority. For me work has always been the 1st priority… And I cannot compromise on that."

Neither does Shikha feel the need to have children.

"The motherly instinct I have for everybody. I nurture everybody… my workplace *is* my family. I am also very close to my sister's kids and my mother – she is my pillar of support."

Apart from work, Shikha makes time for yoga, writing columns and attending professional forums. She has also become more spiritually inclined of late.

"I used to be very short-tempered. I wouldn't show it but I would be boiling inside."

The angry young woman may have cooled, but her passion has not.

"I want to build a company which will last much longer than me… be there even a hundred years from now.

It ain't over till the fat lady sings, or loses that last stubborn kilogram.

ADVICE TO WOMEN ENTREPRENEURS

If you have an entrepreneurial streak in you and you want to do something, please create a good or a service which helps people. Never ever create a business or something where you have to exploit or cheat people because that will never allow you to grow or prosper.

There is an old Hindu theory that there is 'good money' and 'bad money'. Good money is '*barkat*', it brings happiness to you and everyone around you. With bad money, your kids get rotten, relationships get spoilt and there is conflict in the house. So, always stay on the right path and don't cut corners. Make 'good money'.

Secondly, women who want to become entrepreneurs should become free thinkers or self-thinkers. A lot of women tend to depend on the male members of the family. To run a business you have to trust your own judgement, make your own decisions.

Third thing is, you must be sincere to your work. Like, you are sincere to your children, your family. If you have set up something, you are responsible and you have to fulfill your responsibility come what may. Treat your work like a *dharma* and if you don't treat it like your *dharma* then don't fool around with business because it just gives women in general a bad name.

THE PURITAN

Deepa Soman,
Lumière Business Solutions

Deepa started her career at Hindustan Lever but stepped off the ladder as a young mother. She went on to create a market research company whose mission is to employ women professionals on a flexi-time basis.

Deepa Soman works harder than most people and enjoys it. That must be the reason she is meeting me, so well-prepared.

"You asked me about the challenges I have faced, so I created a 'mind map'."

Typical MBA, you might think. But that isn't true. For Deepa has absolute clarity and strength of purpose. So untypical in this world.

Like many women professionals, she dropped out of the rat race early.

Like some of these women, she set out on her own.

The difference is, she took it beyond the dimensions of business. Her company is providing market research services, but creating flexi-work opportunities for women is its true mission.

"My driver is the difference I make to what these women do, what they fulfil, who they become."

Running a mostly virtual organisation is not easy. You have to invest in technology, in creating principles and practices which bind the organisation together. So that there is freedom but also discipline.

"We work with slimmer margins because there is more volatility. But never in 16 years have we missed a deadline."

If Lumière can do it – why not others? Because, it takes effort.

But we must ask for it, we must demand it.

For it is our duty to contribute to the world but our right to live – in harmony, in balance.

THE PURITAN

Deepa Soman,
Lumière Business Solutions

Deepa Soman was born in Matunga in Mumbai.

"My parents had a love marriage, overcoming many obstacles. I grew up in a one-room kitchen home in Sardar Nagar (Sion Koliwada)."

Due to financial difficulties, Deepa's mother pushed herself, took the necessary exams and got a job with the income tax department as a clerk. With both parents working, Deepa went to a crèche after school hours and became a seasoned 'latchkey' kid.

"Growing up, I saw my mother being very professional, ambitious, she worked extremely hard. She also handled all the household chores."

When Deepa was 5 years old she got a baby sister. Soon after, her mother developed a chronic bronchial condition with at least one acute attack every year. Every time she went to the hospital, there was no knowing whether she would return.

"From the age of 9, I learnt to cook and to keep house. Life was so cruel to my mother on a day-to-day basis, I wanted to make her happy in small ways."

Medical challenges continued. Deepa's maternal grandfather suffered from Parkinson's disease while her grandmother succumbed to cancer. Living with them, seeing death at close quarters made Deepa wise beyond her years. But it was not all gloom and doom.

"My father worked for *The Times of India* and the biggest perk was free magazines and newspapers," smiles Deepa.

Writers and poets would often drop by at home. Deepa and her sister Amrita were encouraged to pen down their reflections after watching a movie or on New Year's Eve.

"I was pretty sure I would become a journalist or writer."

A turning point came when Deepa and her family shifted to Andheri and she joined a new school – Canossa Convent – in class 8. On the first day of school, every student had to bring old newspapers as part of a fundraising drive. The newspapers had to be arranged in a pile and left in front of the class.

Some time later, the principal was taking her round. She stopped outside Deepa's class, pointed to her pile and asked, "Who made this?"

Deepa stepped forward, feeling flustered.

The principal remarked, "I want all of you take a hard look at this girl and I want you to know she is going to make something of her life."

Deepa's pile was neatly stacked, with not a single paper out of place. The same way her mother would expect the dining table cleaned – with attention and sincerity. And yet, the principal's words were to have a deep and lasting effect.

"To be praised in front of 50 students was very exciting. I used to be quite casual about studies, I decided to work hard and be more focused."

Despite this resolve, during her prelims, Deepa blanked out during one paper.

"I had developed a phobia for Geometry and just could not write the exam!"

But something positive came out of the incident. There was a girl in Deepa's class called Rose who always stood first in class. She had won a book called *The Power of Positive Thinking* as a prize. Deepa borrowed the book.

"I sat up all night reading it; all my fears and doubts disappeared. It was absolutely transformational."

At the age of 14 Deepa discovered that she was the one in control of her life. And her thoughts.

"I started using creative affirmation and experienced how beautifully it works!"

Deepa had a number in her head – 560 – and that was exactly the number of marks she scored in her SSC board exams. Subsequently, she joined St Xavier's College. Although Deepa was initially keen to try for medicine, on her mother's advice she dropped the idea and took up Arts instead.

"I was a complete bookworm and had lots of fun in college but not in the canteen – in the library."

After graduation, Deepa joined S P Jain for her MBA. She took her classes seriously and fell in love with marketing.

At placement time there was only one company Deepa knew she had to get into – the biggest and the best in the business.

After 7 rounds of interviews, she made it to Hindustan Lever Ltd (HLL). Right after, she got placed. Deepa also met and fell in love with the man she was to marry.

"The first time I saw Milind on campus, I *knew*. This is the guy I want to spend the rest of my life with."

Introduced by a mutual friend, they shared a cup of coffee. Then, right after the exams, he asked if she would like to see the film *Back to the Future*.

"Yes, but can I bring my mother and sister along?" asked Deepa.

He didn't seem to mind at all. After the movie 'date' at Sterling, the gang went to Vithal's for *bhel*. The next day, Deepa proposed to Milind and he agreed. Since he was her junior at S P Jain, they would have to wait – until completed his MBA.

Meanwhile, Deepa joined HLL.

The Lever stint began with a rural immersion where Deepa and another trainee – Mohyna – took responsibility for 5 villages.

"We worked on healthcare and employment and for a brief period I wondered if I should sit for the IAS exam!" she recalls.

The moment passed but the idealistic streak remained.

When the time came for confirmation, Deepa did something unusual – she asked to be put in a field sales position instead of

"Financially things weren't great but love of reading gave me global exposure."

brand management. It took 45 minutes to convince the panel but finally, they agreed. With the desire to stay in Bombay after marriage, Deepa also accepted a transfer to Lipton India, a sister company.

As Lipton sales manager, Deepa had 45 salesmen over 45 years of age reporting to her. She chose her dress and demeanour carefully – saris, *joodas* and a ramrod-straight posture.

"I had this persona of being very approachable but, at the same time, very professional, very no-nonsense. I had absolutely no issues working with men, earning their respect."

Towards the end of her sales stint, Deepa realised she wanted to work in market research. This was with a view to the 'big picture'.

"I had planned to have my first child 3 years after marriage and the second one by age 30. I thought market research would give me more latitude for motherhood."

However, when she returned to work after maternity leave, she wasn't enjoying herself. She decided to avail of the 'career break' open to women managers at Hindustan Lever.

"Everyone at home was scandalised because all the women in my family work. 'What will you do, sitting at home with a baby?' they asked."

Milind had joined an IT company was and travelled extensively. The idea of living in another country intrigued Deepa.

"I was fascinated by Jamaica and said to Milind, 'Let's go there.'"

So on the romantic notion of sun, sand and surf, the Somans shifted to Kingston, Jamaica. Just before they left India, Deepa's mother passed away. Two weeks after her 50th birthday.

"When we were in school, my mother had a 'near death' experience. At that time she said I have made a deal with God – 'let my kids get settled and then I will come to you.'"

The day Deepa's sister got placed was the day their mother went into coma. Thus, keeping her word.

"It was a very difficult time for me because she was my anchor and source of inspiration. Despite all her medical problems, she raised us so well and rose to the top of her profession*."

Deepa felt lost and bereft.

Moving to a new country did not make it any easier. With a small baby to take care of and no intellectual stimulation, Deepa felt 'useless'. She decided to look for some part-time work. But in Jamaica, a degree from S P Jain or experience with Hindustan Lever did not automatically open doors.

"There was no internet back then, so I picked up the yellow pages."

Listed under 'market research' were 3 companies. Deepa applied to 'J A Young Research' because it sounded better than the other two.

Within 3 days, the Managing Director sent a personal reply, apologising for the 'delay' in response. Mr Josh A Young was a veteran of British American Tobacco who had recently set up his own company.

"Mrs Soman, we would be glad to have you work with us," he said.

And that's how Deepa landed her first project. J A Young Research applied for a work permit and more projects followed. Now came the question of how to raise a bill. The chartered accountant explained that, in Jamaica, individuals paid 33% tax whereas companies pay only 25% tax.

Mr Young advised, "Mrs Soman, set up a company rendering services to J A Young Research. It will be better for you."

Now came the question of a 'name'.

"Lumière means light. My name means light. I needed to have a globally accepted name."

And thus, Lumière Consultancy Services was born on 17 February 1995. Work was good and hours were flexible. On days when she didn't have help, Deepa would take her young son with her to the office.

* Deepa's mother (Geeta Samant) rose from a clerical position to Assistant Commissioner of Income Tax.

"At Lipton I demonstrated that you can be gentle and still be tough, get work done."

"Rahul would play with his toys while I would complete my work," she recalls.

With work to anchor her mind and income to boost her security, Deepa's spirits lifted. Her confidence and self-esteem were restored. And then, it hit her.

"How many young mothers must be going through the same emotions – feeling helpless, useless, powerless."

Standing in the verandah, watching the sun set Deepa made a promise to herself.

"If I make something out of my life, I am going to make sure I help other women at this critical juncture."

Professional fulfilment is as important to some women, as a weekly manicure is for others. And both kinds of women should get what they need…

Just as Deepa was beginning to enjoy Jamaica, there was a crisis. Milind's father had a heart attack and there was no one to look after him. Deepa and Milind decided to return home. They chose to live in Nerul (New Bombay), where Milind's father – an ex-BARC employee – had built a two-storey bungalow.

"My daughter, Rhea, was only 6 weeks old when we came back to India. I did not have much of a clue what I would do."

Nerul was a distant, under-developed suburb. Milind was travelling constantly while the kids would keep falling sick with malaria or fevers. There was no support system. Deepa could not commute to an office in South Bombay, or take up a job requiring travel.

"But I couldn't sit idle either. So I thought – let me start something of my own."

Deepa toyed with the idea of setting up a gym. Or a playschool. Then one fine day – in July 1996 – Deepa got a call from Jayadev, a colleague from her Hindustan Lever days.

He said, "We're really strapped for resources – can you work like a research manager from home?"

Working remotely involved a bit of logistics in those days. Milind's driver would pick up the data from Lever House in Backbay Reclamation and Deepa would send the analysis back through him. Billing was based 100% on trust.

"I would log in start time and end time and payment was made by number of hours – no questions asked."

A relationship built not just on need, but mutual respect.

At this time, a new technique was emerging in market research – sequential recycling. The technique involved working with consumers from an early stage in the product-development cycle and produced much better results at a lower cost.

"I got a chance to start working with sequential recycling for Lever's and over time I modified it to suit different categories."

Although it started as a one-woman show, Deepa knew she would grow and need like-minded people to work with her. And instinctively, she felt they should have the same flexibility to work from home, as she did. And it would work, if all these people shared the same vision.

On 15 September 1996, Deepa created a formal document listing 12 'key values'. These included proactiveness, timeliness, responsibility, concern and caring. At this time, Lumière consisted of Deepa Soman, one desk, one computer and one cupboard.

Sitting in a spare room in her house.

But, with a picture of the 'future' in her head. "Even if I went to gym, I was always looking for some young mother who might want to work with me!"

As work pressure grew help came from a family friend – a general manager at UTI who would put in a few hours on the weekend and get paid per project. In 1998, Lumière recruited its first employee.

"Joyce was a young MBA who joined me full-time and I also got a very bright young girl called Sangeetha Dharmaraj who lived in the neighbourhood."

Neither had market research experience but that suited Deepa just fine. Having experienced people would mean a process of 'unlearning'. Better then to train your recruits in the way *you* desire.

"When you are unhappy within yourself, professionally unfulfilled, you can't be a good mother or wife or daughter."

"I taught my girls technical aspects like data collection and moderation. The principle was always to over-deliver, never miss a deadline and never cut corners."

The team continued to grow with two young mothers – Laila Sethna and Trupti Sankar coming on board, working remotely. Then there was Shilpa Ramachandran, who used to do Deepa's travel bookings.

"Each time I would talk to her, I would think she is very organised and would be great to work with!"

As luck would have it, Shilpa got married, shifted to Nerul and joined Lumière. Soon after, Deepa took up an office on rent in the Vashi railway station complex. But that came with its own headaches.

"The loo was unusable and we didn't feel safe, working late at night."

However, to pay for the office Deepa took a personal loan at 11%. And in that sense, it strengthened her commitment level. From 'interesting work' Lumière suddenly became a going concern, a serious business!

The same year – 1998 – Deepa moved from the proprietorship mode to a private limited company.

"I thought it will help me attract talent."

Lumière also invested in building a website, which was quite uncommon at the time.

"Think of the website as your 'headquarters'," advised friend and mentor, Damodar Mall.

A senior at HLL, Damodar had also recently turned entrepreneur. Every 3 months, the two would meet informally – exchange notes and share ideas.

"Entrepreneurship can be lonely, so it was great to have a sounding board and cheerleader."

In 1999, the young company was doing 2-3 projects a month, with 90% of business coming from one client – Hindustan Lever. The repeat nature of work allowed Lumière to go deeper into Lever's business problems and really *understand* different categories. This gave the client added confidence, in the results of the research.

In this endeavour, it helped to have people working in their own areas of interest. For example, Laila had a passion for HR. This helped Lumière conduct several HR projects for blue-chip clients.

"We could speak the language of the client and quickly understand the requirement."

Similarly, Hindustan Lever itself requested Deepa to take on a female manager, Shilpa Mhatre, who had recently quit after having a baby. She had extensive experience with Lakmé and a passion for cosmetics.

"We got a lot of work related to skin and beauty because of her."

The key attraction for such talent was the flexibility of working from home. At the office itself, there were just Deepa and Shilpa Ramachandran, who acted as 'Girl Friday'.

"She handled admin and accounts and could even *sound* like me on the telephone, if need be," laughs Deepa.

In 2001, Lumière's client profile started changing. Hindustan Lever managers were quitting the company for better opportunities. And at their new companies, they continued to work with Lumière.

"That's how we landed a project with Monsanto, a business we knew nothing about!"

But Deepa has this weird sense of confidence – if I have got the project, the person I need to work on it will come. And that's exactly what happened. The team continued to grow – mostly virtually, but a back office with some support staff became necessary as well.

"The back office functioned from the gala in the station while the research team shifted back to the 'home office'."

The company which started from a single room now consumed the entire ground floor of the Soman bungalow. With both qualitative and quantitative research expertise, Lumière started adding 'verticals' or specialisations like healthcare, media, entertainment, and telecom. Over time, managing multiple projects with mostly virtual staff became complicated.

"Earlier Shilpa would get on the phone, *tu aaj kya kar rahi hai, tu aaj kya kar rahi hai.* But this wasn't scalable."

Slowly, a process was put in place for project work allocation and a 'team mail' concept introduced. And yet, the company remained relatively small and 'manageable'.

"I could not imagine working with more than say, 15 employees. In that sense I was becoming a bottleneck."

In 2006, Lumière completed 10 years and conducted a 'visioning' exercise. But year 11 was the real turning point for the company. Deepa's husband Milind decided to quit his job and join Lumière. The reasons were both professional and personal.

For several years Milind had been with i-flex, based in Mumbai/ Pune but handling global responsibilities.

In 2005, i-flex was acquired by Oracle for $909 million. The founding team started to disband and by the end of 2006, Milind decided it was time for him to move on as well.

Earlier that year, Deepa's father had suffered a stroke and their son was now in class 10.

"Trying to grow the business and handle personal commitments had become a challenge. I think I could retain my sanity because Milind came on board," admits Deepa.

Milind himself saw it as a big opportunity.

"I could see that Lumière was growing but there was a lot more that could be done," he adds.

Milind had experience in scaling up operations in the IT industry. With the right technology and discipline, Lumière could also grow manifold.

As soon as he joined, Milind took over some of the 'load' in terms of admin and finance. One of the first things he did was exit TCI and get into a business relationship with Cleartrip. That alone saved the company ₹ 10 lakh a year in travel cost.

"He would joke, 'I have already earned my salary for the first year'!"

Finance was another part of the business Deepa had never really enjoyed.

"I sat with the chartered accountant from time to time but there was lot of inefficiency in terms of delays in billing and receivables. And I would say forget it – let's just concentrate on the next project".

Now, she could do exactly that. Meanwhile, Milind focused on bringing in technology to enhance the virtual workflow. Lumière was an early adopter of Webex, google docs and cloud computing.

"We brought in a lot of best practices from IT project management."

Between 2008 and 2011, Lumière doubled its number of projects and tripled in terms of staff. At present, there are over 40 employees and consultants – onsite and virtual – who work on a fixed retainer plus profit-sharing.

"We hire very carefully, after 3-4 tests and a personal interview. I think we have perfected the art of identifying people who 'fit' our culture."

Lumière also uses 'associates' – freelancers who work as area experts or local partners in cities across India. 90% of Lumière's workforce, however, still consists of women. A fact Deepa is proud of.

"We do have men in some roles and in back office but yes, we are largely an organisation which enables professional women to have a home and a career."

The 'enabling' mission is what remains closest to Deepa's heart. People come, people go, and some grow far beyond their own imagination.

Deepa's executive assistant Shilpa blossomed into a researcher.

Her driver Rajendra Singh assists in the accounts department.

Vaijanti joined as househelp, learnt Tally and moved to the back office.

"I believe there is infinite, unlimited potential in every person," says Deepa.

Every week, she sends out a 'hi mail' with something related to work, something personal, something inspiring. Because leadership is giving your people mental and emotional recharge.

"For me work is play and I enjoy it. I never for a moment feel that I am overworked."

But where does the entrepreneur herself draw strength from?

"I am a spiritually inclined person. I have a little morning ritual of collecting flowers in my garden in a very old basket that belongs to my mother-in-law's mother…"

That ten minutes of personal time is sacred, as is the morning cup of tea she shares with Milind. A swim, a walk, a workout – these are some of the activities that give them a chance to bond. As does the monthly drive to the Ashtavinayak temple in Mahad.

"We leave early, around 6:30 am and have a long conversation on the way. I've got so much clarity on things that way."

Another clear directive in Deepa's life – which came from Milind – is to leave cooking to the cook. Early on, even before the kids came into the picture, he insisted on it.

"You cook out of choice, you cook when you want to, let it not become a chore for you!" was his advice.

Milind was brought up in a home with a cook, where his mother had enough free time to run a small business taking baking classes. As a child he helped both in the kitchen and with his mother's enterprise.

"My mom would always say, when you marry, look for a good human being from an educated family who values women working."

And from a mother's point of view? Is there the usual guilt attached to this entrepreneurial journey?

"Sometimes I do wonder whether you know, I could have done more for my kids, but I know I'm not wired like other mothers, to constantly be around, micro-managing."

With neither her mother nor mother-in-law living at home, Deepa has managed her home and kids with a series of housekeepers and *ayahs*, some part-time, some full-time.

"Luckily we have a large house so we could keep live-in help."

Although there were times, like Ganesh Chaturthi and Diwali, when everyone would take off. And somehow you manage the deadlines and the diapers, you get through it all.

"What we really enjoyed was 'doing' things together – reading a book, playing tennis or practising piano."

Breakfast and dinner are two meals Deepa always had with the children, planning her meetings and client visits accordingly. With both children now in college, and Milind back at home, equations have changed.

"We've all grown up," smiles Deepa.

Lumière too is 'growing up', with a new architect-designed office, new services for clients and new dreams for the future. The company touched revenues of Rs 3.5 crore in March 2012 and aims to cross Rs 10 crore in 5 years time. Hindustan Lever remains Lumière's biggest client but now contributes just 25% of total billing.

"We have constituted a formal Board of Directors and are now looking to expand overseas."

In November 2012, the Singapore Economic Development Board invited Lumière to set up an office in the island state. And more plans for international operations as well.

But there is ambivalence in Deepa's mind. Must ambition come at the cost of quality and cutting corners? Will the work itself remain as exciting, when the driver is more and more billing?

"Money has never been my driving force. What matters to me is that each of us puts heart and mind into every project. And we produce bloody sincere work."

Deepa herself is still very 'hands on' though she doesn't put in 14 hours a day anymore. Just 8-10 hours, which is quite 'chilled' by her standards.

"Actually, I find it hard to just put my feet up and relax... Working hard is what I know best and do best."

But she is becoming lighter and easier, less of a perfectionist. Spending more time on writing, teaching, mentorship. Learning golf and Spanish.

Because there comes a time when you have to let go.

You owe it to yourself.

To explore, to expand, to grow.

ADVICE TO WOMAN ENTREPRENEURS

Find what is that you truly love to do because if you really do something that is very aligned to your interest, aligned to your passion area, chances are you'll do a lot of it and you will do it well.

Take pride in doing well what you do – that's something that I tell my kids as well. If you are willing to work hard and if you are able to keep your butt on the seat... success *has* to come your way.

Paying attention to small things is important.

Be patient with yourself.

Use your family as a resource, a support system. Celebrate the fact that there are in-laws and parents who can look after your kids, express your gratitude to them. You have to keep the balance. You can't be so involved in yourself and your work that you don't nurture your relationships.

As a working woman, learn to delegate your household to reliable help. As a rule of thumb, set aside 10% of your income for the people who manage your home. It will keep you stress-free.

Even in business it's all about relationships. The differentiator will be about how you can build, nurture and grow relationships.

You can and must keep working on your relationship with yourself. I've taught myself to be calmer, manage my temper, choose my words carefully so that I don't hurt people. A lot of these qualities I imbibed from my husband – he's naturally a very gentle and a giving person.

Be open to learning lifelong. I think you owe it to yourself; you owe it to your profession, to know more about it, to be curious, to be reading, to be always on the cutting edge.

Above all, be honest and stay honest. It will get you good sleep at night. And you *will* grow your business.

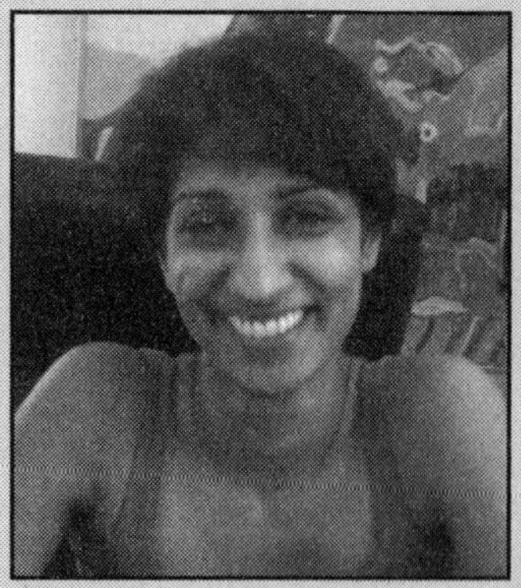

ROLE MODEL

Otara Gunewardene,
Odel

Otara's first 'retail venture' was selling export surplus clothes from the trunk of her car. In 2010, she created history by becoming the first Sri Lankan woman entrepreneur to take her company public.

Every woman has a friend who is really good at shopping. She can wear designer jeans with a roadside scarf and carry off both – with equal aplomb.

Otara Gunewardene is just that girl. But she's used this talent for more than turning heads. Otara is the founder of Odel – Sri Lanka's most famous, most valuable department store chain.

The moment you walk into her flagship store at Alexandra Place in Colombo, you feel the difference. There are bigger shops, but there's nothing unique about them.

At Odel, you will *want* to buy because, somehow, there is still that personal touch.

"I am still very involved in selecting our merchandise," admits Otara. "It's what I enjoy doing the most."

With her high cheekbones and slender figure, you might mistake her for a model.

"No," she shakes her head. "I gave that up years ago."

At the age of 25, Otara walked off the ramp, away from glamour, into the world of business.

And made the business more glamorous.

In 2010, Odel became the first woman-led company in Sri Lanka to go public.

And continues to set a blistering pace in fashion retail.

Making it a model for others to copy.

Even as the Original treads a path all her own.

ROLE MODEL

Otara Gunewardene, Odel

Otara was born in the beautiful city of Colombo.

"I had all the comforts while growing up but my parents weren't born wealthy, they worked very hard."

Otara's father started as a junior executive with Aitken Spence, a blue-chip company in Sri Lanka. He went all the way up to Chairman. Her mother was equally enterprising. She started 'Chitra Lane', a school for children with special needs.

"The school started with two children and today there are over 400."

Otara attended CMS Ladies' College, a private all-girls' school. But she wasn't at all fond of studies.

"I was very athletic, not studious at all. At the sports meets I won a lot of medals for hurdles and high jump. I was also quite good at swimming."

The one thing Otara loved, apart from sports, was animals. She wanted to become a vet but scored poorly in the 'O' level examination. So, she couldn't opt for science.

"I did my A levels privately and then applied to undergraduate colleges in America. I went to Bowling Green University in Ohio because they had a program in Marine Biology."

However, Otara soon discovered she did not like diving. So she switched subjects and eventually graduated with a degree in Biology.

"In my final year in the States, I did a bit of modelling and enjoyed it."

Otara moved back to Colombo in 1986 and became a professional model. Although not as lucrative as the US or even in India, it was attractive enough. Otara walked the ramp, as well as appeared in some print and television ads. But it wasn't really a full-time job.

"My father suggested I start my own business. And I thought ok, why not!"

A company by the name 'Odel' had already been registered – 'O' from Otara and 'Del' from her middle name.

"Dad had also spoken to a friend in Australia to supply me haircare products. So that was really my first step into business."

To receive a consignment of products, Otara needed to pay cash. While her dad could have easily lent her money, instead, he introduced her to the bank.

"I took a loan of $1200 from the bank and I'm glad about that."

There's more pressure to repay the bank than repay your dad. Making you that much more serious about what you're doing!

Otara started making the rounds of hair salons, to market her products. At the same time, she saw another opportunity. Otara had a couple of friends who manufactured garments for export. When she visited their factories, a friend remarked he had a lot of surplus garments.

"Can you help me get rid of this stock?"

Otara picked up some pieces she liked and showed them to friends. This sold out quickly, so she got more stocks. It was all very informal – the 'shop' was literally the boot of her car.

"I had a station wagon and I would park at the back-entry gate, wherever I was doing a fashion show."

During rehearsals, friends and visitors would come around and pick up some items. Or they could drop by at her house and rummage through the stock, kept in a small room next to the garage.

"I also started supplying clothes to some of the stores in Colombo."

Otara also started orders for 'logo' T-shirts. Say, Coca Cola needs 1000 T-shirts to give away during a promotion. Initially, she got orders from companies and executed them through local factories.

"Then I borrowed three machines from somebody and started manufacturing T-shirts myself."

The idea was to also produce original designs. Otara was particularly fond of the elephant, an animal which is very important and very well loved in Sri Lanka.

"I was 22 and just started doing all these things. It was interesting and also kept earning money, so I just kept going."

Otara cannot recall 'how much' money she made in this period. Just that she contributed some of the profit to wildlife organisations. And the rest was invested into buying more and selling more.

"As I started spending more and more time in the business, I decided to quit modelling."

In 1989, Otara started her first shop, a small 500 sq ft outlet on Dickman's Road. She funded it with $50 of her own money and $50 each from two 'investors' – her mother and elder brother.

"I did the interior designing myself, hired a sales assistant and hung an 'open' sign on the door."

This very first Odel outlet quickly caught the eye of the tourist crowd. The 'elephant' T-shirts, in particular, became popular as souvenirs.

"I got more designed and soon we had 20-30 different 'Odel' T-shirts to choose from."

Otara also started the practice of holding 'sales'. During such times, there was so much rush that her mother would come to help out at the cash counter.

Otara's little shop was just one of a hundred similar shops in Colombo. So what made it special?

"You must know what is selling, how much is selling. Or you will never succeed."

"I think I have the ability to buy things that people are looking for..."

But the 'formula' was simple. Otara bought for others the very same things she would like to buy, for herself.

On popular demand, the little shop expanded. Soon it was stocking men's, women's and children's clothing, and had spread from one to four floors.

"I also started opening small stores in other locations."

These were located in malls such as 'Majestic City' and 'Liberty Plaza', as well as hotels. By 1992-93, there were 9 stores bearing the signboard 'Odel' in Colombo.

In the midst of all this, in 1990, Otara married Raju Chandiram, who was to be not just her husband but business partner. While Otara concentrated on buying the right merchandise, he handled the administration and backend side of the business.

"We rented a house and made that into an office-cum-warehouse. Then we hired people to manage the shop operations, to manage the staff and to do accounts."

And Otara was enjoying the whole experience.

"I used to really enjoy thinking of new things to do, like I worked on our advertisements."

Otara would write the copy herself, visualise how it should look and then get a designer to work on it.

Other areas, like finance, were not quite as much fun. But here too, Otara 'educated' herself.

"My brother advised me initially, how to approach and how to talk to the bank. Later we got professional managers."

You don't need to *know* everything but you must have a broad understanding. So you can make the best decision, an informed decision.

But many decisions must be taken simply out of desire, out of a 'feeling in the gut'. In 1993, Otara placed an advertisement in the paper for a property on which we could build a bigger store, a flagship store.

"The moment I saw this crumbling 150-year-old building, I knew this is that place."

Built in 1860, it was an old colonial mansion with wooden floors but very poor maintenance – practically falling apart. But Otara could *imagine* what it could look like.

"We preserved the old-world charm and built the store around it. It worked really well."

'Odel Unlimited' opened shop at Alexandra Place in 1994 and was a huge success. The 10,000 sq foot store offered a bigger range of products and a better shopping experience, with an in-house restaurant and play area for kids.

"We got a lot of tourists and expats because both the products and the ambience stood out."

But it was a trying time, on the personal front. Even as frantic construction was going on for the store, Otara was in the final months of her first pregnancy. But she was at the site, supervising work until the very last day.

"I went back to work four days after Kiran was born, of course, for shorter periods."

Since home and office were close by, Otara could come to work for 2 hours, go back to feed the baby and return to office. More than once in the day.

"I also had my mother who was very supportive, but definitely it was a difficult time. When you are up in the night you get tired and cranky...."

But, this too shall pass. And a baby, or a business, will keep growing, keep growing. At each stage, you must grow with it.

Within a year, the Odel flagship store was in need of additional space. Otara looked out of the window and noticed the building right behind her. She offered to buy it out.

"There are things that a normal, average person does that I am not be able to do. My commitment is to the business and to my family."

"We linked the two buildings together and that's what you see standing here today."

Spread across 33,000 ft, a bigger, better 'Odel Unlimited' opened in 1999. The following year saw the birth of younger son Rakhil. At the same time, trouble flared up on paradise island.

The 2001 LTTE suicide bomb attack at Bandarnaike International Airport was a catastrophic event. Tourist arrivals plummeted, affecting the entire Sri Lankan economy. And companies like Odel.

"Due to the war, we had years when there was hardly any growth but somehow we kept the stores going."

There were times when stores had to be shut for as long as 3 days, due to curfew or bombings. But not once was an Odel store damaged or a staff member injured.

As peace returned, the expansion process continued. In 2010, Odel went public, to raise money for further expansion. The IPO was oversubscribed by a record 63 times. It was the first time that a female entrepreneur had taken a company public in Sri Lanka.

"We started with 1 store, 2 salegirls. Now we have 16 outlets, employing 850 people."

Odel posted sales of Lankan ₹ 380 crore* and profit before tax of Lankan ₹ 26.4 crore for the 12 months ending 31 March 2012. In July 2012, Parkson Retail Asia bought a 41.8% for Lankan ₹ 142.4 crore.

However, Otara retains a 27.88% stake and continues to be the company's CEO. There are plans for bigger stores, more stores, perhaps even overseas. But the one thing Otara remains passionate about is her product mix.

* Sri Lankan rupee = .42 Indian rupee.
LKR 380 crore = INR 160 crore = approx USD 30 million.

"Even though I have a big team of buyers and merchandisers I am still very involved in selecting our products. That's what I love doing, what I am best at!"

Odel stocks more than 1,500 different items, a majority of them sourced locally. Working with more than 1000 suppliers and over 300 factories. Keeping track of 'what is selling' is key.

"In the very beginning, when we started, my mother was the 'ERP'. After 3 years we realised it's not enough and we got software made locally and started using it."

Eventually, the company got a modern ERP system installed which gives up-to-the-minute sales.

"The thing is, I am very impatient. If I ask something I need to know *right* now – I can't wait for three, four days for someone to go and check the shelf!"

And yet, beyond ERP there is ESP. A sense of which way the wind is blowing, what's the 'next big thing' in fashion. What more the customer needs, what she will spend on.

"At the moment we are planning a very large store and no matter how much we research it, the decision to go ahead will always be based on a feeling that 'Yes… it will work'.

Work is all about teaming up with people. How does one handle it, as the company grows in size?

"Till a few years ago, I knew all the staff by name but now we're too big and it's hard to do that."

However, Otara remains very close, very accessible with her key team members. She is also extremely hands-on, which may or may not be such a good thing.

"I am not just a head and not involved in the business… I guide my team in the day-to-day decisions and day-to-day details."

But she's working on changing that, working on letting go.

'Giving back' is another idea Otara is passionate about.

"I've always believed that you must contribute to the community that you earn your money from… so I used to support various organisations."

"Sacrificing yourself for your children is not healthy for them or for yourself. Because you are not at your best either with your children or yourself."

In 2008, Otara decided to focus her efforts on one cause close to her heart –the cause of animal welfare.

"That's why we started 'EMBARK', which is helping street dogs in Sri Lanka."

The initiative started with doing some T-shirts with fun slogans, which became popular. The brand mascot is 'Niko', a street dog adopted by Otara. Every collection is based on a 'story' – like 'Niko the Flirt'.

"We launch each collection with a fashion show and my dream is to take the brand overseas."

With so much on her plate, how does Otara manage it all? Her day starts with getting the kids ready for school and then heading for the gym. By 9 am Otara is in office and it's all systems go until 7 pm, when she heads home.

"I don't see my boys much during the day so I make sure I spend my evenings and weekends with them."

In 2004, Otara and Raju got divorced but remain good friends. As a single mother, Otara is even more conscious of her responsibilities.

"I get invited to a lot of parties and social functions but I choose to attend only a few. "

With house help and supportive parents, who live close by, Otara has maintained her focus on work. Without feeling guilty.

"If I was at home and not working I would be miserable and my children would not like me anyway."

Over the last few years, Otara has also found herself drawn to a more holistic way of life. She practices feng shui, takes only homoeopathic medication and has been attending programs by spiritual teachers.

"They give me different perspectives of how to look at things, how to look at myself..."

Because beyond effort and activity, there is a place of stillness, deep within.

If you can find it and hold on to it, you will make it.

Through anything.

ADVICE TO WOMEN ENTREPRENEURS

I think what is really important is that you enjoy what you do... because unless you enjoy I think you just can't make it successful or bring it to the level that you want. Because you are always battling with yourself and doing something that you don't like doing.

Do not to be afraid to ask people for help, for support and to learn things... I feel some people don't like to ask because they feel they'll look stupid or people will think that they don't know anything. So what if I don't know anything? There are lots of people who are happy to help... you can really use that support to help you grow...

And it's important to keep learning... I am constantly sort of looking at how to improve what I have, how to improve how I am, how to improve what I know.

I am not business qualified, finance qualified or design qualified. So everything I did was basically on gut feel. I think it's essential you maintain that.

When you are strictly figures-oriented and sticking to the book, doing ABCs of a business manual, it's really difficult to succeed, to be different and to make that leap... from being something ordinary to be something extraordinary and memorable.

HOP, SKIP, JUMP

Namrata Sharma,
Krayon Pictures

Moving around the world with two kids, Namrata could not have a conventional career. So she learnt a little of everything and today it's all being put to good use – in the exciting business of animation.

The office is large and buzzing.

The woman running the show is petite and quietly in control.

"I had no clue really, what I wanted to do or where I wanted to go after engineering," admits Namrata.

What she did know was that her career path could not be logical and linear. Because at heart she was a creative person. And, a woman.

"I started my own multimedia company when I was 23, but then I got married and moved to Hong Kong."

Like many women, Namrata moved from city to city, as her husband moved up in his career. But unlike most of those women, she found *something* to do, wherever she went.

Just to learn, just to keep in touch, just to feel energised and alive as a professional. And eventually, it paid off.

"In 2004, we moved to Pune, where I knew we would settle down. And we had a family support-system for the kids."

Finally, it was the right time, the right place and the right opportunity. And Namrata felt she was *ready*, to be on her own.

Today, she heads Krayon Pictures, a major 3-D animation studio with a 150-strong creative team. Alongside she manages hobbies, homework, karate classes, maids and drivers.

All in a day's work.

So no matter where marriage and motherhood takes you, keep your eyes on the road of ambition.

Set your pace, choose the direction and just keep going.

HOP, SKIP, JUMP

Namrata Sharma,
Krayon Pictures

Namrata is a Pune girl.

"I was born in Pune and studied at St Joseph's school, Pashan," she says. "I grew up in a wonderful, supportive family, with one younger sister and one younger brother."

Since childhood, Namrata was very fond of drawing, painting and anything creative.

"My sister would always say, 'Let's do something!' and instead of sleeping in the afternoons we would paint a bedsheet or a paper towel."

After completing class 12 from Fergusson College, Namrata joined the Government College of Engineering, Pune (COEP).

"Actually I wanted to be an architect and my parents were very encouraging. They said – do what you like. But you know COEP is one of the best colleges in Maharashtra…"

So Namrata went with the 'safe' option but even during BE, she remained more of an artist than a geek.

"I was awarded 'Artist of the Year' three times in a row," she grins.

Actually, she admits, there was no concrete plan for the future.

"Luckily I got selected from campus by Thermax."

As a trainee engineer in the electrical engineering department, Namrata worked on cable layouts, but continued to look out for something creative to do. And as they say, seek and ye shall find.

Testing control panels was one of Namrata's duties. The panels were huge and rather ugly to the eye.

One fine day the boss exclaimed, "Can't we make our control panels look nicer?"

Namrata suggested the use of LEDs, to make the panels more colourful as well as easier to use. And subsequently worked on designing it.

"Around this time I also took a course in Photoshop, CorelDraw and DTP – all of which were very new in India back in '93-94," she adds.

Namrata quickly realised that multimedia was basically a nice mix of creativity and technology. The best of both worlds. With just over a year's experience under her belt, the young engineer decided to quit and start her own company.'

The business model was simple.

"My father bought me a computer, I knew the software. I went back to Thermax and said – here is all the stuff I can do for you!"

Namrata's very first project was a computer-based training program for her ex-employer. It brought in a little money and slowly, she got others on board. Friends of friends – all engineers with a bit of a creative streak.

"We saw the advantage of being engineers – we could speak the language of industry. So, clients were comfortable giving us their jobs."

Not that they *knew* everything, but they were willing to learn. So what if it meant nights poring over books and manuals and endless trial and error.

"You start enjoying the process and you realise that there is something new to do on a daily basis!"

The company focused on the business of corporate presentations and architectural walkthroughs. Things were going well, really well. But then came a twist in the road of life, a common one for a woman professional.

"I got married and my life changed in two major ways," recalls Namrata.

Firstly, the pandit said that my maiden name (Archana) and my husband's name (Pawan) was not a good match. He said my name needed to start with 'N'."

On the spot, a few names were suggested and before she knew it 'Archana Arora' became 'Namrata Sharma'. And right after the marriage, Namrata moved to Hong Kong to be with her husband.

"I did not 'quit' work as such, I kept doing small projects from Hong Kong. But the company was no longer *my* baby."

Yet the will to work, to grow, to learn, was strong. And along came a new opportunity.

"The company my husband worked with was developing some software for Disney. So through him I happened to meet this gentleman who saw some of my work and liked it."

Namrata worked on a freelance basis with the Disney studio, as a visualiser for sets and backgrounds. Working in the traditional 2-D style, more with hand drawings than any hi-tech software or technology.

"But yes, I did observe what people were doing and pretty much everything that goes into the making of an animation film. I was here – doing what I always dreamt of doing. There was a huge amount of learning!"

Unfortunately, this too lasted less than a year.

"I was expecting, and I came back to India for my delivery. And while I was in India, my husband got transferred to New Zealand so I never went back."

In New Zealand, Namrata was on a dependent visa, so she could not even look for a job. What's more, she had an infant to take care of. Yet, she could not sit idle. Call it luck, call it destiny – a new and exciting opportunity came knocking.

And it happened through unconventional means.

"My father was a member of Lions Club and I used to be in Leo club as a teen. So I once again joined the Lions Club in New Zealand and I became an active member."

At Lions Club, Namrata befriended many interesting people, including someone working with a large post-production studio.

"A lot of credit of what I am today goes to my husband. Because he has been constantly pushing me – you can do better, you can do better, you can do better."

New Zealand was an exciting place to be at the time, with directors like Peter Jackson filming *Lord of the Rings*.

Due to visa issues, Namrata could not officially work with a studio, but she could certainly 'train' with one.

"This time I was more involved with the production pipeline, so I understood the whole process.

Once again it was an amazing learning experience. But this too was to be a short stint.

"In less than a year my husband moved back to Hong Kong. So once again I started looking for new things to do!"

Namrata got in touch with one of her colleagues from Disney. He mentioned that Johnson and Johnson was looking for someone to build a web portal. The project was exciting but there was one small problem.

"I was confident about the creative aspects but I had no idea how to build the backend!"

She asked her husband for advice and he said, "Well, there are so many companies in India doing software development, why don't you get in touch with one of them?"

Her husband connected her with Mr G K Rao, who was heading a company called Megasoft (an offshoot of Satyam). Mr Rao agreed to stop by in Hong Kong on his way back from the US to discuss the project.

During this meeting they chatted about many things and Mr Rao wanted to understand the Hong Kong market.

"Because of my husband's work, I knew a lot about the IT industry and I could answer most of his queries."

At the end of the meeting, Mr Rao asked Namrata to join Megasoft and handle business development for the company, in Hong Kong. And she agreed.

"Business development was new to me but my husband was a great help at that time. He guided me from scratch – whom should you meet, who should you talk to, how should you write emails..."

All the little things that help you stand out, and quickly achieve your targets.

"I joined in May 1999 and by July 2000 we signed an offshore project. My yearly targets were actually achieved in 6-7 months. So everyone was very happy with my work!"

But what about her young son? Initially, Namrata requested her mother to come down to Hong Kong and help out. Later, she hired a good maid.

"By this time he was two years old and went to playschool in the morning. He could talk, he could express. When I came home I had the satisfaction of knowing what he enjoyed, what he ate – everything about his day."

Megasoft was in expansion mode and that kept the job exciting.

"I helped to set up an office in Singapore, Australia – from Hong Kong itself. We were also overlooking a joint venture in China."

All this was far from the world of animation, but many of Megasoft's clients were in the media industry – with companies like Star TV and McCannErickon.

"I don't know whether it happened just by chance or because of my affinity for media," she laughs.

The learning here was not so much on creative aspects but the *business* side of a creative industry. And project management.

"I was sitting in Hong Kong but there were project managers working here in India, and I had to be a part of that process."

The stint at Megasoft lasted two years. Midway, Namrata shifted to India.

"Star TV wanted to enter India and I was to handle that project, but then 9/11 happened."

Worldwide, markets were crashing and the boss wanted Namrata to look at Hong Kong again. This meant lots and lots of travel. To the head office in Chennai, to Hong Kong – sometimes 3-4 weeks at a stretch!

"There have been times when I have been really frustrated or depressed and said I want to quit. And my husband said, 'Out, go to office'!"

"By this time my son was 4 years old and attending nursery school. He began to understand that while other mothers are coming to school to pick up their kids, my mother is never there."

And slowly, it started coming out.

"At first when I was leaving he used to say, 'Bring me a toy, bring me a watch'. Later he started saying, 'I don't want anything, but *you* don't go'!"

And one day, the matter reached a tipping point. It was the annual day at school and the teachers had put up drawings and charts made by the kids. One of the topics was, 'When am I most happy'.

"There were 40 kids in the class and most of them wrote 'when papa brings ice cream' or 'when we go to the park'."

Janak had written, in inverted commas, in Hindi, "*Jab meri mummy ghar pe hoti hai*".

"That was the moment which really hit me," recalls Namrata. "Next day I went to work and handed in my resignation."

There was a big hue and cry in the office, even Namrata's husband thought she was taking a hasty and emotional decision. But a mother's heart *will* rule over her head.

"I knew I owed it to my son."

Namrata was at home for the next two years, but not *idle*.

"That is when I got into 3-D technlogy, I went to Maya, learnt all the softwares. And I took up some freelancing projects from home."

But her focus remained on the family.

"I saw a great amount of difference in Janak. He was more confident, more outgoing, more happy when I was at home."

Meanwhile, there was a new arrival in the family – a second baby boy in the year 2003. When Galav was 7 months old, Namrata got a call from KPIT in Pune.

"Would you like to start working again?" they asked.

The person calling was an old colleague from Megasoft and he convinced Namrata it was time to get back.

"If you stay at home for too long, you will get used to it," he said. "You will never be able to get back to work!"

At this time, the family was living in Delhi but both Namrata and her husband had always been keen to move back to Pune. Because that's where they belonged.

"Together we sat and brainstormed. We thought that it might make sense if I moved and he eventually follows."

Namrata agreed to take up the job, but on one condition.

"I told them I cannot leave a 7-month-old baby at home. I cannot travel."

The role Namrata took up was in pre-sales – a regular 9 to 5 kind of job. And in Pune, with a super-strong family support structure, it was no problem.

"My mother-in-law, my sister-in-law and my parents are in Pune. So I didn't ever feel guilty or that I was neglecting my son."

When a mother *knows* her baby is in safe hands, she can put all her energy into work, not worry. Like any other professional.

"I was in banking pre-sales and it was again something new for me. This was more backend... how do you connect to people, how do you make proposals, how do you make presentations."

It was an initiation into the world of finance. But eventually, Namrata moved back to the sales department. And though the job was interesting, she was once again itching for a creative challenge.

"I wanted to do something I *liked* doing and I wanted to be independent. I had some thoughts but wasn't sure what to do exactly."

In 2006, Namrata attended a NASSCOM conference on animation and gaming. Just to get in touch with what was happening out there. At the event she met Alok Kejriwal, founder and CEO of contests2win and games2win.

"We started chatting and Alok mentioned he was looking for

"I have not done anything consistently. But the variety of experience is now my biggest asset. It gave me a logical and a creative balance."

someone who could develop flash games for him."

A couple of meetings followed and Namrata decided to quit KPIT to set up Antrix Animation. A company dedicated to developing online games.

"We had one committed client – contests2win – and I knew that I would find other things to do over time."

At the time of quitting Namrata was also reporting to Mr Kishore Patil, CEO of KPIT.

"When I told him I am resigning to to start my own company, he was supportive and wished me luck."

Antrix came into being in April 2006. A small team with an investment of ₹ 10 lakh to cover salaries, advances, some machinery and rental. The company quickly picked up clients like Thermax and Amdocs, growing from 2 employees to 12 in a span of 3 months.

A few months later there was a call from her ex-boss.

"He was keen to learn about the industry, what work I was doing and spent considerable time with me in my office."

One fine day, Mr Patil called.

"There is a movie opportunity. Would you like to take it up?" he asked.

There was much excitement but also rounds and rounds of presentations and discussions. There was the easy option of getting jobwork from foreign companies. Versus the challenge of creating original content.

"We decided to focus on creating our own IP (intellectual property). That means higher risk, but higher returns if you get it right!"

And so, in June 2007, Krayon Pictures came into being. Its very first project was a full-length animation film titled *Delhi Safari*, based on a concept created by Bollywood director Nikhil Advani.

"Nikhil had narrated the story to Mr Nishit Takia (actress Ayesha Takia's father). Nishit knew Kishore Patil and Kishore knew me. That's how we all came together."

Kishore Patil is the main investor* and strategist while Nishit handles business development. Namrata is a co-founder and director of operations. Which means *everything* – systems, processes, infrastructure. And, most importantly, hiring the right people.

"I believe in a top-down approach. My focus is getting the best people at the senior positions."

Because if *they* have competence and commitment, so will the juniors they hire. And creative people in particular are sensitive people.

"Working with the right kind of boss and a mentor is very important for an animator."

The chance to work on an original – not an outsourced – project was another big attraction. Still, getting talented people to shift from Bombay to Pune was a challenge.

"Initially, we had to sell the concept of Pune city. But once they settled in they got used to the place and started liking it."

Liking your job is also a function of the little things. The 'system' should work to make life easier for you, but to do that you need a person who understands the pain points. And *cares* enough to remove them.

You can clearly see, Namrata is one such a person.

"There are many tedious jobs the artist need not really do. We have written our own asset-management tools to take care of them."

Take, for example, 'versioning'. When multiple departments are working on the same file, there are confusions and complications.

* This is a personal venture of Mr Kishore Patil, not MD & CEO, KPIT Cummins.

"Software is available to manage workflow but we wrote our own software, which was cheaper and more efficient."

Cost is a major issue in the animation industry. The production cost of a Hollywood film like *Finding Nemo* or *Despicable Me* is between $70-$100 million. And typically, it would take close to 7 years to complete.

"In Hollywood, the first 2 or 3 years are only spent in R&D. You actually *live* the life of that character, see how it walks and talks. So a lot of time and money goes into designing and pre-production."

The quality standards are so high that an animator will work with less than half a second per day. Which is not feasible in the Indian market.

"The maximum budget we can hope for is $3-$5 million," sighs Namrata. "We have 150 artists working on one and half a seconds a day."

This does mean some compromise in quality but Namrata believes Krayon's films will stand out. Because it is made with passion and commitment, and *for* the desi audience.

"*Delhi Safari* is complete Bollywood. It's out and out entertainment but there's also a message."

Like most animated features, this too is about a bunch of animals. Only the animals are living in Mumbai's Borivili National Park.

"This is one of the largest National Parks within city limits in Asia but every day it's getting smaller," adds Namrata. "The film looks at this problem from the point of view of the animals."

A leopard is teaching his little cub the ways of the jungle. They wander into a quarrying site where the leopard gets shot. This is an emergency situation. Should the animals continue living in the national park or find a new home?

"There are various characters in the film, like a monkey who is a complete rebel and says, 'Let's go kill them all... *sabko maar dalenge... insanon ko*.'"

But how does one *develop* these characters and their quirks?

"It works like this. Once Nikhil Advani thought of the film, he gave us the characteristics of each animal. Like I told you the monkey is a rebel."

So the monkey has to look, act and behave like that. *Zyaada jump karne waala, zyaada gulatiyaan marnewala* – kind of a restless character. The monkey's voice is dubbed by Govinda and he speaks in a typical Bambaiyya style.

Other characters include an anger management guru voiced by Boman Irani and a bratty parrot called Alex dubbed by Akshaye Khanna.

"Nikhil Advani brought in all the actors and he also directed the film. We also have music by Shankar-Ehsaan-Loy."

'Most animation films in India – apart from *Roadside Romeo* by Tata Elxsi – have been mythological stories. And they haven't done too well at the box office. Hence, distribution of animation films is a challenge.

"This film took 3 years to complete and 2 more years to release," says Namrata.

The Hindi version of *Delhi Safari* hit cinema screens in India and the US on 19 October 2012. The film got three and a half stars from critics but failed to break even. Yet, Namrata remains unfazed.

"We expect to recover our money with English and dubbed versions releasing in the US, China, Russia and Saudi Arabia."

What's more, *Delhi Safari* featured among the top 21 animation films competing for nomination at the Oscars in March 2013.

"I know we've managed to create a new benchmark for Indian animation!"

Krayon is now working on two new animation films – *Kamlu* (the story of a camel who wants to fly) and *Auli* (a celestial elephant who lands on earth by mistake).

"We are also doing some jobwork for other companies," says Namrata. "We realised the gestation period of our own films is long and a few outsourced projects help to keep cashflow going."

Cash is the currency of business, energy is the currency of life. And it's the one asset a working mother can never have enough of!

"Part of the reason I wanted to be an entrepreneur was I thought it would be flexible, give me more time for family. However, I soon realised I am working even longer hours."

The first three years saw numerous crises – something would crash and fail and Namrata would be in office late into the night. Many a times the kids would come to the office, do their homework and even drop off to sleep there.

"I believe they sacrificed more than I did… but it was fun."

There were times when they would see the work going on and even offer some great ideas.

"Finally, things settled down and we are partly on auto-pilot," she adds.

A typical day for Namrata begins early. She drops her kids off to school and gets into office by 8:30 am.

"I try to leave at 4:30-5 pm so I can get back and help them with homework, projects and extra-curriculars."

In fact the kids generally come straight to the office from school and they all leave for home together.

"In case I am busy they will go over to either grandparents' place, which is close to the office. So I never have to worry, as such."

But it *is* a complex logistical equation.

"My elder son, Janak, started his karate classes at a place near my office. That made it easier for me to drop him and then come back and work till late evening."

Which was required in the early days.

"Over the years Janak did very well – he got his black belt and started going to international competitions and won many medals*."

The company shifted its office, now the karate class was no longer 'nearby'. Yet Namrata kept her son in the same class. Because he was doing well, and he was attached to a particular 'Sir'.

Now that's a mother's heart speaking over her head.

"There are things that I delegate – like cooking. And there are things I never worry about – like 'have they eaten, have they changed etc.'"

Those are things the family and domestic support structure can take care of. What Namrata does worry about is their studies and all-round development.

* Janak won the first international medal for India in speedball in Japan. Galav is also a national gold medallist in the sport.

"When I put them in tuitions I thought, ok, now they're in safe hands. But there was a drastic drop in Janak's grades."

When asked why he simply said, "I don't want to go for tuitions, you take my studies."

"That means I need to just *be* there, while he studies on his own..." says Namrata.

It's the same with extra-curriculars and tournaments. If you don't go that's fine. But if you are there, it makes that little bit of difference.

"At times I end up doing nothing all day because they have their competition and I just need to be sitting there. You have to do it... as a mother."

While husband Pawan has been a pillar of support, in *these* matters, Namrata carries twice the load.

"Pawan is a very senior IT professional. He is extremely busy during the week."

In fact, Pawan usually gets home only after midnight, long after the kids have gone to sleep.

"When they get up in the morning and are ready to leave, he is still sleeping," she adds.

But, weekends are exclusively for the family.

"I work Saturdays only if it is absolutely necessary and it's the same with Pawan. Weekends are completely for the kids."

Playing games, watching TV, chatting, some sports, some school work.

And in that moment you realise, it's never easy. But if you are determined and daring and willing to stretch yourself – you *can* have it all.

"Recently, I started taking sitar lessons from Ustad Zunain Khan," adds Namrata.

Because life is a glorious raga with many different notes; the instrument is the body, the player is the mind.

We struggle, we strain, we suffer – to master them.

To sway to a rhythm eternal, and divine.

ADVICE TO WOMEN ENTREPRENEURS

If you want to be an entrepreneur you have to know a little bit of everything. So there is no straight route to get there.

If I had worked as an artist, I would eventually became a team leader or even a supervisor. But nothing beyond that. An animation supervisor doesn't know how to sell, can't set up infrastructure or understand finance. The only way you learn all that is by having varied experiences.

So you must go out of your way, out of your comfort zone to get that.

I think perseverance and patience are two things that all women are naturally born with. Have confidence. Have trust and faith in what you want to do. And have the passion to take it forward.

Everyone has stress on the job, having your own company is no different. Juggling between home and work is what makes it more stressful for women, especially Indian women.

But I *have* done it, and I believe you can too.

I thank my mother and mother-in-law for everything I am today. To any woman with a dream I can only say, if these two important women are on your side, anything is possible.

TRIBAL BEAT

Neeti Tah,
36 Rang

Neeti quit a high-flying advertising career to return to her home town in Chhattisgarh and do 'something different'. Combining creativity with commerce, she is bringing traditional tribal arts to the notice of the modern world.

At 26, Neeti had it all.

A job with a multinational agency.

A comfortable life in the big city.

Friends, freak-out and few responsibilities.

But she chucked it all, to move back to Bilaspur, the town she was born in but hardly lived in. All to pursue a vague and uncertain 'dream'.

"In Delhi, I had money, I had glamour but I wanted something more challenging, more creative."

That something is 36 Rang, a platform to promote the hardly known art forms and artists of tribal Chhattisgarh.

Far from the urban jungle, in remote villages connected by dirt road. Here is where Neeti found her hidden gems. She polished their crafts to suit the modern lifestyle, to make them more saleable.

And thus was born 36 (*chhattis*) Rang (colours).

The business is yet very young, like its founder. It is part-hobby, part-social service, struggling with issues commonly faced by young entrepreneurs. Especially those working with handicrafts.

Mass-produce or stay exclusive?

Go commercial or stay social?

Ideally, a mix of both. 36 Rang is still finding its feet, finding its voice but one thing is clear.

Many may have done this work before you, but much more needs to be done.

The artistic and cultural heritage of this country needs young shoulders to carry it forward.

Enter this world of beauty and divinity.

Feel joy, spread joy.

TRIBAL BEAT

Neeti Tah,
36 Rang

Neeti Tah is a small-town girl.

"I was born in Bilaspur in Chhattisgarh. My father is in the real estate and construction business."

Neeti studied at Lawrence school, Lovedale in Ooty, from class 4 to class 12.

"Those were the most wonderful years of my life!" she recalls.

During her schooldays, Neeti took part in and won numerous painting competitions. So when it came to choosing a career, she knew it would have to be something to do with fine arts.

"I was not keen to do a normal BA course, I wanted to do a professional course, something creative."

Neeti joined the National Institute of Advertising in Sainik Farms, Delhi, for a course in design (Graduate Diploma in Design). Although a relatively new institute, the faculty consisted of graduates.

"I was really lucky to have such teachers," says Neeti. "Whatever I am today and anything I know in design, is thanks to them."

On graduating in 2005, Neeti decided to join advertising. With good grades and a great portfolio, she easily landed a trainee position in J Walter Thompson (JWT), Delhi. The stipend was ₹ 8000.

"The training period is 6 months and then it's up to your work – if they like it, they confirm you."

Neeti got confirmed as a Junior Art Director in JWT in 2007, with a package of ₹ 20,000 per month. The following year, she became an Art Director, with a 40% increment.

"At a young age, I got a lot of responsibilities. There were prestigious clients for whom I was handling *everything*."

From concept to designing, executing and presenting the final creatives – and the various stages in between. Making an advertisement is a process, and it's not easy.

"I used to travel quite a bit, especially to Bombay, for shooting, meetings and post-production work."

Some of the campaigns Neeti worked on included Unitech, Hero Honda, Cargill and ESPN.

"I got to work with a couple of Bollywood stars too… that was good."

Another good thing was living in Delhi with siblings. Neeti's older sister was preparing for her civil service examination while her younger brother had completed his schooling and joined Sri Venkateshwara College. On your own and yet 'just like home' – you can't have it better than that.

And yet, Neeti was restless. In 2009, Neeti got a promotion. Three months later, she decided to quit.

"I always wanted to do something of my own, something really creative. I decided that *this* is the time."

But what exactly should she get into? Neeti had no clue. She headed home to Bilaspur and spent 3 months doing 'nothing'. The temptation to go back to Delhi and take up another advertising job was strong, but Neeti resisted.

Because she knew it was the easy way out.

It was then that Neeti got the idea of doing something with tribal art. An art unique to Chhattisgarh yet hardly known outside the state.

"At the most people have heard about Bastar. But there are many other art forms, many talented artists."

Could a platform be created to showcase and promote this talent? To find out, Neeti decided to travel across the state of Chhattisgarh and see for herself what was happening – at the grassroots level.

"I spent 6 months travelling from village to village, getting to know the artists, talking to them, seeing their work."

Neeti found a wealth of art and artisans, unknown and unrecognised by the world at large. One such art form – *bhitti chitra* – had been pioneered by a tribal lady called Sonabai Rajawar. Illiterate and ill-treated by her husband, Sonabai used art to create beauty and meaning in her barren life.

In 1983, her intricate latticework *(jaalis)* and colourful clay sculptures were discovered by officials from Bharat Bhavan, a newly founded museum and cultural centre in Bhopal. An American anthropologist and writer – Stephen Huyler – stumbled upon her work and was fascinated by it. He wrote a book about Sonabai and also shot a documentary feature on her life and work.

"The village people started giving her a lot of respect and she literally became a goddess," adds Neeti.

Sonabai passed away in 2007 but her work lives on through her son and several other villagers whom she trained during her lifetime.

"In business one thing I have realised is that working with family is a good idea. Because there is complete trust in each other."

"It's a pleasant surprise to people that jail inmates can do something that is so beautiful and high-end."

"Madhubani is known all over the world and similarly, I felt that *bhitti chitra* has potential to become a brand in its own right," says Neeti.

But it would need marketing and reorienting the product, for modern times.

"One of the problems with this art is that the pieces made of clay are very heavy. That makes it difficult to transport, especially for exports."

A problem turned on its head, is an opportunity. Could the same art be executed with a different, light-weight raw material?

"We hit upon the idea of *bhitti chitra* using papier mache. But when we made some samples, they developed cracks after some time."

Nothing is as simple as it seems. Through friends in Delhi, Neeti came to know of a papier mache expert.

"I can't pay you fees but will you please help me?" she asked him.

The man agreed to visit Chhattisgarh and hold a workshop for the *bhitti chitra* artists. He stayed in Ambikapur village for two days and trained the artists on how exactly to formulate the mixture. The cracks disappeared.

"We started supplying small shipments – 20-25 pieces – to the US, through Stephen Huyler."

But Neeti realised, the Indian market was different. There was more demand here for small craft items than large, intricate *jaali* work.

"My friends and I brainstormed on what are the modern, funky products we can make."

The end result – *bhitti chitra* jewellery, lampshades and wall hangings depicting tribal life. Common items but with a distinctive touch.

"I also came across a set of tribal ladies who would handpaint their body tattoos on fabric. This is known as *godna* art."

While these artists were creative and spontaneous, their planning and execution skills were poor. Neeti held workshops for them in Bilaspur which resulted in the production of 100 *godna* art stoles.

Like *bhitti chitra* and *godna*, there are other unique art forms in Chhattisgarh such as *dhokra* (metal casting), pottery and wooden craft. But the real challenge was deeper. Since independence, Chhattisgarh had been part of Madhya Pradesh. It was only in the year 2000 that it developed its own identity, when it became a state.

"There was nothing that 'belonged' to Chhattisgarh, like an art form. So the government decided to do something about it."

A style of embroidery known as *marwahi* was chosen and hundreds of men and women across Chhattisgarh were trained in it. This was pioneered by Dr Renu Jogi, wife of the then Chief Minister Ajit Jogi. Initially, orders were procured from Fabindia but over time there was no follow up. A new government came in with its own new schemes.

Trained fingers lay unused and unemployed.

"I realised I can get these people to work with me," says Neeti.

But where does one begin, how does one identify the workers? Neeti approached Dr Jogi and asked her for guidance and help.

"Renu Aunty inspired me to go ahead – without her I could not have gotten so far."

Dr Jogi mentioned that, as part of the government scheme, inmates in jails across Chhattisgarh had received training in embroidery. So Neeti approached the superintendent of Bilaspur central jail and made an offer of jobwork. Ten inmates were eager and willing to participate. But, there was a twist to the stitch.

"I want 36 Rang to look like a global brand but made by the local artisans."

"I got them to embroider funky tribal motifs on T-shirts, something which had never been done before!"

Although enthusiastic, the inmates had to be retrained. And they could not work with great speed.

"The first 500 T-shirts took 10 months to complete," says Neeti. "It was a learning experience for both the artists and for me."

Meanwhile, Neeti also found some local block printers and got 20 saris as well as some dupattas made with tribal motifs. With adequate stock of craft and clothing items, Neeti decided it was time to go to the market.

"I held my first exhibition on 23 October 2010 by Concern India Foundation at Epicentre in Gurgaon."

The saris did very well, quickly selling out at ₹ 8000 a piece. The bright T-shirts with tags declaring 'hand-embroidered by tribal groups of Chhattisgarh' were also appreciated.

"A lot of awareness was created about 36 rang and our mission of promoting tribal art."

Confident about her products, Neeti took up stalls at more exhibitions. Meanwhile a couple of stores like Loose Ends, Bliss in Mumbai and Yellow Button in Bangalore agreed to stock 36 Rang T-shirts. But entering the retail market has its own challenges.

"Stores work on consignment basis and pay only after sales are made, which can be as long as 6 months. That makes it tough for people like us!"

Online sales is another avenue 36 Rang is exploring. Here again, some of the bigger websites have their own requirements – say ten pieces in each design.

"We don't work with large volumes. My saris in particular, are one of a kind."

These are the kind of issues every entrepreneur working in the handicrafts sector grapples with. Especially those working for the benefit of artisans. While it makes business sense to mass-produce, it's not practical. Artisans in rural areas don't work by the clock.

"It's as much about their convenience as mine!"

Uncertainty creates stress. Neeti deals with this by marketing her goods only when she has all her stock in hand. In the first year, she commissioned 500 T-shirts, in year 2 the number went up to 700. As a matter of principle, she does not repeat her designs.

Because it's as much for the kick of art as it is about commerce.

"It's a thrill when people enter my stall, see the quality, design and workmanship of our T-shirts and say 'wow'!"

The 'wow' factor was strong enough for 36 Rang to clock sales of ₹ 12 lakh and 'break even' in its first year of operation. Artisans are getting work and costs are getting covered but profits are notional.

"Touch wood, I have managed to sustain this idea. Whatever we make, we put back in – the business is standing on its own feet."

Also standing on her own feet is Neeti herself – she handles everything from sourcing of raw material to manufacturing, designing and even the accounting. Neeti's younger brother Nirav, who recently graduated from Delhi University is also chipping in.

"Wherever I go for my exhibitions Nirav is accompanying me, he's a great support and he's learning about the business as well."

Nirav handles the marketing and PR for 36 Rang as well as much of the physical work required at exhibition venues. Whether it's a phase in his life or he decides to get into the business long term remains to be seen.

As important as working support is moral support. And here, it's the entire family which is by Neeti's side – her father, her sister and her brother-in-law.

"Unfortunately I lost my mother in 2007, but I know I continue to receive her love…"

"I want that surprise element also to be there. You should feel happy that '*haan* I did something different!' "

With all these blessings, the venture is slowly but surely moving forward.

36 Rang runs a rural centre for *marwahi* embroidery, supervised by two employees based in Bilaspur. However, as with any small business, getting committed employees is not easy.

"There was a girl from National Institute of Fashion Technology (NIFT) who worked with me for 8 months and then she got some other job. *Yeh sab chalta rehta hai*."

In October 2011, Neeti went international with an exhibition in UAE. Encouraged by the response, she returned some months later to set up a stall at Dubai's Global Village. Exhibitions in Kuala Lumpur and Mauritius and Singapore followed.

Saris top in popularity, followed by T-shirts and embroidered kurtas. There is also huge demand for traditional Chhattisgarhi *dhokra* (gunmetal) art.

"I am working with a few *dhokra* artisans for small orders. I can understand what the client wants and get them a better price."

A retail store in Raipur, online sales and more international exhibitions are on the cards. But Neeti has no plans to expand suddenly or take too much onto her plate.

"Basically I want to have a good balance in life."

Will marriage and all that it brings, upset this balance? Neeti is confident that when the time comes, she will be able to handle it.

"I will sit down and make it very clear to my husband – whoever he is going to be – that listen, I love what I do and I not going to leave this."

Although never the 'social worker' type Neeti finds a lot of peace and satisfaction working with and helping her artisans. Bringing them money, as well as recognition.

"When a travel magazine interviewed me I talked about Atmadas, he is one of our most talented artistes in *bhitti chitra*. I can't wait to see the smile on his face when I show him the article!"

Feeling good about what you do, and who you are.

Aim to be there and you will.

Better sooner, than later.

ADVICE TO WOMEN ENTREPRENEURS

Believe in yourself, believe in your dream. Stay focused and no matter what, make it happen for you.

Nothing is impossible. If there are some obstacles, don't be disheartened. Just keep moving… keep moving forward.

Family support is really important, it gives you the confidence to be who you want to be.

I had a lot of freedom while growing up and this gave wings to my dreams. I thank my parents for bringing me up to think and take responsibility for myself. I wish parents everywhere give this valuable gift to their daughters.

DUST WORTHY

A Ameena,
PJP Industries

Clad in a burqa, she works with heavy machinery, in the unusual industry of sawdust. Her daring and determination resulted in a partnership with Godrej, leading to further growth and expansion.

We are standing next to a Very Big Machine.

There is dust everywhere, but not by accident.

It is the very substance Ameena is proudly pouring through her fingers.

"Very fine, very fine 85 mesh we are making."

A Ameena is the owner and operator of PJP Industries, makers of fine sawdust, exclusively supplied to Godrej Consumer Products Ltd.

This is not a woman-friendly industry. It involves grease and grinding chambers and maintenance of a 115 hp motor. But this tiny burqa-clad woman, mother of three, does all of it – quite effortlessly.

"My husband working in Saudi, so most of the time I am in my industry. I working not for money, but to be a lady entrepreneur."

Competition was rough, conditions were tough, but Ameena pulled through. She proved herself and won a contract to exclusively supply Godrej. Subsequently, the company helped her scale up the operations with both monetary and technical assistance.

"I do all my works very sincerely," she says in a voice so soft I can barely hear her.

Like a whisper in the stillness of morning, like a cloud in the brilliant summer sky.

Ameena's is an uncommon achievement.

It speaks volumes without need of words.

DUST WORTHY

A Ameena,
PJP Industries

Ameena was born in Villupuram, Tamil Nadu, but calls Pondicherry her 'home'.

"I completed my schooling in 1983 and my higher secondary in 1985. The same year I got married, when I was 17 years old. My husband was related to me and working in Gulf."

Ameena became a housewife, with two lovely daughters. But at the same time she was different from other housewives. She completed her graduation and post-graduation after marriage, after having children.

"I always wanted to study more and more."

Even after MA, Ameena joined the government-run Small Industries Service Institute in Pondicherry. She wanted to do 'something special' in life, something in business. But what?

"My father and brothers were having an industry – Amin Chemicals – so they said I can join that and help them."

After 30 years in business, Amin Chemicals had gone 'sick' due to imposition of vehicle tax in Pondicherry. This increased costs and made it difficult to compete. Ameena joined the company in 1991 to look after the administration work. In the 7 years she spent there, she learnt everything about the business.

"I learnt how is the industry run, what are the problems faced by a businessman? By learning all this I could also help to turn around the company."

Slowly but surely, Amin Chemicals came back on track. Turnover increased to over ₹ 1 crore per annum and two new units – A R Industries and A S Industries were set up to do jobwork. All this kept Ameena on her toes.

"I used to work full-time, from morning to midnight. In between I will take my scooter and go home for cooking and looking after children when they come from school."

At the time, Ameena didn't have anyone to help her at home. But she managed, and she wanted 'more'.

"I told my father I have learnt the business and will manage my own industry which is now PJP Industries."

But why take on a new headache and bigger responsibility?

"I wanted to do something differently and achieve something. Then only I started my own industry, taking my own decision where I will give others pay."

PJP Industries was started in 1998 as a proprietary concern. Since she had experience of the pulverising industry at Amin Chemicals, Ameena decided to enter the same line of business. However, getting the permission to open the plant was a challenge.

"When I went to Pondicherry Municipality they did not take me seriously."

No one could believe that a lady clad in a burqa could be desirous, and capable, of running a pulverising plant.

"They made me wait for many months."

The machine itself cost ₹ 17 lakh, which Ameena bought with family savings. For the first 4 years, she did jobwork for various companies, including Hindustan Lever. The work was mostly grinding of starch and also aluminium sulphate.

The company made a profit from its very first year, on a modest turnover of ₹ 25 lakh.

"Whenever or whatever I touch the business, is going to profit. I don't make any loss."

In 2002, Ameena entered the sawdust industry. According to an estimate by *Outlook Business* magazine, the annual requirement of sawdust is 50,000 tons (worth ₹ 40 crore). And one of the major challenges is procuring a regular supply of the raw material.

"To make sawdust we need the wood powder. It is a by-product of sawmill industry."

Pollachi town, on the border of Tamil Nadu and Kerala is a major sawmill hub. Many years ago, Ameena made a visit to Pollachi and found a supplier. Come rain, come shine, she has her supply of wood powder.

"We are having a good understanding and co-operation."

This is no easy task, because there is tough competition. Some of it, unfair.

"One person beat other... they are always ready to beat others. To get my material, to try to reject my material, to try to send the raw material from other sides...so many problems we are facing."

And yet, the supplier is loyal to Ameena, because she is good for his business. She pays on time, she keeps her word. Sincerity is an uncommon virtue but it pays.

The next aspect is quality control. The '5 mesh' and '10 mesh' coarse wood powder* must be ground to a fine dust of '85 mesh'. This is not easy as the wood powder itself varies in texture.

"We are maintaining the quality because I'm doing the machine very sophisticated, it's very secret. So, we are not facing the variations and we are getting the good product finally."

It was the quality of her work and the unusual aspect of a female entrepreneur in this heavy industry that brought Godrej to Ameena's doorstep. Sawdust has an application in mosquito coils**, which are manufactured by Godrej and marketed under the brand names 'Good Knight' and 'Jet'.

In 2008, Ameena signed an agreement to supply exclusively to the company. And there has been no looking back since.

* Mesh is the 'scale' used to describe the size of powders and granular materials. '5 mesh' means particles can pass through a sieve of 3.35 mm (coarse powder) while '85 mesh' means the particle can pass through sieve of 0.178 mm (a very fine powder).

** 60% of the raw material used in mosquito coils is sawdust.

"Whenever or whatever I touch the business, it is going to profit. I don't make any loss."

From a turnover ₹ 25 lakh in 2002, PJP Industries crossed ₹ 85 lakh in March 2010. Apart from Ameena, the factory employs 12 people, mostly labour.

"In administration and operations and management… all work is myself only."

Ameena is not an engineer and it's a 20 ton pulveriser we are talking about. So how does she manage this mean machine. By observation and determination.

"I'm learning in my father factory. I thoroughly know my machine because those who know maintenance, that person only success in this field."

Ameena is a 'doctor' of her own machine. So that she does not have to depend on quacks. With this kind of confidence, it was but inevitable that she would expand the business. In 2010, Ameena began putting up her second unit at Bahour, 18 km from Pondicherry.

"My first factory we have capacity of 150 tons per month. Second one is 500 tons per month*."

The new factory with 4 machines was commissioned on 6 November 2012. Godrej has supported the venture from start to finish by investing ₹ 40 lakh as well as committing to buy the entire output.

"Godrej people are very much appreciating and they are like my family."

Ameena has also put in ₹ 30 lakh of her own – from earnings in the business. And Indian Bank has extended a loan of ₹ 1 crore.

The new unit employs 20 persons and Ameena travels back and forth between the two factories.

"I drive two-wheeler and four-wheeler also, so it's not a problem."

Ameena's husband worked in Saudi Arabia as a housekeeping

* Godrej requires approx. 1500 tons of sawdust per month, of which Ameena supplies 650 tons.

supervisor from 1992 to 2003. Since the last 3 years, he is involved with the business. But he gives her all the credit for what she has achieved.

"99% this field development, industry development only my Mrs. I only helping."

Ameena admits this entire venture is unusual.

"Normally most of the girls from my caste, most 99% all are housewife. But my father and husband's family co-operating with me."

Since her husband was mostly away, he may not have felt her absence from the home. But what about the children?

"Sometimes they are misunderstanding. Now they are understanding that our mother is doing some good work, so do not disturb her."

While she married young, Ameena was particular that her daughters complete their education and only then think about settling down. Her elder daughter Mansura has completed her MBA in Biotechnology while the middle one Nazeera is a BTech IT from Anna University.

Ameena's youngest daughter Hawiyya was born in 2006. After 17 days of rest, she was back on her feet and in the factory. Business, as usual.

"Only one difference is that now I have a maidservant for cooking work."

Meanwhile Ameena wants to move beyond sawdust – her 'dream project' is to start manufacturing premix powder for mosquito coils. For a person with her tenacity, it's not a tall order.

Strength lies in quiet conviction.

"In the problem time when we get angry, it is not very good results. That time I am thinking about how can I manage the problem. How to remove it…Yes, quite a lot I am praying."

Prayer is universal

God is universal.

Pray to the Universe and God *will* hear you.

ADVICE TO WOMEN ENTREPRENEURS

Work hard, this is the success of the industry.

You are the woman, we should make happy in the home also and also seeing how is the family's way. My daughters or children or sons, they should be disciplined. That is very rare and important in my success.

Simultaneously to be hardworking and sincere with full efforts and interest in their work, then only the women entrepreneur will success.

M Abdul Wahab (husband):

She is very intelligent.

After I working abroad, she studying in Tamil Nadu University, through correspondence.

First she pray to God, then look after family, next only business. Also relations like father and mother and some poor people coming, she help them.

25 years completed marriage, not going one time to cinema theatre. This is record.

Before she used to do cooking and company and jobwork, very difficult. Pondicherry jobwork very difficult, lot of competition. But now, only Godrej working very good.

Pondicherry government full supporting. I am proudly saying – "She is first acting lady enterprepreneur in Pondicherry."

She very dedicated. Since from morning wake up at 6 o'clock, do prayer, after thinking business... company good... I got any time any problem, I am going to remove the problem. Any problem or work start, first prayer. After that full success, not failure.

99% working my Mrs. 1% I do marketing and any help she needs, I go to help.

START UP RESOURCE

If you would like to contact any of the entrepreneurs featured in this book for help/ advice, here are their email ids. Do try and be specific in your queries and a little patient in getting a response!

1. **Meena Bindra** – *meena.bindra@bibaindia.com*
2. **Manju Bhatia** – *manju.bhatia@vasuli.net*
3. **Rajni Bector** – *c/o akshaybector@sify.com*
4. **Nirmala K** – *nirmala@vivamgroup.co.in*
5. **Ranjana Naik** – *ranjunaik@gmail.com*
6. **Leela Bordia** – *Info@neerjainternational.com*
7. **Han Qui Hua** – *1016335307@qq.com*
8. **Premlata Agarwal** – *premlata.ag@gmail.com*
9. **Patricia Narayan** – *petty_patty@yahoo.com*
10. **Sudeshna Banerjee** – *sudeshna@digitech-hr.net*
11. **Jasu Shilpi** – *info@jasushilpi.co.in*
12. **Dipali Sikand** – *dipali@lesconcierges.co.in*
13. **Paru Jaykrishna** – *parumj@asahisongwon.com*
14. **Binapani Talukdar** – *pansydry@yahoo.co.in*
15. **Ela Bhatt** – *bhattela@sewa.org*
16. **Shona McDonald** – *shona@shonaquip.co.za*
17. **Nina Lekhi** – *nina@baggitindia.com*
18. **Sangeeta Patni** – *spatni@extensio.com*
19. **Satya Vadlamani** – *murlikrishnapharma@gmail.com*
20. **Shikha Sharma** – *drshikha@drshikha.com*
21. **Deepa Soman** – *deepa.soman@lumieresolutions.com*
22. **Otara Gunewardene** – *otara@eodel.com*
23. **Namrata Sharma** – *snamrata@gmail.com*
24. **Neeti Tah** – *mail@36rang.com*
25. **A Ameena** – *hawiyya@yahoo.com*

HELPING HANDS

You need practical and emotional support in this journey of life, and entrepreneurship. Here are some educational institutes and organisations that you might want to look into:

USEFUL COURSES

These are short duration courses which equip you with specific skills to start/ scale up your business.

Management Program for Women Entrepreneurs (MPWE) at IIM Bangalore: A unique 25-day program held in April/May every year, both aspiring and existing entrepreneurs can apply.

Email mpwe@iimb.ernet.in

Management Development Program for Women Entrepreneurs at IIM Udaipur: A 6-week program (April and May) with focus on developing a viable business plan

http://www.iimu.ac.in

Goldman Sachs 10,000 Women Entrepreneurs Certificate Program with Indian School of Business (ISB): A16-week program with 3 weeks of classroom sessions and 13 weeks of mentoring support on the job.

For women running a business for more than a year, with revenues of ₹ 5-50 lakh and looking to scale up. Held in Hyderabad. Bangalore, Mumbai, Delhi, Pune, Mohali and Indore.

http://10kwomen.isb.edu/

Start Your Business Program at S P Jain, Mumbai

Held over 12 weekends in Mumbai, for aspiring and early stage entrepreneurs – both men and women.

http://www.spjimr.org/syb/ or email: msrao@spjimr.org

NETWORKING

Life is a series of connections, and so is business. You learn from others who are on the same path.

TIE Stree Shakti: A platform which connects and enables enterprising women through mentoring, education and on-ground activities.

http://www.tiestreeshakti.org or email: zee@tiemumbai.org,

WEConnect: Empowers women business owners by providing certification, resources, mentoring and peer/corporate connection.

email: sucharita@weconnectinternational.org

POST-MOTHERHOOD CAREERS

Women who take a 'break' often don't know how to get back to work. These women-led organisations are making it happen.

Avtar Career Creators: Offers career services for professionally qualified women who wish to create part-time or flexi-time careers.

http://www.avtariwin.com or email: sr@avtarcc.com

Fleximoms: Work from home, project based, part-time or full-time jobs for women professionals + advisory and mentoring.

http:// www.fleximoms.in or email sairee@fleximoms.in

CORPORATE INITIATIVES

Tata Second Careers Internship Program: Women professionals who have taken a break of 6 months or more for any reason can apply for flexi-hour assignments with various Tata group companies.

http://www.tatasecondcareer.com

Learn the art of writing with Rashmi Bansal
(All workshops held on Zoom, on weekends)

For dates visit: https://rashmibansal.in/workshops

Short Story Writing Workshop (3 hours)

If you want to start telling your stories, register for this hands-on workshop. The goal is to have a complete story written by you at the end of just 3 hours. The best stories from the workshop get published on my website

Deep Dive Non- Fiction Workshop (2 days/3 hours each day)
This workshop is designed for anyone who is keen on writing an impactful non-fiction book. The workshop is practical in nature and features hands-on exercises as well as Q & A. I also cover 'how to get published' and provide a review for 3 chapters of your book.

Personal Story Telling Workshop (3 hours)
Whether you are a CEO, or a junior manager, stories will help you energise your team and build your personal brand. Learn how to tell your personal story with confidence and flair.

All workshop attendees also become part of a virtual writing community.

Discover the Power of Storytelling

Customised workshops for schools and colleges
Team building and leadership workshops for organisations
Coaching CEOs in the Art of Storytelling.

If you want Rashmi Bansal to conduct a hands-on worksho
write to: enquiry@rashmibansal.in with your requirement.